HISTORY OF ENGLAND

VOLUME THREE

GEORGE MACAULAY TREVELYAN was born in 1876 and educated at Harrow and Trinity College, Cambridge. He was Regius Professor of Modern History at Cambridge from 1927 to 1940 and Master of Trinity College from 1940 to 1951. He is the author of *England under the Stuarts, British History in the Nineteenth Century, Six Centuries of Social History, England under Queen Anne,* and A HISTORY OF ENGLAND, which was first published in 1926.

HISTORY OF ENGLAND

Volume Three: From Utrecht to Modern Times: The Industrial Revolution and the Transition to Democracy

by G. M. TREVELYAN, O.M.
Master of Trinity College, 1940–1951. Formerly Regius Professor of Modern History in the University of Cambridge

Doubleday Anchor Books
DOUBLEDAY & COMPANY, INC., GARDEN CITY, N.Y.

First Edition, June 1926
Second Edition, July 1937
Second Edition revised, April 1942
Third Edition, October 1945
Reissue (with minor corrections), 1952

PRINTED IN THE UNITED STATES OF AMERICA

DESIGNED BY DIANA KLEMIN

A History of England was originally published by Longmans, Green and Co., Ltd. in 1926. The Anchor Books edition is published by arrangement with Longmans, Green & Co., Inc.

Anchor Books edition: 1953

CONTENTS

BOOK FIVE

From Utrecht to Waterloo. Sea-Power and Aristocracy. First Stage of the Industrial Revolution

MAPS

HISTORY OF ENGLAND

VOLUME THREE

BOOK FIVE

From Utrecht to Waterloo. Sea-Power and Aristocracy. First Stage of the Industrial Revolution

INTRODUCTION

The Eighteenth Century in England starts politically from the Revolution Settlement of 1689, on which it may be said to be a gloss or comment. The accession of the House of Hanover in 1714 was only a confirmation and extension of the principles that had placed William and Mary on the throne twenty-five years before.

The Revolution Settlement had the defects of its qualities. It was inevitably too conservative, or so at least it appears to modern eyes. It would have been better, some think in the retrospect, if the opportunity had been taken to redistribute the Parliamentary seats more nearly according to population. In the elections to Cromwell's Parliaments the rotten boroughs had been abolished as being under the influence of the local gentry, and the county representation had been proportionately increased. But the old constituencies had been restored with Charles II, and the men of 1689 left the unreformed representation to grow ever more corrupt with years, bringing thereby many evils on the country, possibly among others the quarrel with America. But the merit of the Revolution lay in being a settlement by consent, and consent could only be obtained by avoiding as far as possible the disturbance of vested interests. Now, one of those vested interests was the power of certain nobles and gentry to influence elections to the House of Commons in certain boroughs. A

Reform Bill had no place in the minds of either Whigs or Tories in that era.

Indeed the ostensible object of the Revolution was not change but conservation. James II had illegally attacked a number of vested interests and chartered corporations—the Church, the Universities, the town Municipalities, the electoral rights of the parliamentary boroughs, the property of freeholders,—and he had denied the efficacy of the laws of the land. By inevitable reaction, the Revolution, in its just defence of these interests against illegal assault, gave to them a sacrosanct character which helped to protect them against wise and legal reform for a hundred and forty years to come. The outrages that provoked the Revolution had engendered an ideal enthusiasm for vested interests as such, because the action of James II had for a while identified vested interests with the cause of British freedom. And this ideal enthusiasm survived the occasion that had called it forth. The existing laws, which James II in his tyranny had over-ridden, became a fetish to Judge Blackstone and the men of the Eighteenth Century.

The Revolution was a triumph of the lawyers over the executive, the close of a long struggle begun by Coke and Selden to subject the legality of the King's actions to the free judgment of the courts that administered the Common Law. The victory of law over irresponsible and arbitrary power was a splendid triumph for civilization, but it made the lawyer's point of view somewhat too predominant in the Eighteenth Century. The Revolution which had been made in order to oppose illegal changes attempted by an arbitrary monarch, was appealed to in retrospect by Blackstone and even by Burke, as a fixed standard, a criterion by which legislative reform of a popular character was to be condemned beforehand.

Partly for this reason, the period of Walpole and the Pitts was the heyday of unchallenged abuses in all forms of corporate life. Holders of ecclesiastical, academic, charitable and scholastic endowments had no fear of enquiry or reform. Schoolmasters could draw their salaries without keeping school. Universities could sell degrees without holding examinations or giving instruction. Parliamentary boroughs and municipal oligarchies could be as corrupt and ridiculous as they liked; it was enough that they were old. 'Whatever is is right—if it can show a charter' seems the watchword of the Eighteenth Century.

It is not, therefore, surprising that the greatness of England during the epoch that followed the Revolution is to be judged by her individual men, by the unofficial achievement of her free and vigorous population, by the open competition of her merchants and industrialists in the markets of the world, rather than by her corporate institutions, such as Church, Universities, Schools, Civil Service, and town Corporations, which were all of them half asleep. The glory of the Eighteenth Century in Britain lay in the genius and energy of individuals acting freely in a free community—Marlborough, Swift, Bishops Butler and Berkeley, Wesley, Clive, Warren Hastings, the Pitts, Captain Cook, Dr. Johnson, Reynolds, Burke, Adam Smith, Hume, James Watt, Burns, William Blake, and a score of others, to whom our later age will find it hard to show the equals, though we have indeed reformed and rationalized our corporate institutions.

After the prolonged political and religious crisis of the Stuart epoch, an equally long period of stability, under laws of a generally liberal character, was no bad thing even at the price of some stagnation. And, indeed, the sudden vigour put forth by Britain at Chatham's conjuring, the conquest of Canada and the founding of the Indian Empire, showed that the political stagnation did not mean national decadence; the British State and Constitution were the most efficient as well as the most free of the governments of the world in those last days of the *ancien régime*. There followed, indeed, the loss of the American colonies, partly owing to the defects and corruption of our home constitution, partly for more general reasons concerned with the relations of America to England. In imperial and foreign affairs the British aristocracy both succeeded and failed on the grand scale, proving at least far more successful than the contemporary despotism of Bourbon

France. On the whole, Britain flourished greatly in the Eighteenth Century, and her civilization struck roots both deep and wide.

But mischief lay in the fact that this period of immutable institutions and unaltered law coincided in its later years with the period that saw the beginning of economic and social changes of great rapidity and of yet greater import for the future. The Industrial Revolution began first in our island, and may for convenience be dated from the early years of George III. Throughout his long reign [1760–1820.], new forces of machinery and capitalized industry worked their blind will upon a loosely organized, aristocratic society that did not even perceive that its fate had come upon it.

The highly civilized and well-established world of which Dr. Johnson and Edmund Burke are the typical minds, could think only in terms of politics and literature; men failed to observe that a revolution, more profound than the political changes overseas that they discussed and deprecated, was taking place daily in their own midst, and was sapping the old English order without any proper readjustment being made by public authority. Indeed, just when the Industrial Revolution was making reforms in our political and municipal institutions more imperative than ever, the reaction against Jacobin propaganda from abroad drove the governing classes to refuse, on principle, any political change at all, while nothing was done either to check or to guide economic change in its fullest flood. On the top of all this came twenty years of Napoleonic war, necessarily distracting the nation's attention from its own grave internal affairs, and complicating the Industrial Revolution at its most critical stage by war-time abnormality in trade, prices and employment.

After this fashion the quiet and self-contented England of the Eighteenth Century slid unawares into a seething cauldron of trouble, whence a very different world would in due time emerge. Yet even in that confused and desperate crisis, such was the energy latent in the individual Englishman, such were the advantages of the island position to the Mistress of the Seas, such was the power in war time of the new industrial machinery, that Britain, though so recently stripped of her American colonies, emerged as the chief victor of the Napoleonic wars and the mistress of a new Empire. And even while the war was raging, her creative spirit, sheltered behind her fleet, blossomed as in the age of Elizabeth. The era of Nelson and Wellington, of Fox and Pitt, of Castlereagh and Canning, was also the era of Wordsworth and Coleridge, of Scott and Byron, of Shelley and Keats, of Turner and Constable, of Cobbett and Wilberforce, of Bentham and Owen, and many more. The men of that day seemed to inhale vigour and genius with the island air. Though the social order was much amiss and the poor suffered, among the more favoured classes the individual reached a very high point of development during the early stages of the Industrial Revolution, in its first contact with the old rural life and the still surviving culture and freedom inherited from the Eighteenth Century.

CHAPTER ONE

Early Hanoverian England. Character of the Aristocratic Government, Prime Minister, Cabinet and Parliament. The Spirit of the Eighteenth Century. John Bull and French Influences. The Church and the Wesleyan Movement. Scotland. Universities and Schools. Village Life. Decay of the Yeoman Begins. The Underworld. Humanitarianism. The Eve of the Industrial Revolution

KINGS: George I, 1714–27; George II, 1727–60; George III, 1760

The coming over of William of Orange had confirmed the doctrine of the Whigs and confused that of the Tories, but it gave the Whigs no mechanical advantage over their rivals. Throughout the reigns of William and Anne the two parties continued to share power evenly; the Crown and the electorate favoured first one side and then the other, according to the circumstances of the hour; the party contest continued to be vigorous, sometimes to fierceness, and in the main fortunate in its outcome for the country's interests. It is only in the reigns of George I and II that we find a state of things that may, with reserves and explanations, be picturesquely described as a 'Whig oligarchy.' Nor would it have come into existence even then, if half the Tory party had not been so gravely compromised with Jacobitism.

Partly for this reason, partly because George I was ignorant of English language and customs, the first two Hanoverians abandoned to the Whig leaders certain prerogatives of the Crown which William III and even Anne would never have let out of their own hands. The formation of Ministries, the dissolution of Parliament, the patronage of the Crown in Church and State, all passed, in effect, from the monarch to the Whig chiefs. In that sense a political oligarchy was indeed established after 1714. But in another aspect the change was a further development of the popular element in our constitution, by the establishment of the omnipotence of Ministries dependent on the vote of the House of Commons, and by the reduction of the power wielded by the hereditary monarch.

Later on, George III attempted in the first twenty years of his reign [1760–80.] to take back the patronage of the Crown into the royal hands, in consonance with the undoubted intentions of those who made the Revolution Settlement. But as soon as he had recovered the patronage of the Crown, he used it to corrupt the House of Commons even more systematically than Walpole and the Whig oligarchs had done. Neither the Whig oligarchs nor George III ever tried to stand on the unparliamentary ground of the Stuarts. They never ventured to deny that the executive could only exercise power in agreement with a majority of the House of Commons. But it was possible in the Eighteenth Century to corrupt the members through the distribution of patronage, because the rotten boroughs were becoming less representative of the country with every year that passed.

Under the first two Georges the power of the House of Commons increased, while its connection with the people diminished. The long hibernation of the Tory party and the deadness of all serious political controversy damped public interest in Parliamentary affairs, other than the distribution of places and bribes. The Septennial Act, passed in 1716 to secure the House of Hanover against Jacobite reaction, prolonged the normal life of a Parliament; by rendering political tenures more secure, it further deadened political interest in the country and increased the readiness of members to enter the pay of government.

Under George III there was a great revival of public interest in politics, but no increase in democratic control over Parliament. But when, by the Reform Bill of 1832, the middle class recovered more than their old power over the House of Commons, they found in the modern machinery of Parliament and Cabinet a far more effective instrument of government than any which had existed in Stuart times. The Parliamentary aristocracy of the Eighteenth Century had forged and sharpened the future weapons of the democracy. It is doubtful whether nobles and squires would ever have consented to concentrate such powers in the Lower House, if they had thought of it as a strictly popular body. But they thought of it as a house of gentlemen, many of them nominees or relations of the Peerage, as the 'best club in London,' as the 'Roman Senate' to which the highest interests of the country could safely be committed.

Under these conditions, the aristocratic Eighteenth Century made a great contribution of its own to the growth of British political tradition. The aristocrats devised the machinery by which the legislature could control the executive without hampering its efficiency. This machinery is the Cabinet system and the office of Prime Minister. By the Cabinet system we mean in England a group of Ministers dependent on the favour of the House of Commons and all having seats in Parliament, who must agree on a common policy and who are responsible for one another's action and for the government of the country as a whole. Neither Prime Minister nor Cabinet system was contemplated in the Revolution Settlement. They grew up gradually to meet the country's needs in peace and in war. The first approach to a united Cabinet was made by William III merely to fight the war against Louis, but he remained his own Prime Minister and his own Foreign Minister. In Anne's reign Marlborough acted as the head of the State in wartime for all military and diplomatic affairs, but he left to his colleagues the management of Parliament. It was Sir Robert Walpole, the Whig peace Minister from 1721 to 1742, who did most to evolve the principle of the common responsibility of the Cabinet, and the supremacy of the Prime Minister as the leading man at once in the Cabinet and in the Commons. It was significant that, unlike his Whig and Tory predecessors in power, Sir Robert remained undazzled by the lure of peerage, and refused to leave the Lower House so long as he aspired to govern the country. When he consented to become Earl of Orford he was retiring for ever from office.

In effecting these changes in the custom of the constitution, Walpole acted not a little from love of personal power, but he did the country a great service. In driving out from his Cabinet all colleagues who did not agree with his policy or would not submit to his leadership as Premier, he set up the machinery by which Britain has since been ruled in peace and war. The Cabinet system is the key by which the English were able to get efficient government by a responsible and united executive, in spite of the fact that the executive was subject to the will of a debating assembly of five or six hundred men. They solved this problem, which many nations have found insoluble, not, as was often contemplated in William III's reign, by excluding the Ministers from the Commons, but on the contrary by insisting that they should sit in and lead the House of Commons, like Sir Robert Walpole. The Cabinet is the link between the executive and legislative, and it is a very close link indeed. It is the essential part of the modern British polity.[1]

It was well for England that the Revolution Settlement did not supply her with a brand-new, water-tight, unalterable, written constitution. A sacrosanct written constitution was necessary to achieve the federal union of the States of North America after they had cut themselves adrift from the old Empire. For England it was not at all necessary, and it would certainly have proved inconvenient. If England had been given a rigid constitution when James II was deposed, the Crown would have had assigned to it, in perpetuity, powers which within thirty years of the coronation of William and Mary it handed over to be exercised by its Parliamentary advisers. It is probable, also, that a rigid constitution, drawn up according to the lights of 1689, would have excluded the King's Ministers from sitting in the House of Commons.

A written constitution, as distinct from the sum of ordinary law and custom, is alien to the English political genius. One of the worst signs of the straits to which Cromwell was driven by his inability to find a basis of national agreement, was the fact that he promulgated written constitutions dividing up by an absolute line—never to be altered—the powers of Protector and Parliament respectively. These expedients were contrary to the real method of English progress. The London fog which decently conceals from view the exact relations of executive and legislative at Westminster, has enabled the constitution to adapt itself unobserved to the requirements of each passing age.

[1] The English in those days were better politicians than political theorists. They permitted the French philosopher, Montesquieu, to report to the world in his *Esprit des Lois* (1748) that the secret of British freedom was the separation of executive and legislative, whereas the opposite was much nearer to the truth. Partly on account of Montesquieu's error, confirmed by Blackstone, partly for better local reasons, the Federal Constitution of the United States was drawn up on the idea of separating executive from legislative.

When we speak of the Whig oligarchy under the first two Georges [1714–60.], we mean (so far as we mean anything definite) about seventy great families, who, in alliance or in rivalry among themselves, exercised the power and patronage of the State, on condition of retaining the constant support of the House of Commons. The Heads of the great Whig families mostly sat among the Peers, and their cadets in the Commons. The Peers were able to keep the confidence of the Lower House, partly because they never seriously opposed themselves to its political ideas, and partly because they owned many of the rotten boroughs that returned so many of its members. These great noblemen had therefore no temptation to set up the claims of the more dignified but less powerful chamber in which they themselves sat. The Peers were unofficially but very effectually represented in the House of Commons, and had no objection to the constant increase of its power.

It was not until the Nineteenth Century, during and after the Reform Bill of 1832, that the Peers thought it necessary to assert the direct power of their own chamber. It was only then that they had cause to question the prescriptive right of the House of Commons to legislate at will for the nation. But in the Nineteenth Century such resistance, though by no means wholly ineffectual, came in the main too late. Englishmen had been so long accustomed to be ruled by the House of Commons when it was an aristocratic assembly, that they would not allow its power to be curtailed when it began to be more truly representative of the nation at large.

Although from 1714 to 1760 the patronage and executive power of the State rested in the hands of the Whig magnates, they were as far as possible from being absolute and arbitrary rulers like the 'Venetian oligarchs' to whom Disraeli compared them. It was the era of the rigid reign of law in England—law that had triumphed over executive power in 1689. And in the days of Blackstone the laws of England closely limited the power of those who governed the State. The citizen had many strong bulwarks to protect him against government, and enjoyed an amount of personal freedom that was the envy of all Europe. Anything less like the arbitrary and inquisitorial government of the Venetian Republic it is difficult to imagine. If there was tyranny in the land in the mild years between 1714 and 1760 it was not the political tyranny of Parliament and Cabinet, but the social tyranny of the squires in the countryside.

All through Tudor and Stuart times the unpaid Justices of the Peace had administered and judged the English village and the English county, partly by virtue of their local importance as landlords, partly by virtue of their commissions as Justices granted them by the central government. Shakespeare has drawn such a country-bred agent of the Crown in Justice Shallow of Gloucestershire, Falstaff's friend. Addison's Sir Roger de Coverley is another. Government relied for its working not on a paid and dependent bureaucracy, but on a political understanding with the local gentry, who acted as its unpaid agents.

Such had been the machinery of Tudor and Stuart rule. It required, like so many things English, tact and mutual understanding to ensure the co-operation of the central and the local authorities. James II broke it to pieces. He tried to bend the will of the gentry to serve the camarilla at Whitehall on the question of Roman Catholicism. But there was no organization available for such an unwonted assertion of the central power. It was impossible to use the country gentlemen against themselves, and there was no paid bureaucracy. The Revolution of 1688 in one of its aspects was a revolt of the localities against the central government; in other words, of the squires against the Privy Council. The victory of the local gentry over the King was so resounding that thenceforth they were emancipated for a century and more from all effective central control, in social and economic no less than in political and religious matters. The central power learnt to identify itself with the country gentry to such an extent that the Privy Council never again attempted to control the squires in the interest of the community in general, as had been sometimes done under Elizabeth and the early Stuarts in such matters as the Poor Law.

This part of the lesson taught by the Revolution was not forgotten. When in their turn the Whig oligarchs came to wield the power of the Crown, they were careful to leave the countryside to be administered and judged by the local squires, Tory and Whig alike. In *Tom Jones* Squire Western is a strong Tory, but he holds his commission as Justice of the Peace by the good will of the Whig Lords and the 'Hanoverian rats' whom he is always abusing. The Justices of the Peace held their commissions from the Crown, through the selection of the Lord Chancellor, but they were not paid by the Crown, and their wealth and local influence came to them from their landed estates which the Government could not touch. Thus the political power of the Whig oligarchy at the centre was effectually limited in the localities by the oligarchy of the squires, who were mainly Tory. But there was nothing to limit the social power of the landed gentry, Whig and Tory together. It was the rural landlords who formed the true oligarchy, no longer controlled by the central power, which rather they themselves controlled. In England there was no democratic township; and elected County Councils were first set up by Lord Salisbury's Government in 1888. Until that date, the aristocratic Justices of the Peace ruled the English countryside.

Thus rural England was aristocratic, and that meant in the Eighteenth Century that most of England was aristocratic. So things remained until the Industrial Revolution made England democratic by converting her from a society mainly rural into a society mainly industrial and urban, where aristocracy had no natural power.

Two things specially distinguished the government of Britain from the governments of the *ancien régime* on the continent—Parliamentary control, and freedom of speech, press and person. Of these advantages Britons were very conscious and very proud. They looked with contempt on French, Italians and Germans as people enslaved to priests, Kings and nobles, unlike your freeborn Englishmen. Freedom had been so lately acquired in Britain and was still so rare a thing in Europe, that our ancestors prized it high among their blessings.

Nevertheless, political and social power in that easy-going century was concentrated too much in one class, the landowners. The time was coming when that defect would greatly enhance the social evils of the Industrial Revolution. But under the first two Georges, before the coming of great economic change, the wage-earner, both in town and country, scarcely seems to have resented at all his want of social and political power. The British working man, then called the 'honest yeoman' or the 'jolly 'prentice,' was quite happy drinking himself drunk to the health of the 'quality' at election time. And even if he had no vote, he could stand cheering or hooting in front of the hustings, while the candidate, possibly a Peer's son, bowed low with his hand on his heart and a rotten egg in his hair, addressing the mob as 'gentlemen,' and asking for their support as the chief object of his ambition. The sight filled foreign spectators with admiration and astonishment. The spirit of aristocracy and the spirit of popular rights seemed to have arrived at a perfect harmony, peculiar to the England of that epoch. There have been worse relations than that between rich and poor, between governors and governed. There was no class hatred, and though highest and lowest were far apart, there were infinite gradations and no rigid class barriers as on the continent. But this careless, good-natured state of society could not outlast the coming of the Industrial Revolution.

It was the special function of the Eighteenth Century to diffuse common sense and reasonableness in life and thought, to civilize manners and to humanize conduct. The century that began with the universally approved *Asiento* treaty for supplying South America with slaves, ended with the capture of national opinion by Wilberforce and the Anti-slave-trade Committee. That movement, which saved civilization in three continents, was the product of the religious and rationalist peculiarities of the epoch of Wesley and Voltaire, of Beccaria and John Howard.

When the Stuarts ceased to reign, the English upper-class could still be represented in fiction by such widely divergent types of culture and manners as Squire Western on the one side and Squire Allworthy and Sir Roger de Coverley on the other. By the end of the century, when Jane Austen began to write, there was a regularized standard of manners and speech among gentlemen.

The reign of Beau Nash [DIED 1762.] at Bath taught the rules of polite society to the country squires who resorted thither with their families, and hastened the disappearance of the sword as the proper adornment of a gentleman's thigh. Largely for this reason, there was a great reduction in the number of killing affrays, and after-supper brawls of fatal issue regretted in the morning. But the regular duel with pistols did not fall into disuse until the bourgeois and Evangelical influences of the Nineteenth Century completed the work of humanity and common sense. Meanwhile, among humbler folk, the passion for pugilism made stabbing and murder 'taboo,' and the custom of making a ring to see two disputants use their fists according to rule fostered the national sentiment for 'fair play,' and tended gradually to discourage the promiscuous and barbarous melees of which we read too often in Smollett and Fielding and in memoirs of their time.

As patrons of art and letters, the English upper class reached in the Eighteenth Century a point that they had never reached before, and have since scarcely maintained. Not only great country seats like Holkham, Althorp, and Stowe, with their libraries and art treasures, but many smaller houses of the gentry focussed for rural society the art, science and polite letters of the day, with which the dominant landlord class identified itself hardly less than with sport, agriculture and politics. The country houses and the world of fashion did more for culture and intellect than the dormant Universities. The upper class, under the guidance of Dr. Johnson and Garrick, imposed the worship of Shakespeare, as the greatest of mankind, on a public not very intelligent, perhaps, of Shakespeare but most obsequious to his noble patrons, and consequently very respectful to literature.

It was during the Eighteenth Century that a process, begun in the Stuart period, was brought to completion,—the establishment among the learned of the custom of writing in English instead of in Latin. This change had important consequences: British scholars became more than ever separated from their continental brethren; thought and learning became more national, more popular, and more closely allied to literature. Bentley, Blackstone, Gibbon and Adam Smith all made appeal to the general intelligence of their countrymen at large, rather than to a professional learned audience scattered over all the countries of Europe.

On the other hand, one of the peculiarities of the movement of English culture in the Eighteenth Century, as compared to the Elizabethan era, was the deference to foreign models. Aristocratic leadership partly accounted for this. The patrons were 'milords' accustomed to make the Grand Tour of Europe, mixing with the society of foreign courts and capitals as tourists seldom do to-day, and bringing back statues, pictures, objects of virtù, French literary and philosophic ideas, and Italian standards of music and poetry. The link with the continent was the stronger because it was reciprocal: foreign admiration of British institutions and British thinkers was a chief original cause of the 'Encyclopædist' movement of rational philosophy in France. 'Le Grand Newton,' Locke and Hume were names as highly honoured in Paris as in London and Edinburgh.[2]

[2] Voltaire, the dictator of continental opinion, wrote: 'La nation anglaise est la seule de la terre qui soit parvenue à régler le pouvoir des rois en leur résistant; où les seigneurs sont grands sans insolence et sans vassaux, et où le peuple partage le gouvernement sans confusion.' 'En Angleterre communément on pense, et les lettres y sont plus en honneur qu'ici. Cet avantage est une suite nécessaire de la forme de leur gouvernement.'—*Lettres sur les Anglais.*

It is indeed a singular fact that, during the hundred years after the Revolution of 1688, when England was in violent reaction against French religion and politics, when English and French armies and navies were in constant conflict in both hemispheres, and when the common people despised and hated everything French with a fierce ignorance and prejudice, our taste in letters, in architecture and in house decoration was to an unusual degree subjected to French and Italian ideas. In the reign of Charles II we had, like the rest of Europe, begun to submit to the cultural influences of the Court of Versailles, and we did not cease to do so after La Hogue and Blenheim. There was gain as well as loss in this temporary 'academizing' of our literary standards,—gain to English prose and loss to English poetry: gain to clearness of thought and expression, loss to imagination and native vigour. The 'romantic' and 'naturalist' movements begun in the last decade of the century by Scott, Coleridge and Wordsworth, were a revolt from foreign standards back to native traditions and native freedom. But even in the full Eighteenth Century the native English novel had been progressing freely, with little deference to foreign models, from Defoe through Smollett and Fielding to Miss Austen. Nor did our drama ever accept the French 'unities' of time and place.

Neither must it be forgotten that during this period, when upper class poetry and literature were least 'romantic,' most rationalized and most academic, the imagination of the common folk was still being nurtured not only on the Bible but on ghost stories, fairy stories, ballads and tales of romantic glamour, of which their everyday rustic life seemed a part. Indeed it was precisely when 'romance' made its Nineteenth Century conquest of literature proper, that the school textbook and the newspaper began to take the place of the traditional romantic lore of the cottage fireside. It is even arguable that the Eighteenth Century, which produced William Blake and Burns and Wordsworth, was in its true nature more 'romantic' than the following century with its efforts to escape by feats of imagination from the drabness of its real surroundings.

However that may be, the artificiality of our Eighteenth Century culture was strong enough to impose an alien regime on the world of music. Handel and the Italian Opera largely took the place of our native music, which had once been reckoned the best in Europe. But the 'Beggar's Opera,' [1728.] that took the characteristically English form of a satire on the victorious Opera from overseas, produced a line of English popular operas, lasting into the Nineteenth Century. These operas with dialogue, of which Gilbert and Sullivan came in the end, were truly national work in a period of strong foreign influence.

Painting gained most and lost least by the close association of fashionable English society with the culture of the continent. Indeed the age of Reynolds and Gainsborough was the first notable efflorescence of a native pictorial art in the island. Its arrival to serve the 'great families' was a fortunate coincidence in time. The portraits of the native English aristocracy in their heyday of power, prestige and happiness, look down from those perfect canvases in Olympian calm, over the heads of the so differently featured art-patrons of to-day.

The improvement characteristic of the Eighteenth Century was more marked in manners and intelligence than in morals and the stricter virtues. Gambling raged among the wealthy even more than in our own time, and drinking deep was scarce thought a blemish. The best of the upper class aimed at the full and rational enjoyment of this life, rather than at preparation for the next, of which they spoke seldom and then with a cheerful scepticism.

The accession of the House of Hanover, followed by nearly fifty years of Whig rule, left the Anglican Church with all its exclusive civil and political privileges, but imposed on its spirit the moderating influence of latitudinarian appointments to Bishoprics and other benefices in the gift of government. The Jacobitish sympathies of the High Church party, and its desire to persecute Dissenters as revealed in the last years of Anne's reign, made latitudinarian appointments necessary to keep the peace and preserve the dynasty.

The intellectual strength of the Latitudinarian party and the rational and tolerant spirit of the new century rendered this policy on the part of Government successful. Until the French Revolution and the Evangelical movement raised new issues, the clergy of the Anglican Church ceased to be zealots, whether political or religious. Goldsmith's 'Vicar of Wakefield' teaches his flock, by precept and example, those simple virtues which the pious of all denominations are too prone to under-value unless they are joined to some form of religious 'enthusiasm.' For a while the parish clergy were content to inculcate morality with little stress on dogma, and none on emotionalism, sentimentality or party spirit. The 'reasonable' character of Christianity was emphasized, and the miracles recorded in the Bible were regarded as historic proofs of a system agreeable to the philosophy and common sense of all times. The Classical learning of the period between Bentley and Porson, of which the clergy had their full share, harmonized well with this comprehensive attitude. The great philosophical works of Bishops Berkeley and Butler defended Christianity by the appeal to reason. In the England of the Eighteenth Century the Church remained on terms with the scientific and latitudinarian spirit of the age. The English spirit of compromise was suited, and the more advanced 'deism,' though it began in England early in the century, flourished only in France and was not regarded as 'respectable' over here.

The clergy, while thus inspired—or uninspired—were in certain respects in closer touch with the great body of the laity than at any time before or after. Indeed, by modern standards, the parish priests of this era became too much identified with their flocks. They rendered frequent and useful service on the magisterial bench, for the most part in a pure spirit of good citizenship. The parson as Justice of the Peace had often more law, more humanity, and a less invincible hatred of poachers than the squire at his side. The black coat in the hunting-field was little criticized prior to the Evangelical movement.

In Stuart times there had been a certain proportion of men of gentle birth among the parish clergy, but under the Hanoverians the identity of the social class of squire and parson became more close. As the value of tithe rose, the squire found it proper to put his younger son into the family living and to enlarge the parsonage into a lesser manor-house by throwing out a bay-window or two. These family arrangements were part of the great business of making life pleasant for the upper class, in which the men of the Eighteenth Century were such adepts. But the system had also its uses for the community: for, if there was any merit in the Anglican ideal of having 'an educated gentleman in every parish,' this was how it came nearest to realization. Gilbert White [B. 1720, D. 1793.], a country clergyman, observing his birds, season after season, at Selborne, taught men to feel that

He prayeth well, who loveth well
Both man, and bird and beast.

Such a clergy and such a squirearchy together were able to put down popular superstitions like witch-hunting that had flourished horribly in Stuart days, particularly under the Puritans.

Thus the Established Church took an integral part in the civilizing work of the Eighteenth Century. The two leading defects of its qualities were its discouragement of all forms of zeal, and its neglect of the poor, especially in the great towns, the collieries and the industrial districts. The old parish divisions of England, no less than municipal government and Parliamentary representation, answered ill to the real distribution of population in a country that had been in constant economic change for two hundred years, and was now changing much more rapidly than ever before. Moreover, audiences as completely uneducated as were most of the English of that day, were not likely to be much impressed by arguments based on Butler's *Analogy* and by the sweet reasonableness of a learned religion.

The Dissenting bodies of the Bunyan tradition, which

had been founded in the heat and zeal of the Cromwellian era and had survived the period of persecution under Charles II, still served the needs of the poor in some districts, but even they were becoming more 'respectable,' less 'enthusiastic' and more bourgeois. The Presbyterian body had largely become Unitarian. The Quakers, ceasing to be popular revivalists, became spiritually 'quiet' and economically prosperous.

These wide gaps in the social field left by the existing religious bodies, were filled by the full flood of John Wesley's uncompromising ardour for the salvation of souls. [B. 1703, D. 1791.] One of the greatest missionaries and the greatest religious organizers of all history, Wesley chanced to be contemporary with one of the greatest of popular orators, George Whitefield, who may be regarded either as his supporter or as his rival. [B. 1714, D. 1770.]

The zeal of these first 'methodists' was opposed in every respect to the characteristic faults and merits of the Eighteenth Century attitude of mind. For this reason their separation from the Established Church of the day was, perhaps, unavoidable, although Wesley to the last regarded himself as her faithful son. But the corner-stone of religion as he preached it was neither 'reason' nor sacramentalism, but the doctrine he had borrowed from the Moravians that conversion comes as a sudden personal assurance of salvation, bringing new birth and dominion over sin. This revivalist doctrine, in the mouths of Wesley and Whitefield, had enormous power. But the indecorous field-preaching to vast audiences, the convulsions, agonies and raptures of the converted were at least as odious to the 'respectable' classes, clerical and lay, as the early proceedings of the Salvation Army in the latter years of Queen Victoria. It was very natural that the Bishops and clergy should ostracize these Methodist proceedings, and since the Toleration Act only tolerated registered Dissenters, the Wesleyans had to choose whether they should register as Dissenters or cease to save souls. Their design to form a Church within the Church proved impossible in the circumstances of the age.

In this way it came about that the revival, after it had taken a permanent institutional form, swelled the numbers, not of the Establishment, but of the Dissenting bodies, very greatly to the future advantage of the Liberal Party in the Nineteenth Century. But early Wesleyanism, founded by a consistent Tory, was a conservative influence socially and to some extent politically. In the days of Jacobin and early Radical propaganda, Methodism proved a powerful counter-attraction among the poor. It directed into other channels the first rebellion of the uncared-for millions, for it gave them other interests and ideals besides the material, it fostered in them self-respect as citizens of another world whose franchise was not confined to the well-to-do, and it provided them with a democratic religious and educational organization of their own. But, as time went on, working-class religion became more often identified with working-class politics, and the local preacher was often a Radical agitator as well.

It was only at the very close of the Eighteenth Century that something of the spirit of Methodism began to react upon the Established Church and upon the upper classes themselves. The greater seriousness induced in those quarters by the prospect of the French Revolution, helped this change of temper. But though Evangelicalism then gained a formidable party among the Church clergy, its strength lay among the Church laity, in Wilberforce and the anti-slavery 'saints,' in Shaftesbury and the philanthropists of the new century, and in many conquerors and rulers of India and the Empire.

In the days of George II, the Wesleyan movement was carried by its founders to the American Colonies, and in the future United States it became a force of great potency and numerical strength. In Wales, Methodism swelled to full tide a national revival springing from a native Evangelical movement. Only in Scotland it failed, because there the people already had a popularly governed Church of their own, and were well educated and deeply interested in a native system of theology.

But although Methodism, which leaped the Atlantic,

was stopped on the banks of the Tweed, the religious history of Scotland in the Eighteenth Century bears a close family likeness to that of England. The middle years of the century saw the victory of a latitudinarian movement known as Moderatism, rebelling against the harsh and bigoted rigour of the older Presbyterian dogmatists. The historian Dr. William Robertson, [B. 1721, D. 1793.] Principal of Edinburgh University, is the chief figure of the movement. Even 'deistic' philosophers like David Hume [B. 1711, D. 1776.] were at least tolerated in the land, and Adam Smith [B. 1723, D. 1790.], as Professor at Glasgow University, helped to give Scotland a new intellectual preeminence. The rapidly increasing wealth of town and country speeded the mental liberation and growth of the society that produced Robert Burns and Sir Walter Scott.[3]

But the common people in many a rural parish never liked these modern sermons with their 'cauld clatter of morality' instead of the old zeal and dogma. The Moderates depended dangerously on the revival of 'patronage,' by means of which individual patrons appointed ministers without regard to the wishes of the congregation—a system unchallenged in England but irregular and unpopular in the Scottish Church. In the early Nineteenth Century a great Evangelical revival in the Presbyterian body was destined to lead to renewed religious ardour and eventually to the 'Disruption' of the Church under Chalmers on the question of patronage. [1843.] But by that time Moderatism had done its work in Scotland in destroying the spirit of intolerance and enlarging the intellectual outlook of the whole community.

The slumbers of the English Universities in the Eighteenth Century were more scandalous than the lighter and more broken slumbers of the Church. There were practically no

[3] There are two fascinating books on the great changes in Scotland in this period—H. G. Graham's *Social Life in Scotland in the 18th Century,* and Galt's *Annals of the Parish.*

examinations held at Oxford, and few at Cambridge.[4] Our own over-examined generation may think that deficiency a blessing, but the poor quality and quantity of the teaching were deplorable, taken in conjunction with the low output of valuable works of learning by communities so rich in leisure.

There were still only the two Universities to serve all England and Wales, and they had shrunk to something like half the number of students as compared to early Stuart times. In 1750 Oxford matriculated 190 and Cambridge 127 freshmen. Many of these were noblemen and gentlemen not intent on serious study; others were poor scholars, either seeking to enter the Church, or at Cambridge with its North-country connection to pursue the study of mathematics after the Newtonian traditions of the place.

In the midst of a generation full of intellectual vigour and specially devoted to antiquarianism and science, the decadence of the Universities may seem very strange. It is to be explained in part by the exclusion of Dissenters; in part by the legal reservation of University and college posts, with a few exceptions, to the clergy, in a time of great scholarly enthusiasm among laymen. Another evil was the assumption of almost all the prestige and functions of the University by the individual Colleges, at a time when each College was inspired less by academic ideals than by the spirit of a relaxed monasticism. There was no fear of investigation or reform in that era of security for all corporate institutions. Warned by the outcome of James II's conflict with Magdalen, the Whig governments did not even attack the notorious Jacobitism of Oxford, or the not less notorious

[4] Lord Eldon, then plain John Scott, graduated at Oxford in 1770; he used to relate that he was asked only two questions by way of examination for his degree—'What is the Hebrew for the place of a skull?' and 'Who founded University College?' By replying 'Golgotha' and 'King Alfred' he satisfied the examiners in Hebrew and History. At Cambridge the better men stood the test of the very serious Mathematical Tripos, still partly conducted by *viva voce* disputations. But there was no examination in Classics.

Jacobitism of certain Cambridge Colleges. *A fortiori* there was no fear of a demand for scholastic reform.

In the school world, there was both loss and gain in Eighteenth Century England. On the one hand many of the old endowed schools became inefficient and corrupt. On the other hand Dissenting Academies and various private schools taking in scholars for fees provided a good modern education fairly cheap. And as regards the poor, the movement for founding Charity Schools which began in Queen Anne's reign, followed by the Sunday School movement about 1780, was the first systematic attempt to give primary education to the working classes as such, as distinct from the selected clever boys to whom the old Grammar Schools gave the opportunity to rise out of their class. (Miss M. G. Jones, *The Charity School Movement*, 1938—an important study in eighteenth century social history.)

But if the characteristic benefits of our modern systematized education were absent, so too were its defects. Neither upper nor middle class education moulded the individual after a stereotyped pattern. The old-fashioned Grammar School for farmers' sons at Hawkshead would not have borne modern inspection, but it allowed the shy and tender plant of Wordsworth's genius to grow naturally and in its own queer way, as would not have happened if the boy's every hour had been mapped out for organized athletics and instruction.[5] Very different from Hawkshead were the 'public schools' of the aristocracy; they suffered from indiscipline and bullying, but their very want of organization encouraged individual eccentricity and power. The product of genius per head of population in Eighteenth Century England seems, by comparison with our own day, to have been in inverse proportion to the amount of education supplied.

The discipline of the home, though milder than in former ages, was still very strict for the child; parents and schoolmasters still believed fanatically in the virtues of the rod.

[5] See his *Prelude*, Books I.—II., for an Eighteenth Century Grammar School at its best.

To some extent the want of facilities for secondary education was made good for young people by the apprentice system. Apprenticeship was not as universal as it had been in Tudor and Stuart times, but it was still very general, affording domestic discipline and thorough training in a craft to a large number of youths, during that critical after-school age for which so little provision is made in our day.

Here again there was no inspection of domestic conditions of service. The evil-minded and avaricious master could misuse his apprentice with little fear of anything beyond a bad reputation among his neighbours. Pauper children, apprenticed to the lower type of master or mistress, perished as miserably as the same class of child in the worst factories of a later generation. So far from originating cruelty to children, the factory system called attention to the evil by concentrating it where all could see, and so stimulated indignation that brought it to an end. The fate of the unfriended child under the old apprentice system may be read in Crabbe's story of Peter Grimes, and in authentic records of the doing to death of apprentices by Mrs. Brownrigg and others, which fully justify the poet's harrowing tale.[6]

On the other hand an even more common type was the 'jolly apprentice,' *alias* the 'industrious apprentice,' living with his master as one of the family, and hoping to marry his daughter and succeed him. And the paid journeyman was also part of the manufacturing tradesman's 'family.' Industry was to a large extent based upon these arrangements, humanly so admirable, before the coming of the factory system segregated the classes.

These domestic industries were not all collected in towns

[6] 'Peter had heard there were in London then,— / Still have they being!—workhouse-clearing men, / Who, undisturbed by feelings just or kind, / Would parish-boys to needy tradesmen bind; / They in their want a trifling sum would take / And toiling slaves of piteous orphans make.' (*The Borough*, xxii.)

Grimes kills one apprentice after another. See also Mrs. George's *London in the Eighteenth Century*, pp. 231–33.

or industrial districts, but were many of them seated in villages, amid all the amenities and traditions of old rural life. Not only did the village manufacture largely for its own needs, but the national and international markets were supplied to a considerable extent from rural England. Besides the 'spinsters' and the weavers of cloth both coarse and fine, a great variety of the most elaborate arts and crafts, such for instance as clock-making, were carried on in small country places. Iron and wooden implements and vessels of all sorts were produced by the blacksmith, wheelwright and carpenter, and many villages were still quite able to build their own houses. The 'village shop' dealing in every variety of article was not yet common, for that system implies the regular supply of village needs from the town. The pedlars walking their rounds normally sufficed for that.

This was the last era in our island history when the village was the normal unit of society. Under the first two Georges, most men and women, including many not engaged in any form of agriculture, were in the full sense of the word 'villagers.' They were interested, not in the political, athletic and scandalous chronicle of the world at large, of which they heard seldom and little from the news-sheets of the day, nor in the life of town, factory or trade-union, but simply in the daily human drama of their own village set amid its surrounding fields and woods, with its traditions, its ghost stories, its neighbourliness, its feuds, and its shrewd, ignorant rustic comment on the mysterious world beyond. From that frugal but digestible dish of ideas our ancestors still drew the food for their thoughts on the eve of the Industrial Revolution. What they knew of sport was what they saw and took part in for themselves at the covert side, or on the village green, or on the squire's new cricket ground.

The early Georgian village represented, on the whole, a healthy economic and social order, but with the defect that the power of the great landowners was on the increase, instead of yielding to a more diffused system of landownership and a larger measure of village autonomy.

Even in the reigns of the first two Georges, the small yeomen freeholders[7] and the small squires were declining in numbers. The great period of the yeomen freeholders and of small, compact estates was the Tudor and Stuart epoch. In Anne's reign the acquisitive tendency of the large landowners was becoming more than ever marked. The squires were jealous of the small freeholders as being politically and socially independent of their sway. The rage for game-preserving characteristic of the epoch made them look askance at a fellow without a coat-of-arms who had the impudence to shoot partridges on his own patch of ground. Indeed, the squirearchical Parliaments of the later Stuarts had most tyrannically passed game laws which excluded all freeholders of under a hundred pounds a year from killing game even on their own land.[8]

To buy out the small freeholder was an even more satisfactory way of disposing of him. For his part, he often thought he might do better in the modern world than by staying on his farm. All through the Eighteenth Century yeoman families were drifting to the towns, often to become the founders of the great business firms of Modern England. Often, too, they became large tenant farmers, gaining more perhaps in wealth and importance than they lost in independence.

The movements of humanism and rationalism were for a long period more observable in the educated classes than among the lower orders. The underworld of the times of Gay and Hogarth, when Wesley and Whitefield first took

[7] The word 'yoeman,' used in Tudor and Stuart times to include tenant farmers as well as freeholders, was used by Arthur Young for freeholders only, and came to have that narrower sense in the Nineteenth Century. But many Eighteenth Century writers, including Adam Smith, used it in the older and larger sense.

[8] Even the good Sir Roger de Coverley does not quite like the yeoman of a hundred pounds a year, 'just within the Game Act, and qualified to kill an hare or a pheasant; he knocks down a dinner with his gun twice or thrice a week; and by that means lives much cheaper than those who have not so good an estate as himself.'

it in hand, was as barbarous as it was full of life and character. Long before the Industrial Revolution, governmental and social neglect were producing grave evils,—the uncared-for state of the poor in London and other rapidly growing cities; the want of provision for popular education south of the Scottish Border; the displacing of the Englishman's time-honoured diet of ale and beer by the cheap and deadly gin.[9]

To deal with the unsorted masses of humanity huddled together in the towns, there was no better police than the old watchman with his rattle, and police-magistrate Fielding's 'Bow Street runners,' fit but few. As late as 1780 the Lord George Gordon mob fairly set fire to London before the troops were called out. Mounted highwaymen beset the roads converging on the greatest capital in the world with a scandalous impunity, and were popularly regarded as the representatives of careless English valour and freedom:

Six highwaymen shall carry me
With good broadswords and sweet liberty;

such was the ballad-maker's idea of a noble funeral.

Since the Revolution, trials, whether political or criminal, were more fairly conducted, and the rules of scientific evidence were gradually beginning to be understood by lawyers for the first time in history. But the prisons, still farmed out to a base type of gaoler to make his profit out of the prisoners, were, in Wesley's opinion, worse than anything 'on this side hell,' and the innocent debtor often

[9] Gin was not seriously taxed till 1736. The yearly average of British spirits distilled rose from about half a million gallons in 1684 to nearly five and a half million in 1735. In the early Eighteenth Century, mortality and crime among the poor were increased by the new taste for gin. The retailers invited customers to come inside and get 'drunk for a penny and dead drunk for two-pence.' On the other hand tea, imported in great quantities by the East India Company, was beginning to rival alcohol as the drink of the people. As early as 1742 complaint was made that 'the meanest families, even of labouring people' in Scotland, 'made their morning meal of tea,' to the disuse of ale.

fared the worst of all. Hanging for innumerable minor crimes against property was on the increase; public flogging of men and women was not yet abolished. But with the last decades of the century the humanitarian movement under Howard and others had set about its task so long overdue. Humanitarianism was an Eighteenth Century product, whereas the evils it sought to remedy were, with the exception of gin, as old as civilized man.

Life under the first two Georges, though not in itself of the type we associate with the Industrial Revolution, moved under conditions that were bound to hasten that great change, if certain mechanical inventions should chance to be made. The peculiar laws and customs of Hanoverian England allowed an unusual freedom to the individual, and did little to discourage private initiative; religious toleration left Dissenting merchants in perfect liberty to devote their energies to money-making, while they were prevented from taking part in public life; foreign Protestant refugees, rich in trade secrets and industrial skill, were made free of the economic citizenship of the island; commerce and manufacture were impeded by relatively few restrictions of State, municipality or guild; a free trade area extended from John o' Groats to Land's End, in contrast to the innumerable customs barriers then dividing up Germany, Italy and the Kingdom of France; the lords and squires who ruled the land were, unlike the French and German *noblesse,* in close personal relations with the mercantile and industrial magnates, and were often barely distinguishable from them;[10] science in the land of New-

[10] It was the Duke of Bridgewater who was called 'the father of Inland Navigation,' and 'the first Manchester man.' And are we, for instance, to count a man like Sir Walter Blackett, who died in 1777, as a squire or as a merchant and capitalist? He was the greatest man in Newcastle and on Tyneside, but he also developed a large agricultural estate in the heart of rural Northumberland, with all the appurtenances of a country house, grouse-shooting, tree-planting, etc. A law passed by the Tory Parliament of 1711, and not repealed by the Walpole Whigs, had closed

ton was honoured and exploited by the more enterprising merchants and their aristocratic patrons, on the look-out for a good thing to improve mining operations or manufacture; capital had been accumulated as never before in the world's history, and the English moneyed men, accustomed to invest it in commerce on the grand scale, would readily apply it to industry on a scale equally profuse, if once new inventions gave capital a fresh opening there; the markets for English goods already existing in America, Europe and the Orient could be indefinitely developed by our merchant service, to dispose of any increase in the quantity of goods manufactured at home. In all these ways the England of that era was the predestined cradle of the Industrial Revolution.

An iron industry of immemorial antiquity was still dependent for fuel on the rapidly diminishing forests of the Sussex Weald, the Midlands and the Severn Valley; any day the shortage of timber might suggest to ingenious minds a method of smelting iron with coal. Since the days of the Plantagenets, coal, then easily won near the surface, had been much used for domestic purposes, especially in London where it was known as 'sea-coal' after its voyage from Tyne to Thames mouth. Wheeled traffic for heavy goods was still exceptional. Where water-carriage was not available, the coal sacks were slung across the patient pack-horses, breasting the passes of the Welsh hills. In that primitive way the textiles of Yorkshire, Lancashire and the Cotswolds had still to travel when Walpole was Prime Minister. And when Josiah Wedgwood began his career as a master-potter in the year of the taking of Quebec [1759.], the clay and the finished crockery still entered and left the Five Towns on the back of the donkey or the horse.

Indeed, the one great remaining obstacle to the initia-

the House of Commons to all merchants, however wealthy, who were not also landowners. Whatever the intention of the Act, its effect was to compel merchants to become landed gentlemen also, rather than to exclude them from Parliament. Many landed estates in the Eighteenth Century, besides Sir Walter Blackett's, were improved and embellished with money made in industry or commerce.

tion of an Industrial Revolution was the badness of transport in old England. The making of canals only began with the reign of George III. Yet the roads in winter were often quagmires wherein loaded pack-horses sank to the girth, and waggons could not be moved at all. On portions of the main roads, indeed, toll-bars were being set up by private companies, with Parliamentary powers to tax the traffic and keep the surface in repair. But during the Seven Years' War most of the mileage, even on the main roads of England, was still free to those who could force their way through the mud. The heavy coaches lumbered along in the ruts in a very different style from that in which their light-timbered successors in the years following Waterloo scoured the same roads remade by Macadam. In 1754 the Flying Coach advertised that 'however incredible it may appear, this coach will actually (barring accidents) arrive in London in four days and a half after leaving Manchester.' It took a week to travel between York and London; and in the days of Porteous riots and the rising of 'forty-five,' Edinburgh had no regular service running from the British Capital whence Scotland was supposed to be governed.

Society on the eve of the Industrial Revolution had many features most attractive to us in the retrospect: a rural population attached to the land and its labours and recreations, to the village and its traditions; great variety and independence of type and character among men; individual training, skill and taste in arts and crafts as a normal part of the economic life of the people. But in judging what the Industrial Revolution did to our island, it is necessary to remember that a fuel famine due to the using up of our timber was already settling down on various parts of the island in the Eighteenth Century, until relief came through the distribution of coal by canals, and afterwards by railways. The fuel famine was already putting an end to our old iron industry and was on the point of lowering the standard of comfort in domestic life. A well-to-do tradesman in Launceston was reduced to paying threepence to a neighbour for use of his fire to cook a leg of mutton; and his poorer neighbours, like most of the South English peasantry outside coal or peat districts, lived on bread and cheese, and too seldom knew the joys of a fire. And apart from the question of fuel, it is safe to say that the population of Great Britain could not, without the great industrial and agricultural changes of George III's reign, have risen much above seven millions without a lowering of the standard of life to something nearer the level of contemporary Ireland.

CHAPTER TWO

George I and II. The Whig Oligarchy. The 1715 and the 1745. Social Consequences in Scotland. Walpole and the Elder Pitt. Great Britain in Peace and War. Annexation of Canada and Foundation of the Indian Empire

KINGS: George I, 1714–27; George II, 1727–60

During the reigns of George I and II, the policy of British Ministers at home and abroad was guided by the necessity to maintain the House of Hanover on the throne. This was held to involve the continuance in office of the Whig party, on condition that political power was enjoyed only by conformists to the Anglican worship, and that the Tory squires in the countryside were given no personal ground for discontent with the rule of their political rivals. The Tories, disaffected to the House of Hanover but unwilling to take an active part in restoring a Roman Catholic Stuart to the throne, were unable to join either side in the rebellions of 1715 and 1745, or to assert themselves in a united and effective manner at elections or on the floor of Parliament.

While in England the descendants of the old Cavaliers had become, for the most part, law-abiding and home-staying Tories, who occasionally drank the health of 'the King over the water' with a sigh and a shrug, in Scotland the Cavaliers had to a much greater extent become Jacobites, prepared to take up arms at a favourable opportunity. The habits of obedience to government and the dread of civil war were of much later growth in Scotland than in England. The Union of 1707 was still unpopular, and a Jacobite restoration might, it was hoped, mean a revival of Scottish independence. The Episcopalian Church, established and privileged south of the Tweed, could only hope to recover power in North Britain by the sword. Finally, the chiefs of the Highland tribes opposed to the hegemony of the tribe of Campbell, were longing to carry on that ancient feud after the old Highland fashion. For these reasons the rebellions of 1715 and 1745 were revolts of Scottish origin, which failed for want of English support.

In 1715 the English rising scarcely spread beyond the Roman Catholic section of the squires of Northumberland, under their leader the young Earl of Derwentwater and their Protestant stalking-horse Mr. Forster. Picking up some Scottish allies in the Borderland, they rode through Cumberland into Lancashire to rouse the Roman Catholics there. The little force surrendered to the royal troops in the streets of Preston, where Cromwell had cut off a more formidable Cavalier invasion coming south by the same route. The 'fifteen' in England was the last Pilgrimage of Grace, the dying effort of the old feudalism and Romanism of the Northern Counties which received the *coup de grâce* from the confiscations that followed the revolt. Wesleyanism and Industrialism were soon to make a new world between Trent and Tweed.

In Scotland the 'fifteen' was a more serious affair. The tribes opposed to the Campbells, joined with the Episcopalian congregations of the east coast, raised an army more formidable in numbers than the similar forces that followed Prince Charles Edward thirty years later. But the Whigs showed more energy and promptitude in defence of the throne upon this earlier occasion. A rising had been expected as a result of the accession of George I, and government was not taken by surprise as in 1745. John Campbell, the Duke of Argyle of the day, who commanded the royal forces in Scotland, was a better General than

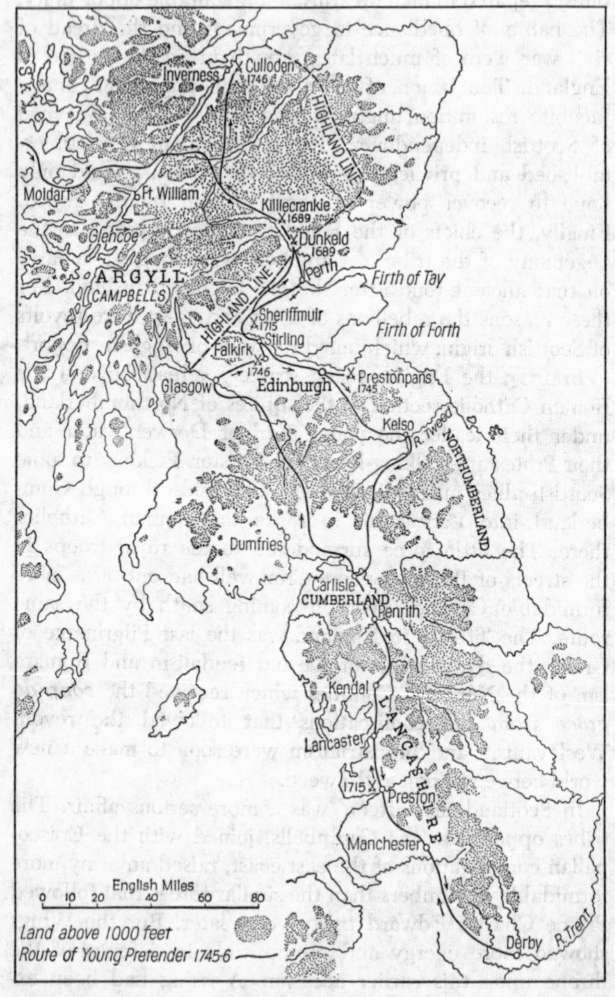

Map 1 Scotland and North England in the time of the Jacobites

poor Sir John Cope who lost Prestonpans. Argyle's influence, paramount in part of the Highlands and great throughout all the Lowlands, was ably exerted at this crisis. The Presbyterians south of the Forth followed their Whig clergy; and the burghs, with few exceptions, showed a warlike readiness in the Hanoverian cause, which was wanting in 1745, after thirty years of profound peace had relaxed the old fighting habits of the Lowlanders and disintegrated the militia of the towns. The Earl of Mar, who led the Scottish Jacobites in 1715, had no ability either as statesman or as General. The battle of Sheriffmuir [NOV. 1715.], where 3500 men under Argyle held up 8000 under Mar, though indecisive at the moment, had the effect of checking the advance of the revolt and so sealed its doom. Moreover, when James, 'the Old Pretender,' son of James II, came to Scotland too late in the affair, he had none of the gifts for rousing enthusiasm which distinguished his son Charles Edward in the 'forty-five.'

It was fortunate for the stability of the new order that this first effort of the Jacobites had taken place before the House of Hanover had had time to attain its full measure of unpopularity. George I, though not the worst, was perhaps the least generally attractive of monarchs. Unable to speak English, with blowsy foreign women for his mistresses, with a grim domestic tragedy in the German background, he made no appeal to the admiration or the fancy of his new subjects. He was, indeed, a great promoter of our constitutional liberties, because he knew and cared so little about things English that he left to his Ministers all questions of domestic policy and all patronage in Church and State. He insisted only that his Ministers must be Whigs, and fortunately had the good sense, after a little experience, to decide that Walpole was the Whig under whom the governance of England would prove least troublesome. For even under the first two Georges the King still shared with the House of Commons and with the Whig oligarchy in the selection of the chief Minister.

That Jacobitism failed to overthrow even such a King as

this, was due to the admirably obstinate refusal of the exiled Stuarts to pretend to be Protestants and play Charles II's game over again. Moreover, the danger to George I's throne was reduced by the value which the French Regent Orleans, in the early years of Louis XV, placed on England's friendship. Foreign menace to the dynasty came first from the unexpected quarter of Spain, long moribund but galvanized into a brief vitality by the rule of an Italian of genius, Cardinal Alberoni. That remarkable adventurer revived the Spanish fleet and army, and entered upon schemes, somewhat too ambitiously conceived, for restoring Spain to power in Italy and the Mediterranean, and the Stuart family to the throne of Britain. His ally against Hanover was that unquestionable Protestant, the wild warrior King, Charles XII of Sweden, who

> left the name, at which the world grew pale,
> To point a moral or adorn a tale.

Charles and his lifelong rival Peter the Great of Russia were agreed in nothing save hostility to the House of Hanover, and the warlike Swede was looked to as the head of the next Jacobite invasion. But his death before a petty fortress in Norway [1718.] followed close on the destruction of Alberoni's new Spanish fleet by the British off Cape Passaro in Sicily; together, these two events confirmed the throne of George I and the British naval dominion in the Mediterranean, based on Gibraltar and Minorca.[1]

The next danger to the Hanoverian settlement came from within. [1720.] A mania of speculation, known as 'the South Sea Bubble,' swept over all classes with peculiar

[1] The British Government had been so anxious for peace that it had suggested giving Gilbraltar to Alberoni as the price, which he had the folly to refuse. After Passaro, Captain Walton, who followed the flying enemy, reported progress to Admiral Sir George Byng, in a letter that ends with the often quoted words: 'We have taken and destroyed all the Spanish ships which were upon the coast, the number as per margin.' This concluding sentence was long mistakenly believed to have comprised the whole letter.

ease in that first era of stock-jobbing. The government itself was carried into the whirlpool. State interests and obligations were most foolishly embarked in the schemes of the South Sea directors. The King's German mistresses and the Prince of Wales were deeply involved in projects which in retrospect appeared deliberate plans to exploit the widow and the orphan. When the crash came, the outcry of the disillusioned and ruined filled the land. The Jacobites never had a better chance, but their momentary good fortune proved their permanent undoing, for the South Sea affair brought Sir Robert Walpole to power, and once he had grasped the helm of the tempest-tossed State, he never let go of it for twenty years. [1721–42.] At the height of the South Sea madness he had warned his colleagues and the public, and had prophesied the end. Therefore, in the hour of distress he was called upon to restore the national credit and confidence.

Hitherto the new century had been one of violent party and dynastic feuds. It was Walpole's long rule that gave to the Eighteenth Century in England that peculiar sense of domestic peace and stability which is often regarded as its chief characteristic. Rest after three generations of strife was Sir Robert's gift to Britain.

Apart from bitter factions arising from personal rivalry among the Whigs themselves in Parliament,—Pulteney, Carteret and Townshend against Walpole,—the real opposition to government was Jacobitism in the country. Fear of a dynastic counterrevolution acted as a constant check upon the actions of the Cabinet. It inspired Walpole's 'moderation' at home, and the peace policy which he adopted abroad, lest the land-tax pressing heavily on the squires in time of war should goad them to disloyalty. The same fear of Jacobitism led him to bow before the foolish storm raised against his Excise Bill, for the sake of which, as he wisely said, he was not prepared to govern by force of arms. [1733.] Great Parliamentarian though he was, he never valued his ascendancy in Parliament at more than it was actually worth, and always calculated the effect upon public opinion of everything that he did or decided to leave undone. With a very small army and no effective police, the British State might at this period have been defined as aristocracy tempered by rioting.

To reconcile the politically disinherited Tory squires to the House of Hanover, nothing was needed but the lapse of time without provocation or crises, and that Walpole procured. Apart from politics, the Eighteenth Century world, in its laws and social customs, was perfectly constructed to suit the squires and the Anglican clergy. The House of Hanover meant security for that world of established custom, whereas a Stuart restoration would mean putting out again on a sea of chance and trouble. By the time George III came to the throne [1760.] this had become apparent to all, and squires and clergy became once more the chief supporters of the throne. In the interim, unity of spirit had been taught to Englishmen of all classes and denominations by Walpole through peace and prosperity, by Pitt through war and glory. Both Walpole and 'the great Commoner' ruled the Empire from the floor of the House of Commons, and through the machinery of a Cabinet dominated by a Prime Minister.[2]

[1721–42.] To be governed by Walpole personally was no hardship to the Tory squires. A Norfolk landowner of old family and moderate wealth, who even when Prime Minister was said to open his gamekeeper's letters first of the batch, who hunted with his beagles in Richmond Park when he could not get home, who drank steadily and told the broadest of stories over the bottle, was clearly a good fellow at bottom, no Presbyterian, no City upstart, no haughty and exclusive nobleman. An entirely loyal Whig, Walpole ruled by alliance with the Whig Peers, the moneyed men and the Dissenters, but in his own person he represented the squires of England.

[2] The Prime Minister's famous residence in Downing Street dates from this period. George II presented it to Walpole, but he would only accept it as an official gift to be passed on to his successors. For Walpole's contribution to the growth of the Cabinet system and the office of Prime Minister, see pp. 17–19, above.

His royal masters found him equally to their mind. He could sit by the hour with George I, drinking punch and talking dog-Latin as their only available medium of conversation. George II, a man greatly superior to his father, was almost a model constitutional King in his dealings with Walpole. Unfaithful as he was to his paragon of a wife, Caroline of Anspach, he valued her far above any of his mistresses, and, greatly to the advantage of his subjects, took her advice on public affairs. She was Sir Robert's wisest counsellor and staunchest friend.

Walpole's mind and character were peculiarly adapted to the work of pacification at home and abroad. His genius lay in the arts of management, both in the good sense and the bad. No strain of idealism or romance tempted him to venturous or warlike policies. Good sense and kindliness were his dominant virtues; cynicism his fault. The good-natured smile on his broad face was half a sneer. He would never govern by bayonets or by any form of terror, but saw no harm in allowing power to rest on the obvious and traditional basis of Parliamentary corruption, instead of making appeal to the national pride and conscience. When the elder Pitt, in the following generation, [1757.] tried to rule solely on the strength of that nobler appeal, he fell at once, and had to make terms with the arch-corruptionist Newcastle before he was permitted to win the Seven Years' War for England. Walpole, from the first, took Parliament and the world as he found them. If he laughed at the 'patriotism' of the 'boys' in opposition and thought that most Honourable Members had their price, the facts of the time bore out the judgment. It was not through Walpole that moral regeneration was to come.

His love of peace abroad was genuine. It is not by idealists alone that the cause of peace has been upheld through the ages. Coarse and cynical though he was, Walpole had the humanity to keep England out of the war of the Polish Succession, in spite of the desire of his colleagues to revive the old Whig feud against the Bourbons. [1733–38.] 'Madam,' he said to Queen Caroline in 1734, 'there are fifty thousand men slain this year in Europe, and not one

Englishman.' Britain could safely stand aside from that aimless scuffle among the Powers of the continent, because the Marlborough wars had removed the danger of French hegemony. Our abstention enabled us to recruit our strength, which we would need ere long for more serious ends. Walpole took an active and successful part as 'honest broker' in bringing about the general pacification that at length ended the war.

Sir Robert's peace policy was brought to an end by a great movement of opinion in favour of maritime war with Spain. The movement, though neither well informed nor well directed in 1739, was the same ground-swell of democratic patriotism which twenty years later bore William Pitt to power, and overwhelmed the French in India and North America. Even in 1739 the popular instinct was right in looking across the ocean for its objective. It was no question of European boundaries that excited the mob, and only the King had the interests of Hanover at heart. Popular passion was aroused by the old claim of the English, dating from Hawkins and Drake, to trade freely with South America, and by the insistence of Spain in limiting that trade to the clauses of the *Asiento* Treaty.[3] The wrongs of Jenkins and his ear, said to have been torn off by irate Spanish custom-house officials, brewed such a popular storm that Walpole yielded and unwillingly drew the sword. In his hand it seemed a clumsy weapon.

As usually occurred when England went to war after a long peace, the operations of the united services were ill-conducted, and the attacks on Porto Bello, Carthagena and Cuba left the question of South American trade very much where it had been before. But warfare on the Spanish Main had its repercussions both in England in Europe. Walpole fell from power in 1742, as a result of an adverse vote in the House of Commons, though he still retained the favour of King and Lords; he would have done better to resign three years earlier, instead of attempting to wage a war which he did not believe could be conducted to any decisive or profitable close.

[3] See Vol. II., p. 295

The other consequence of the maritime war with Spain was continental war with France. The 'family compact' between the Bourbons ruling on the two sides of the Pyrenees, dismally prophesied by the Whigs as the sure consequence of the Treaty of Utrecht, had hitherto borne no practical fruit. But as a result of the War of Jenkins' Ear against Spain, Walpole's successors inevitably drifted into hostilities against France, when the War of Austrian Succession had again set Europe ablaze. The thirty years of peace with France came to an end. The breathing space had served England well, secured her free institutions and enhanced her prosperity and power. But other men and other measures were now needed to decide new issues, drawing to a head in America and India.

The quarrel of English and French colonists in the Ohio valley for the empire of the New World, and the quarrel of the English and French companies for supremacy in the Carnatic and the Delta of the Ganges, each arose from the nature of things as an irrepressible conflict between the communities on the spot. These issues were not the outcome of the intrigues or ambitions of European statesmen, but for their solution a man very different from Walpole was required at the head of affairs in England. It was fifteen years after Walpole's resignation before he was found in William Pitt; as Frederic the Great said, England was long in labour, till at last she brought forth a man.

Yet Walpole had been right in his warning that renewed hostilities with the French and Spanish Bourbons would mean the launching of another Jacobite attack on the dynasty, which his wisdom had so long staved off. The year of Fontenoy, a lost battle wherein our battalions of infantry distinguished themselves against the French in the Netherlands, was also the year of Prince Charles Edward's astonishing adventure in Britain. [1745.] He found an island almost denuded of troops, utterly unaccustomed to war or self-defence, and so selfishly indifferent to the issue between Stuart and Hanoverian that the inhabitants let 5000 Highlanders with targe and broadsword march from Edinburgh to Derby, gaped at but equally unassisted and unopposed. [SEE MAP 1.] The weak side of Walpole's regime of negations and management was shown by the low level of British public spirit in 1745, whether regarded from a Jacobite or Hanoverian standpoint. Such sloth compares strangely with the zeal and the sacrifices which William Pitt conjured out of these self-same Britons and their children a dozen years later.

Nothing but a fantasia of misrule could have resulted from a change of dynasty effected by Highland clans in defiance of Parliament and the laws, through the mere lethargy of the civilized world in defending its own institutions. Parliamentary government, deeply corrupted and not yet based on a wide franchise, could scarcely have survived the repeal of fundamental statutes by kilted swordsmen. The Stuarts, restored on these terms, must have attempted to secure their power by renewed persecution of the Dissenters, who would certainly have remained loyal to the House of Hanover; and the conquerors must needs have proscribed every statesman, churchman, soldier and sailor who was not prepared to swallow the loyalties of a life-time—for by 1745 a whole generation had grown up in the Hanoverian allegiance. England would perforce have been governed by Irish and Scottish adventurers who knew nothing of her needs, and by a Prince whose later life became as ignoble as his youth had been gallant and brave. We might soon have been engaged in a new cycle of civil wars, fatal to civilization and industry at home, and to commerce and empire overseas.

Precise speculations are indeed idle, but the consequences of a *coup d'état* by wild Highlanders in London must in any case have been both tragic and absurd. Britain was saved from them by her small but excellent army, summoned home in haste from fields of fame abroad. In face of these gathering hosts, the veterans of Dettingen and Fontenoy, it was impossible for Charles Edward, whose ranks had only been swelled by 300 Manchester men since he crossed the Border, to persuade his officers to march on from Derby to almost certain destruction. [FRIDAY, DEC. 6,

1745.] Yet the destruction towards which the Jacobites marched back into Scotland was more certain though less immediate. The advantage of surprise had been theirs, and once it was spent they had no resources in reserve.

Like Prestonpans at the beginning of the rebellion, Falkirk after the return from Derby was a victory for the Highlanders. But a few months later the last charge of the tribal swordsmen in Scottish history was broken on Culloden Moor by cannon loaded with grape-shot, and by the volleys of the long red line, three deep. [APRIL 16, 1746.] After the battle, the Duke of Cumberland stained a good military reputation and great public services, by cruelties against the Highland population, then approved by the scared and angry English, but ever since held in detestation. The facts have been exaggerated, but they are bad without exaggeration. The government had throughout shown a lethargy and an incompetence which were the main cause of the rebellion. Lord President Forbes alone had shown spirit and wisdom; if his advice had been taken earlier, there would have been no rising; if it had been taken at the end, the poor Highlanders who had only followed their chiefs would have been treated with clemency and justice.

In England the consequences of the 'forty-five' and its suppression were merely negative and merely political, involving the further decline of Jacobitism; but in Scotland the results were positive and deeply affected the institutions of the country. The Jacobite rising had been formidable, because of the power of chiefs, lords and gentlemen over their vassals. It was, therefore, an obvious measure of policy to do away with heritable jurisdictions in Highlands and Lowlands alike. The feudalism that had so long survived in Scotland was abolished, to give the central government greater security and power. But the abolition had also the effect of further liberating the democratic and equalitarian spirit of that peasant society into which Burns was born in 1759, where 'the man's the gowd for a' that.'

It was of even greater importance that Scotland was at last enabled, with the help of the English armies, to settle her Highland question. If civilization was to go forward in the north of the island, it was essential to put down the warlike organization of the tribes and the extra-legal allegiance to the chiefs. The King's writ must run in the glens. An Afghanistan could no longer be tolerated within fifty miles of the 'modern Athens.'[4]

This most necessary change was at last accomplished, but not in the best way. Lowland law was applied to Highland tenures and customs with harsh uniformity, and with all the customary ignorance of civilized man in his dealings with a primitive society of which he despises the appearance too much to study the reality. The chiefs became landlords, on terms very disadvantageous to their late tribal followers, transformed into tenants at will. Forgetful of ancient ties, they turned the crofters off their little farms on the hillsides and transformed the glens into sheep-runs; even before the American Revolution as many as 30,000 Highlanders are believed to have emigrated across the Atlantic.

Yet the land obtained peace, when the Highland Line ceased to have political meaning and became a geographical expression. The making of roads and the safety of travellers upon them, soon linked up all Scotland into one community. Devoted Presbyterian missionaries converted the Highlanders to the common stock of the nation's religious and educational ideas. One of the happiest and most characteristic policies of the elder Pitt was the raising of Highland regiments to fight for Scotland and the Empire in Canada and over the wide world. Modern Scotland, —the Scotland of Burns and Sir Walter Scott,—emerged as a result of these changes, and of the great economic progress that accompanied them. There was evolved a united people, proud of itself and of its whole history; proud alike of Celt and Saxon, of Covenanter and Jacobite; with a national hagiology extending from Wallace and Bruce,

[4] Besides the well-known works of Scott and Stevenson, there is an excellent picture of old Highland society and intrigue between the '15 and the '45 in Mr. Neil Munro's novel *The New Road.*

through John Knox to Flora Macdonald, representing that singular blend in the national psychology of the dour and rational with the adventurous and romantic, of the passion for freedom with loyal devotion to a chief. Scotland became more prosperous in agriculture, industry and commerce than she had ever hoped to be in the sad days of Darien. Yet, for all her new material welfare, she remained full of reverence for the things of the mind and the spirit, sending out her well-schooled sons to develop and govern the British Empire in every clime. When the century of progress closed, Scotland was a good neighbour and friend to England, as she had never been before and has never ceased to be since.[5]

[1748–56.] The period of European peace dividing the War of Austrian Succession from the outbreak of the Seven Years' War, roughly corresponded in England to the rule of the Pelhams,–Henry Pelham and his brother the Duke of Newcastle, the greatest borough-monger England ever produced. They may be said to have reverted to the traditions of Walpole, in an age when those traditions were ceasing to be enough. Within the island, these years were the culminating moment of Eighteenth Century contentment and repose, for Jacobitism was no longer a danger, and politics had ceased to be enlivened by the epic contests between Walpole and his personal rivals. In the House of Commons, Pitt's restless and haughty spirit was subject to the calming influences of the time, and he was content to leave Ministers unscathed for awhile by the thunderbolts of his oratory. He was even content to act in the office of Paymaster of the Forces. But in India and North America warlike operations were taking place in time of nominal peace, that would soon cause slumbering Britain to awake.

Both in India and America the offensive was taken by the French. The dissolution of the Mogul Empire and the consequent independence of the Indian Princes of the Carnatic, had suggested to Dupleix the idea that the

[5] See p. 32, above, for the Church movements in Scotland at this period.

French Company, hopelessly inferior to the English in trade, should enter into military alliance with some of the native powers, raise Sepoy regiments under French officers, and extirpate the stations of the British East India Company at Madras and elsewhere. In Canada the French were carrying out a well-conceived plan of a line of military posts all the way from the mouth of the St. Lawrence to the Lakes, down the Ohio valley to the Mississippi, and thence to the mouth of the great river in the Mexican Gulf. [SEE MAP 8, VOL. TWO.] From this chain of river communications they intended to appropriate to France all America north and west of the Appalachian and Alleghany mountains.

In India the English Company was older and richer than the French, and more deeply rooted in native life. In North America the two million colonists on the English-speaking seaboard far outnumbered the French Canadians. The French, therefore, must depend for success on greater unity, more vigorous leadership, and ampler naval and military support from the home government. The Island of Mauritius, on the route from the Cape, was their naval base for the defeat of the English in India, and Louisburg in Cape Breton would serve the same purpose for their conquest of North America. [SEE MAP 5.] At first the energy of Dupleix carried all before him in the Carnatic, till Robert Clive left the counter for the field, and seized and defended Arcot. [1751.] Grim hand-to-hand fighting went on along all that coast in time of peace, gradually turning to the advantage of the English, whose resources on the spot were much greater than those of the French owing to their superiority as a trading community. When the Seven Years' War broke out the French power was already on the decline in India.

It was otherwise in North America, where the English Colonies, except Massachusetts, were unwilling to strike in defence of their own interests and seemed incapable of uniting in a common policy. Physical communications between the English settlements were difficult, and concerted action was prevented by the rivalries between Colony and Colony, between Assembly and Governor, and by the intense individualism of a raw new world that had never been under feudal or royal discipline.[6]

The French settlements, on the other hand, that had never known freedom from Church, State and seigneur, were united in loyal obedience to their government. And they were strung together like beads on the line of the St. Lawrence and Mississippi waterways. Fine royal regiments and leaders from France were there to aid and command them. Moreover, the French were in close contact with the Red Indian tribes, whom they treated well, but used without scruple or humanity against their European foes. In 1753 they drove the English traders out of the Ohio valley and erected Fort Duquesne to prevent their return. Two years later, General Braddock's expedition, sent out by Newcastle's government to re-establish English rights beyond the Alleghanies, was cut to pieces in an ambush of French and Red Indians. [1755.]

After the Seven Years' War began in form in 1756, success still shone upon the French efforts everywhere, except in India where the genius of Clive was already paramount. In face of the world-crisis, it became apparent that the Whig oligarchy was past its work. Its days were numbered, its mandate exhausted, its mission fulfilled. Jacobitism was dead, and the old Whig scheme of things was therefore, if for no other reason, moribund. It was out of touch with the new live forces in the nation which it had, in its better days, helped to nurse into life. It lived by corruption and 'management.' But Newcastle could not bribe the French armies out of Canada, or induce their Admirals to abandon the sea by giving Irish Bishoprics to their brothers.

But if the old Whig party was spiritually dead, the old Tory party no longer existed, and the new Tory party had not yet been born. The British were sheep without a shepherd, or rather the shepherds were playing cards while the wolf was in the fold. When William Pitt said 'I know that I can save this country and that no one else can,' he was speaking the modest truth. He alone was trusted by

[6] For the character of the English and French settlements in North America see Vol. II., pp. 225–232.

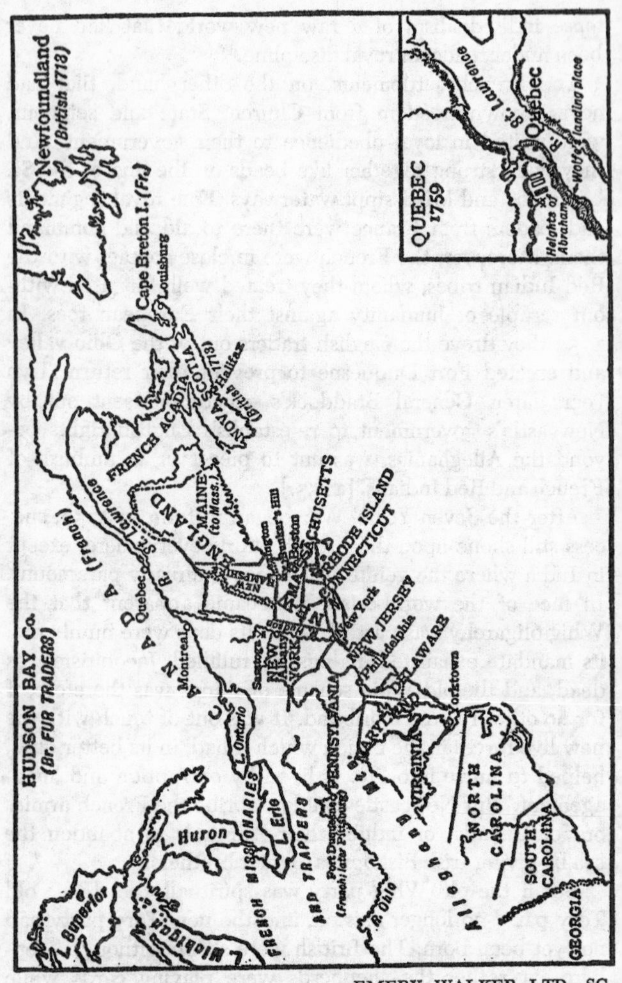

Map 2 French and English Colonies, 1755, see Map 8, Vol. one for Mississippi, etc.

the middle and labouring classes, as the one disinterested politician, who had, when Paymaster, refused to take the customary toll from the moneys that passed through his hands. He alone of British statesmen carried the map of the Empire in his head and in his heart. He alone understood the free and impatient spirit of the American colonials, and he alone knew how to evoke and use it for the common purpose. He had been the favourite grandson of a great Anglo-Indian. He was the personal friend of London merchants and aldermen. 'The Great Commoner,' as he was called, openly displayed contempt for the ruling Whig aristocracy, but revived the living part of the old Whig tradition that could still inspire the mass of his countrymen by whatever party name they called themselves—pride in the free Constitution secured by the Revolution of 1688; faith in Parliament because it represented, however imperfectly, the people; faith in the people as a whole, of all classes and all denominations; dread of the power of Roman Catholicism and despotism overseas, and the determination to prevent the ocean and North America from falling under the control of the Bourbons; faith in the future of the English race.

Such was Pitt's creed, to which the British people responded at his call. The House of Commons also was fain to respond, for Pitt's oratory wholly quelled and half inspired Honourable Members who had sold their souls to Newcastle for some mess of patronage. Pitt's manner was justly criticized as artificial, but it represented great realities of power and passion; he was ever an actor, but his voice and gesture dominated the auditory and the stage.

Besides his powers, never perhaps equalled as orator and leader of Parliament and nation, Pitt possessed in addition the qualities of a great minister of war. He was a master of world-strategy, an adept in the proper combination of Britain's fleets and armies, wherein her greatest war-strength has always lain; he chose the right men for command by land and sea, filled them with his spirit, and sent them on the right errands with adequate forces. As a war minister he surpassed Lincoln; as national leader in time of crisis the two men may be compared and their methods contrasted.

The world-wide conquests of 1758–60 cannot be set to the credit of the Whig oligarchy, though they can to some extent be regarded as the final triumph of the old Whig foreign policy. But the Whig oligarchy so mismanaged the early stages of the Seven Years' War, and brought the country into such danger, that Pitt was called in as the People's Tribune to save the country from defeat. By an arrangement that suited both parties, Parliamentary corruption and public patronage were left to Newcastle, and power to Pitt. [JUNE 1757.] His appeal was made to the popular elements latent in the British Constitution at home and more fully developed in Massachusetts. He evoked the spirit of freedom to save the Empire.

To glory we call you, as freemen, not slaves,
For who are so free as the sons of the waves?

So chants the naval war-song of the period. Truth to tell, the recruitment of the Navy by the press-gang was then the one strikingly unfree element in the relation of government to the citizen. Nevertheless, the song gives the spirit in which the Navy and the Empire won the decisive war against France on the high seas, in Canada and in the Ohio valley. That victory decided that free institutions instead of despotic institutions were to dominate North America.

Pitt's ally was Frederic the Great of Prussia. That two million peasants scarcely yet emerging from serfdom, together with a few score thousand Huguenot refugees, inhabiting certain sandy regions of North Germany, should have enabled their King to defy for seven years the onslaught of Austria, Russia and France, may seem a miracle. It was due not merely to Frederic's genius in war, but to his own and his rough old father's nursing and drilling of a docile people in time of peace. Frederic stood for the principle of a scientific, military autocracy, personally controlled by a self-sacrificing, laborious King, his people's stern but careful tutor. Against him were arrayed, with the blessing of the Pompadour, the self-indulgent eaters of the people's bread who presided over the decadent governments of this *ancien régime* upon the continent. Meanwhile Pitt demonstrated the power of British liberty in time of war. That Pitt and Frederic were allies against the world explains their success. The English people idealized, after their fashion, the alliance that had sprung up from the needs of the hour. They dilated warmly on the bond of common Protestantism, and saw in Frederic the Protestant champion defying the persecuting Catholicism of Austria and France.[7]

During the Seven Years' War, Frederic was engaged in defending against the three great military powers of Europe the Silesian province, which he had seized in the War of Austrian Succession in spite of his pledged word. The heroism of the defence covered the baseness of the original robbery. Yet even Frederic must have succumbed but for Pitt's subsidies and the British troops who helped to defend his Western flank against France, and in doing so won the victory of Minden. [1759.] To England, the collapse of Frederic would have meant a continent united against her. Pitt's policy was 'to conquer Canada in Germany' and he did it. Though he had formerly headed the popular outcry against Continental and Hanoverian entanglements, he now succeeded in making even the European part of the war popular. Innumerable public-house signboards were dedicated to 'The King of Prussia,' and to the gallant 'Marquis of Granby' who charged at the head of our squadrons on the battlefields of Germany.

The object for which Pitt fought upon the continent of Europe was nothing more than safety and the *status quo*; his real objectives lay overseas. The re-establishment of naval supremacy was essential to the warfare he meditated. In 1756 there had been serious fear of French invasion, and something approaching a panic in England. [1756.]

[7] In spite of the growing influence of Voltaire the judicial murder of the Protestant Calas took place in France as late as 1762. An interesting comparison might be made between the position at this time of Protestants in Austria and France and of Catholics in Ireland.

Minorca had been lost and the unsuccessful Admiral, John Byng, had been shot, to save Ministers from the popular indignation, in spite of the manly protests of Pitt. Under Pitt's government, naval supremacy was rapidly recovered in a series of vigorous actions, culminating in Hawke's great victory off Quiberon, the Trafalgar of the war. [1759.]

Canada, which then consisted of French settlements scattered along the banks of the St. Lawrence, could be best approached and conquered by land forces conveyed and covered by the fleet. The perfect co-operation of the two services led first to the capture of Louisburg, commanding the entry to the great river [1758.], and next year [1759.] to Wolfe's daring ascent of the Heights of Abraham from the river bank and capture of Quebec itself from the French royal army. [SEE MAP 2.] Wolfe and his magnanimous rival, Montcalm, were mortally wounded almost at the same moment in that memorable day, which decided the fate of Canada. Meanwhile in the Ohio valley, Scottish Highland regiments and American Colonials, working together as everyone seemed able to do under Pitt, had crossed the Alleghanies, driven out the French and renamed Fort Duquesne as Pittsburg. Before the end of the Seven Years' War, the French power had disappeared from North America. The unexplored West was the Great Commoner's present to the English-speaking race.

In the course of the war many French possessions in West Africa and in the West Indian archipelago were seized, and a great Empire was founded in the East. In India, indeed, another genius than Pitt's was at work in the field of war and government. The six to nine months' voyage round the Cape prevented our organizer of victory in Downing Street from planning campaigns for the Ganges as he planned them for the St. Lawrence. Indeed the battle of Plassey [1757.], leading to Clive's conquest of Bengal as the first extensive British-ruled territory in India, took place during the months when Pitt's great Ministry was painfully coming into existence.

[1760.] When George III succeeded his grandfather, the name of Britain was held, perhaps, in higher esteem by the nations of the world than ever before or since. Her free institutions, imperfect as we know them to have been, were regarded with envy by the European nations of that day. No 'anti-English' tradition had yet arisen: the Irish were quiet and forgotten; the American colonies were still united to the mother country and devoted to Pitt. England and 'the Great Commoner' were as much admired as they were feared by the French themselves, a generous and philosophic nation, at that time thoroughly out of love with their own despotic institutions which had brought them to such a pass. The English race was at the top of golden hours. It owed its position mainly to its own fortune and conduct over a long period of time, but latterly to one man who had raised it in three years from danger and disgrace. Yet in another twenty years our fortunes were destined again to fall low in either hemisphere. And in that decline the defects of the admired constitution and of the admired man would play no inconspicuous part.

BOOKS FOR FURTHER READING: Lecky's *England*, Vol. II.; John Morley, *Walpole*; F. S. Oliver, *The Endless Adventure* (3 vols.), a study of Walpole; Basil Williams, *Life of William Pitt, Earl of Chatham* (2 vols.); Macaulay's *Clive* and first Essay on *Chatham*; Grant Robertson, *England under the Hanoverians*; Hume Brown's and Andrew Lang's *Scotland*; P. E. Roberts, *India* (Vol. II. of Clarendon Press *Historical Geography of British Dependencies*); Egerton, *History of British Colonial Policy*; Parkman, *Montcalm and Wolfe*; Ramsay Muir, *History of the British Commonwealth*; Corbett, *England in the Seven Years' War* (2 vols.).

CHAPTER THREE

Personal Government of George III. The American Question. The Disruption of the First British Empire. Restoration of Government by Party and Cabinet. The New Whig and New Tory Parties. Burke, Fox and the Younger Pitt

KING: George III, 1760–1820

Before George III came to the throne in 1760, the conflict between executive and legislative, which had hampered government in the Stuart era, had been laid completely to rest by the novel device of a responsible and united Cabinet, led by a Prime Minister, but dependent on a majority vote of the House of Commons, and with all the Cabinet Ministers seated in Parliament. This system went several steps further than the negative settlement of 1689 towards rendering free government practicable. It has since been adopted in the self-governing Dominions and in many countries of Europe, and stands as England's chief contribution to the science of political mechanism.

The system had served well in peace-time under Walpole, and in war under the elder Pitt. His son, as head of the revived Tory party [1783–1801.], was destined to stereotype this method of government, by which Britain has been ruled ever since his day. But between the great Ministry of the elder Pitt and that of his son, intervened twenty years when government by responsible Cabinet and Prime Minister was in confusion, if not in abeyance. [1761–82.] That break in the smooth development of our constitutional history was caused by the able attempt of George III to recover the powers of the Crown as they had been left by the Revolution Settlement of 1689, to make the Prime Minister a mere instrument of the royal will, and to reduce the Cabinet to a group of the 'King's servants' in fact as well as in name. All this he temporarily achieved, after fierce and complicated struggles in the 'sixties. He succeeded because he resumed into his royal hands the patronage of the State, wherewith he bribed the House of Commons himself, instead of leaving patronage and corruption as the perquisite of the Whigs.

Obviously George III would not so far have succeeded, if Cabinet government had then rested on democracy instead of on aristocracy, on opinion instead of on 'management.' The Parliamentary and Cabinet system of the mid-Eighteenth Century, excellent as machinery, lacked moral force and popular support. It is true that, when the Seven Years' War began so ill, the Whig oligarchy had bowed to the popular demand and allowed Pitt to become Prime Minister to meet the crisis. But there was no regular method of exerting popular pressure on the House of Commons, owing to the large proportion of 'nomination boroughs' where members were returned at the bidding of an individual. Nor had the elder Pitt any personal hold over the curious political machinery of the day. Though he had sat for Old Sarum, where sheep grazed over the mound that marked the ancient city, he was not a great borough-monger or a friend of borough-mongers. He despised, and in his haughty humour insulted the Whig oligarchs, and they feared and disliked him in return. 'Fewer words, my Lord, for your words have long lost all weight with me,' he said to Newcastle himself. It was, therefore, impossible, when the national danger had been averted by Pitt's victories, for the arrangement between him and the Whig lords to become the basis of a permanent system of government.

The other circumstance that gave George III his chance of restoring royal power through Parliamentary corruption, was the absence of a strong Tory party, capable of keeping both Crown and Whigs in check. The Parliamentary Cabinet system requires for its healthy functioning, two rival parties to criticize each other and to offer to the nation a choice between two alternative governments. Under William and Anne the Whigs and Tories, though often violent and factious, had performed that service well. But under the first two Georges there had been no real Tory opposition, owing to the ground being occupied by Jacobitism. But Jacobitism, moribund after the 'forty-five,' expired when the popular young Englishman, 'farmer George,' who 'gloried in the name of Briton,' succeeded his German grandfather. Former Jacobites and high Tories like Dr. Johnson willingly fixed their wandering and famished loyalty on so respectable a figure. The revival of a new Tory party, reconciled to the Revolution Settlement, was long overdue. But twenty years passed after the new reign had begun, before the resurrection was accomplished under the younger Pitt.

[1760–82.] In the interval, George III governed 'without party,' making the Cabinet a mere instrument of the royal will and Parliament the pensioner of the royal bounty. The 'King's friends' in the Commons were his hired mercenaries, at best his personal devotees–not proper Tory partisans. The result was by no means in accord with Bolingbroke's prophecies of the golden age, that was to follow the advent of a 'patriot King' independent of all political factions. That ideal had caught the imagination of George himself, of Chatham, and of many others weary of government by the Whig aristocrats. But as soon as the idea was put in practice, the land was filled, not with the benisons of a grateful people on a benevolent monarch, but with the noise of unseemly conflict between rulers and ruled. The characteristic episode of the period was the martyrdom and deification of the scandalous Wilkes, turned by government persecution into the champion of popular rights, against an encroaching executive and a House of Commons claiming to override the choice of the Middlesex electors as to the man who should represent them in Parliament. [1763–69.] Abroad, the prestige and admiration won by England in the Seven Years' War were thrown away, first by the methods which Bute used to secure the Peace of Paris in 1763, and later by the ill-conducted quarrel with our own Colonies. When the domestic crisis of the Empire came to a head, Britain was left face to face with a hostile Europe where she had many enemies and no single friend. [1775–82.]

That affairs went so ill at home and abroad during the first twenty years of the new reign, must not be ascribed wholly to the faults of the King and his enemies, the Whig aristocrats. Part of the blame must be shared by Pitt himself,—or the Earl of Chatham as he became in this unhappy period. Though without a regular Parliamentary following of his own, he held the balance between King and Whigs, because he represented in some degree the spirit of the nation for which the House of Commons so very inadequately spoke. But Chatham, though popular in his political sympathies, had a personal pride that was more than aristocratic. He could be a noble and liberal-minded autocrat, but he could never be a colleague. His faults of temper and understanding made him, who should have been the umpire and abater of the strife, further confound confusion. He could work neither with George nor with the Whigs, still less effect an arrangement between them.

[1766–69.] At one moment the government was again put into Chatham's hands, and he was called upon to form a Cabinet 'above party,' and to save the State once more, this time from its internal maladies. But at that moment his physical and mental powers gave way. The gout, which he had been fighting with heroic constancy ever since his Eton days, at last overcame the resistance of a lifetime. For months together he lay in a brooding melancholy, refusing to see his bewildered colleagues, fierce and unapproachable as a sick lion in its lair. His Ministry, which had no principle of cohesion save his leadership, staggered to ruin, carrying to limbo the last hopes of the country and the Empire.

By 1770 George III had triumphed over all his enemies —over the 'Whig connection,' and over Chatham whom he detested as he did all save the second-rate statesmen who were willing to serve him without a policy of their own. 'Trumpet of sedition' was his name for the man who had saved and enlarged the Empire that he himself failed to preserve. To criticize the royal policy was 'sedition' in the eyes of George III, who judged the merit of all statesmen by their attitude towards himself.[1] He was not likely to be more gracious in his dealings with the colonials of New England, where 'sedition' of a more serious nature than Chatham's was endemic in the soil, and where a problem of Imperial relations of the utmost nicety and danger was coming up for solution.

The disappearance of the French flag from the North American Continent as a result of the Seven Years' War, led to the disruption of the first British Empire. For it relieved the English colonists of the dangers which had made them look for protection to the mother country. At the same time the expenses of the late war and the heavy burden of debt and land-tax with which it had saddled Great Britain, suggested to her statesmen, in an evil hour, that the colonies might be made to contribute something towards the military expenses of the Imperial connection. An attempt to levy contributions towards the future upkeep of royal forces in America was first made through George Grenville's Stamp Duty on legal documents in the colonies. It was passed in 1765, but repealed next year by the Rockingham Whigs on account of the violent opposition which it had aroused beyond the Atlantic. In 1767 indirect taxation on tea and certain other articles was imposed on America by Charles Townshend. Chatham, the strongest English opponent of the policy of taxing the colonies, was then Prime Minister in name, but in actuality he was far removed from the political scene by gout and melancholia. Of these unpopular taxes the tea duty alone was maintained in a much modified form by George III's henchman Lord North in 1773, for the sake of principle only, as the profits were utterly negligible. Unfortunately, eight years of controversy on the taxation question had so worked

[1] In 1778 he complained that Chatham's public funeral in Westminster Abbey was 'an offensive measure to me personally'; it never occurred to him that his subjects remembered that the dead man had won the Seven Years' War, and were momentarily indifferent whether he died on good or bad terms with the King.

upon the average colonial mind, that the overthrow of that principle was regarded as worth almost any disturbance and sacrifice. 'No taxation without representation' was the cry, and every farmer and backwoodsman regarded himself as a Hampden, and North as a Strafford.

It was natural that the Americans should object to be taxed, however moderately and justly, by a Parliament where they were not even 'virtually' represented. They had always acknowledged an indefinite allegiance to the Crown, though Massachusetts had made very light of it at certain times in the Stuart era, and had even gone to war with France without consulting the Crown in 1643. But Americans had never admitted the supremacy of Parliament, in the sense of conceding that the two Houses sitting at Westminster could vote laws and taxes binding on the Colonies, each of which had its own Assembly. On that issue, as on most issues of constitutional law that have divided the men of our race at great historical crises, there was a good legal case pleadable on either side. But as a matter of political expediency it was most desirable that the colonists should be taxed for Imperial purposes by their own representatives rather than by the British Parliament.[2]

Unfortunately they made no move to tax themselves, partly from thrift and partly from indifference to the Imperial connection. When once the French danger had disappeared, the Empire seemed a far-off abstraction to the backwoodsman of the Alleghanies, like the League of Nations to the Middle West to-day. And even on the sea coast, where the Empire was better known, it was not always better loved: it was represented by Governors,

[2] On the issue in constitutional law, see *The American Revolution, A Constitutional Interpretation*, by C. H. McIlwain (Macmillan, 1923), and a criticism of it by Professor Pollard in *History*, October 1924, p. 250. The Americans, going on precedents prior to the Revolution of 1688, distinguished sharply between the Crown, whose authority they admitted within limits, and the Westminster Parliament, which they regarded as a local assembly. To the English, this distinction was impossible, because the 'Crown in Parliament' was for them the supreme authority.

Colonels and Captains of the British upper class, often as little suited to mix with a democratic society as oil with vinegar. Futhermore, the Empire was associated in the mind of the Americans with restrictions on their commerce and their industry, imposed for the benefit of jealous English merchants, or of West Indian sugar and tobacco planters who were then the favourite colonists of a mother country not yet disturbed about the ethics of slavery.

Chatham, or rather that more formidable person, William Pitt, had made the Imperial connection popular in America in time of war, and might have made it tolerable even in time of peace. But Chatham had ceased to influence the politics of the Empire, except as a Cassandra prophet warning George III in vain, and being called a 'trumpet of sedition' for his pains.

In theory,—or at least in the theory that was held in England,—the Empire was a single consolidated State. In practice it was a federation of self-governing communities, with the terms of federation undrawn and constantly in dispute. Such a situation was full of danger, the more so as the situation and the danger were alike unrecognized. The defunct Whig oligarchy can hardly be said to have had a colonial policy or any clear ideas about the future of the Empire. Pitt's great Ministry had come and gone. And now, to meet the pressing needs of Imperial finance, George III's Ministers had advanced partial and one-sided solutions that proved unacceptable, while the Americans refused to propose any solution at all. A way out could have been found by men of good will summoned to a round-table conference, at which Britain might have offered to give up the trade restrictions, and the Americans to make some contribution of their own to the military expenses incurred by the mother country on their behalf.

But such a conference was outside the range of ideas on either side the Atlantic. England was still in the grip of 'mercantile' and protectionist theories of the old type. She still regarded her colonies primarily as markets for her goods, and the trade of the colonials as permissible only so far as it seemed consistent with the economic interest of the mother country. As the historian of our British colonial policy has remarked, 'That the measures of 1765 and 1767 precipitated the crisis is obvious enough; but that the crisis must sooner or later have come, unless Great Britain altered her whole way of looking at the colonies, seems equally certain.'[3]

As to the hope that America might voluntarily contribute to the Imperial expenses, 'America' did not exist. The thirteen colonies were mutually jealous, provincial in thought, divided from one another by vast distances, great physical obstacles and marked social and economic distinctions. They had failed in 1754 at Albany to combine even for the purpose of fighting the French at dire need, and they were little likely to unite in time of peace for the purpose of negotiating with England on an Imperial question which they denied to be urgent.

And so things drifted on to the catastrophe. On one side was the unbending stubbornness of George III, who dictated policy to Lord North, that easy, good-natured man, so fatally unwilling to disoblige his sovereign. On the other side was the uncompromising zeal of the Radical party among the Americans led by Samuel Adams, to whom separation gradually began to appear as a good in itself.[4]

[3] Egerton, *The American Revolution*, p. 4. Adam Smith's *Wealth of Nations*, advancing Free Trade ideas, only appeared in 1776, the year of the American Declaration of Independence.

[4] The temper and programme of the party which overcame the American 'Tories' and effected the separation from Britain is best described as 'Radical' to English readers, whatever meaning that term may now bear in America. The Revolutionists were not 'Whigs' in the English sense of the word, for they savoured neither of aristocracy nor of moderation. They were not 'Liberals,' for they did not wish to allow liberty of speech or opinion to their opponents, whom they eventually expelled from the country. They were not 'Socialists,' for they had no designs of redistributing property, and were individualists in economic theory. They were democrats, with less than no reverence for any authority not derived directly from the people: they sought to enforce the will of the majority on the minority and to

The general causes rendering it difficult for English and Americans to understand one another were then numerous and profound: many of them have been removed by the passage of time, while on the other hand the difference of race is much greater to-day. English society was then still aristocratic, while American society was already democratic. Six or seven weeks of disagreeable ocean tossing divided London from Boston, so that personal intercourse was slight, and the stream of emigration from the mother country had run very dry ever since 1640. In England politics and good society were closed to Puritans, while Puritanism dominated New England and pushed its way thence into all the other colonies; it was Anglicanism that was unfashionable in Massachusetts. English society was old, elaborate and artificial, while American society was new, simple and raw. English society was based on great differences of wealth, while in America property was still divided with comparative equality, and every likely lad hoped some day to be as well-off as the leading man in the township. In England political opinion was mainly that of squires, while in America it was derived from farmers, water-side mobs, and frontiersmen of the forest.[5]

In two societies so widely set apart in the circumstances and atmosphere of every-day life, it required people with imaginative faculties like Burke, Chatham and Fox, to conceive what the issues looked like to ordinary men on the other side of the Atlantic. George III had strength of mind, diligence and business ability, but he had not imagination.

[1773.] After the famous outrage on the tea-chests in Boston harbour, the English Government, naturally and deeply provoked, made its fatal mistake. It hurried through Parliament Penal Acts against Massachusetts, closing the port of Boston, cancelling the charter of the colony, and ordering political trials of Americans to be conducted in

make the poor man count as much as the rich man in politics. They can, in fact, be best described, in English political terminology, as Radicals.

[5] For some previous remarks on American society and the influence of the frontier, see Vol. II., pp. 232–34.

England. These measures rallied the other colonies to Massachusetts [1774.] and ranked up behind the Radicals doubtful and conservative forces for whose support the English Government might still have played with success. The Penal Acts meant in fact war with the colonies. [SEE MAP 2.] They were defensible only as acts of war, and if adopted should have been accompanied by preparations to ensure armed victory. Yet in that very year the British Government reduced the number of seamen in the Navy, and took no serious steps to strengthen their forces in America. When the pot boiled over at last, and hostilities broke out of themselves at Lexington [APRIL 1775.], Burgoyne wrote thus from Boston:

> After a fatal procrastination, not only of vigorous measures but of preparations for such, we took a step as decisive as the passage of the Rubicon, and now find ourselves plunged at once in a most serious war without a single requisition, gunpowder excepted, for carrying it on.

During the twelve months preceding Lexington, while the British authorities, having defied New England to the arbitrament of force, contented themselves with the inactive occupation of Boston, the Radical party in the country outside had used the respite to organize revolutionary power and terrorize, or expel, its opponents. Indeed, ever since the original passage of the Stamp Act, the 'Sons of Liberty' had employed tarring-and-feathering and other local methods of making opinion unanimous. Even so, the Loyalists in most of the thirteen colonies remained a formidable body. Few, if any, had approved the measures by which the British Government had provoked the war, but they were not prepared to acquiesce in the dismemberment of the Empire, and for social and political reasons of their own they disliked the prospect of Radical rule. Their strength lay among the mercantile and professional men and the large landowners of the coast, and they were stronger in the Middle and Southern Colonies than in New England. Against them were arrayed the humbler folk in most sections, the small farmers and the frontiersmen of the West, organized under leaders of amazing audacity and zeal. The Loyalists were slower to move, more anxious for compromise than war, and they got little leadership either from their own ranks or from the British, who too often treated them very ill and drove them by ill-usage or neglect to join the rebel ranks.

Yet the Radicals would never have overcome the trained soldiers of George III and their own Loyalist fellow-subjects, had they not been led by a statesman of genius who was also a first-class soldier, organizer and disciplinarian. George Washington belonged by temper and antecedents rather to the Loyalist than the Radical classes. But, although he was first and foremost a gentleman of Virginia, he was also a frontiersman who had seen service against Indians and French beyond the Alleghanies, and who knew the soul of young America as it could only be known in the backwoods. Good Virginian as he was, he was no mere provincial, with feelings and experience limited to his own colony. He had a 'continental' mind, and foresaw the nation he created. Some well-informed vision of the astounding future of his country westwards, helped to decide George Washington to draw his sword for a cause which was bound, in the stress of war, to become the cause of American Independence. The American militiamen brought to the ranks qualities learnt in their hard struggle with nature, —woodcraft and marksmanship, endurance, energy and courage. But they grievously lacked discipline, save what the Puritan temper supplied to the individual, and what Washington imposed upon the army. His long struggle, as Commander-in-Chief in the field, with the exasperating ineptitude of the Continental Congress, was a war within the war. Fortunately for him, the British army, in spite of its fine fighting qualities, made mistake after mistake not only in the military but in the political strategy of the contest.

It was a civil war, not a war between two nations, though when the battle smoke at length subsided two nations were standing there erect. Because it was a civil war, and because its issue would decide among other things whether England should in future be ruled by the King acting through Parliament or by Parliament acting through the King, opinion was divided in England no less than in America. Once fighting began, the bulk of the British people supported their government, so long as there was any hope of reconquering the colonies. But they showed so little enthusiasm for the fratricidal contest that recruiting was very difficult, and the government largely employed German mercenaries whose conduct further incensed the colonists. Moreover in England there was always a strong minority, speaking with powers as diversified as those of Chatham, Burke and young Charles Fox, that denounced the whole policy of the war and called for concession to save the unity of the Empire before it was too late.

Military operations were as ill-conducted by the British as they had been rashly provoked. The troops, as Bunker's Hill showed [JUNE 1775.], were not inferior to the men of Blenheim and Minden. But the military mistakes of Generals Burgoyne and Howe were very serious, and they were rivalled by those of the government at home. Lord George Germain in England planned the Saratoga campaign as Pitt had planned the taking of Quebec, but with very different results. His plan gave the Americans the advantage of acting on the inner lines, for he sent Burgoyne to Canada to march down the Hudson and isolate New England, but without making sure that Howe moved up to meet him from the South. The result was that, while Howe lingered in Philadelphia, Burgoyne and his 5000 regulars were cut off in the wilderness beside the great river, and surrendered at Saratoga to the American minutemen. [OCT. 1777.]

After Saratoga the French despotism felt encouraged to come to the aid of liberty in the New World. This remarkable decision dismembered the British Empire, but it did not thereby achieve its object of restoring the House of Bourbon to world power. For it turned out that the idea of revolution, if once successful in America, could traverse the Atlantic with unexpected ease. And no less unexpectedly, from the broken eggshell of the old British Empire emerged two powers, each destined to rapid growth—a new British Empire that should still bestride the globe, still rule the seas and still hold up its head against the Powers of the continent; and a united American State that should spread from Atlantic to Pacific and number its citizens by scores of millions, in the place of thirteen little, mutually jealous colonies upon the Atlantic coast.

It was well that America was made. It was tragic that the making could only be effected by a war with Britain. The parting was perhaps inevitable at some date and in some form, but the parting in anger, and still more the memory of that moment's anger fondly cherished by America as the starting-point of her history, have had consequences that we rue to this day.

The War of American Independence ended as a war of Britain against half the world. The Bourbon 'family compact' of France and Spain fought her by sea and land as of old; the French ships under Suffren seriously endangered her communications with India; Russia, Prussia, Holland and the Scandinavian Powers united their diplomatic and naval forces in the 'armed neutrality of the North' to defend the rights of neutrals against the Mistress of the Seas. [1780.] In Ireland, for the first and last time in history, Protestants and Catholics united to overthrow the system by which their common interests were sacrificed to England.

In the hour of need, to which her fools had brought her, Britain was saved by her heroes. Among the statesmen, Carleton saved Canada, and Warren Hastings saved India; among fighting men, Eliott defended the Gibraltar Rock against the armaments of France and Spain, and Rodney's victory recovered the mastery of the seas from de Grasse. [1782.]

But the recovery of the thirteen colonies, already become the United States of America, was for ever impossible. Chatham died before he had given up hope, but three years later all King George's subjects acknowledged the fact. But nothing would bend the King's will save the positive refusal of his Ministers to proceed any longer with a task in which they had long lost faith and heart. They had even lost sure hold of their majority in a House of Commons paid to vote for them. As early as April 1780, the House had voted, by 233 against 215, in favour of Dunning's Resolution, 'that the influence of the Crown has increased, is increasing, and ought to be diminished.' It was significant that the county members who best represented any genuine body of electors, voted sixty for the Resolution and only eight against. After the surrender of Cornwallis to Washington at Yorktown [OCT. 1781.], the war in America was virtually at an end, and the news of Yorktown in England brought the system of personal government by the King to an end too.

The House of Commons accepted without a division a strongly worded motion against the continuance of the war in America. From the day of Lord North's resignation, in March 1782, Britain has never been governed save by a Prime Minister and Cabinet responsible not to the King alone but first and foremost to the independent judgment of the House of Commons. It was a matter of great importance that, owing to the catastrophe in America, the attempt to regain political power for the Crown came to an end when it did. If the personal government of George III and of his children after him had been protracted into the next century, the democratic and Reform movements of the new era, finding themselves opposed by the King as their chief source of conservative resistance, must have become anti-royalist and very probably Republican.

With the restoration of full Parliamentary government its necessary accompaniment, party government, was restored too. George III had set out to abolish party, according to Bolingbroke's prescription, but the net result of his activities, over and above the loss of America, was to bring into being a new Whig party and a new Tory party, and to arouse a democratic interest in politics which, though it failed for fifty years to carry Parliamentary Reform, served to put the life of public opinion into the Whig party led by Lord Rockingham, Burke and Fox, and into the Tory party created by the younger Pitt, and to fill the sails of Wilberforce's Anti-Slave-Trade Crusade.

[1782.] Immediately on the fall of North, the King's open enemies, the Rockingham Whigs, came into office for a few months. They were no longer the unregenerate Whig oligarchy of Newcastle, for, though still under aristocratic leadership, they appealed first and foremost to public opinion, and seriously intended to diminish Parliamentary corruption. Their long misfortunes had taught the Whigs many things, and they had sat at the feet of Edmund Burke. His deep, sagacious insight as a political philosopher was the more powerful and the less reliable because its vehicle was a magnificent oratory, and because his Irish temper, fiery almost to madness, prevented him from seeing more than one side of a case at any stage of his career, whether as Whig, as anti-Jacobin, or as Indian reformer. When his patron Lord Rockingham took office in 1782, his political creed was still in its earlier period of liberal emphasis. The short Ministry of the Rockingham Whigs that summer, left a deep impression for good on our public life, because it passed Burke's Economic Reform Bill, which greatly reduced the patronage of government in sinecures and places, and rendered it impossible for anyone ever again to bribe Parliament wholesale, as Walpole, Newcastle and George III had done. The Augean stables were half swept out.

When, on Rockingham's death, the Whigs quarrelled among themselves over the mysterious personality of Lord Shelburne, Fox outraged the nation's sense of decency by coalescing with Lord North, against whom he had for so many years been addressing his heated Philippics. On the fall of the Fox-North Ministry, which the King actively helped to bring about, young Pitt took the reins of power as the head of the revived Tory party. [1782–83.] He had strongly opposed the King's personal government and American policy, but he was ready to make an alliance on his own terms with the Crown. George, since he could no longer rule in person, greatly preferred Pitt to the Whigs.

[1783–93.] The first decade of Pitt's Ministry, before the French Revolutionary wars came to confuse the issues, was a Ministry of peace and reconstruction, no less wise and more active than that of Walpole. Pitt reconstituted the finances of the country, restored its prestige at home and abroad, began to rebuild a new British Empire on the ruins of the old, modernized and secured the governments of Canada and India.[6] After Walpole's example, he reconstituted the power of the Prime Minister in the State as the true governor of the land, not the mere instrument of the royal will. He finally fixed the British conception of the Cabinet, as a responsible and united body, dependent on an independent House of Commons. The work of his precursors in office, the Rockingham Whigs, in re-establishing the party system, was happily rounded off by Pitt. The Tory party, as revived under his leadership, was no longer a name for the 'King's friends,' but an independent Parliamentary connection, with rotten boroughs and election funds of its own, and with roots of affection in great classes of the community. Though its heart of hearts was still the squirearchy and the Church, its young leader earned the confidence of the mercantile community, as Charles Montagu and Walpole had earned it, but as no Tory chief had ever done before. Pitt unlike the Foxite Whigs understood political economy and finance, subjects little studied in Brooks's. As a boy at Pembroke, Cambridge, he had sat long hours reading Adam Smith's *Wealth of Nations* when it first appeared, and a few years later, under further instruction from Shelburne, he was putting the new doctrines into practice at the Treasury. Like his father he was at home among the aldermen in the Guildhall, and the City trusted and loved the son as it had trusted and loved the father.

Owing to the personal ascendancy of Pitt, the revived Tory party became for a while an instrument of progress. By doing things which the Whigs might well have done themselves, he drove Burke and Fox round in a dance of factious opposition to liberal measures. But it was in the nature of things that the leader of the party containing the

[6] On Canada and India, see pp. 121–28, below.

great conservative forces of the nation, should not be allowed to go indefinitely far down the path of change. When, answering to a strong movement in the country that had arisen out of the disasters of the American war, Pitt proposed a mild measure of Parliamentary Reform, his own followers would have none of it. [1785.] Burke had scotched the snake of Parliamentary corruption with his Economic Reform Bill, but neither he nor his Tory adversaries wished to kill it by reducing the number of rotten boroughs. The magnificent reptile had still a long and honoured life before it. For, with the French Revolution and the wars that followed, an end was put to all political changes in England for thirty years. They were terrible years though glorious, and we might never have survived them at all, had it not been for what Pitt had already done in the first decade of his Ministry.

[1793–1801.] As a War Minister at grips with Jacobinism and its fleets and armies, Pitt had to rely not only on the strength and confidence of workaday England, which he had himself rescued from prostration after the American war and nursed back to vigorous life, but he had also to rely on the political vested interests which he had attempted in vain to reform. And when a man, in defending his country from foreign conquest, has to rely on certain forces, he ceases to be capable of criticizing them. He becomes subdued to the material in which he works. Nor, perhaps, would the triumph of ultra-conservatism during the Napoleonic wars have done much permanent harm to the country, but for the reaction of those political habits of mind on the social and economic aspects of the Industrial Revolution proceeding all the time in our midst.

BOOKS FOR FURTHER READING: Egerton, *The American Revolution* (Oxford, 1923); Lecky, Ramsay Muir and Grant Robertson, as before; Basil Williams, *Chatham*, Vol. II.; Winstanley, *Chatham and the Whig Opposition*; Sir G. O. Trevelyan, *The American Revolution* and *Early Life of Fox*; Rosebery and Holland Rose for the younger *Pitt*.
AMERICAN WORKS: Channing, *History of the United States*; Van Tyne, *Causes of the War of Independence*; Truslow Adams, *Revolutionary New England*; Professor

Morison (Harvard and Oxford), *Sources and Documents illustrating the American Revolution, with Introduction*; L. B. Namier, *Structure of Politics at the Accession of George III*, and *England in the Age of the American Revolution*.

CHAPTER FOUR

The Tory Oligarchy and the Beginnings of the Democratic Movement. Tom Paine and the Anti-Jacobin Reaction. Burke, Fox, and the Whig Schism

After the defeat of George III's attempt to revive the power of the Crown, there had been a full restoration of aristocratic, Parliamentary government. Under the wise statesmanship of the younger Pitt, a Tory oligarchy became as firmly seated as the former Whig oligarchy of the Walpole-Newcastle era. Government depended once more, not on Court favour, but on the free judgment of the Houses of Parliament; reference to outside public opinion was secondary though not wholly neglected. Both Walpole and the younger Pitt, though supported by the Peers, were in the fullest sense House of Commons men; their power rested on the rotten borough system more than on the House of Lords. Indeed Pitt cheapened the prestige of the Peerage by lavish creations, particularly to reward owners of rotten boroughs for their support. The traffic in sinecures and pensions was still very brisk, although the means of corruption were more limited and less flagrant under the younger Pitt than under Newcastle or North, because of Burke's Economic Reform Bill.[1]

The old Whig and the new Tory oligarchies were much the same, in spite of the change of political label. The monopoly of power by the landowning class remained as before. The religious and political system with which the new Toryism was identified, was none other than the 'Hanoverian' scheme of things which had been saved by

[1] See p. 78, above.

the prudence of Walpole and the energy of Pitt's father. But there was a change, not indeed of aim, but of emphasis, because the constitution was challenged no longer by Jacobites but by Jacobins. The Whig oligarchs had defended the existing system against Stuart reaction supported by the French Bourbon despotism. The Tory oligarchs defended the same system against a new democratic movement at home and against armed French Revolution abroad. Burke's transition from Whig to Tory, in face of the changed situation, was, therefore, no more 'apostasy' than Fox's opposite choice to move the mass of the 'Whig connection' forward onto ground not wholly out of touch with the new democracy.

The Tory party, taught by Burke in his later anti-Jacobin mood, learnt to pride itself on being the true heir and protector of the English Revolution Settlement against the false lights of the French Revolution. Toryism stood for Parliamentary government against the 'direct action' of the Jacobins and against the popular autocracy of Napoleon. In making that stand it did the world a great political service, as became fully apparent after the long wars were over, when Canning's version of Toryism became synonymous for awhile with European liberty. But this Parliamentary constitutionalism of which the Tories were the champions was not, according to their own definition, either 'democratic' or 'representative' government. It was a 'mixed constitution,' mainly aristocratic, but with a popular element, and with scope left for occasional interference by the King.

At the same time the active revival of Roman Catholic claims to civil rights in England and Ireland completed the reconciliation of the Tories to the principles of 1689. In opposing the Catholic claims, George III and the great majority of his unenfranchised subjects were in hearty agreement with the rank and file of the Tory party. The appeal to Protestant fears ceased to be a Whig and became a Tory cry at election time. Royalist and popular sentiment, which it was an object of Toryism to unite, were happily reconciled on the basis of a double fear of the

French Revolutionists and of the Roman Catholics. The Wesleyan movement without and the Evangelical movement within the Church, strengthened the nation's hostility to 'the infidel philosophy of Tom Paine,' and to the 'Popery' of the Irish rebels. The fact that Jacobinism and Roman Catholicism were cutting each other's throats in Europe, did not prevent our insular conservatism from condemning and dreading them both, as fundamentally alien to the English spirit, and irreconcilable with our 'happy constitution in Church and State.' In Tory cartoons, any time between 1790 and 1830, 'Magna Carta,' the Bible, and the King's Crown on the top of those two sacred volumes, are pictured as the basis of our national 'liberties,' which the Foxite Whigs with their infidel and Popish allies were accused of desiring to destroy. This simple creed was deficient in its analysis of much that was going on in the world, it was exploited by selfish politicians and classes, and it wrought mischief in industrial England and in political Ireland; but it served to beat Napoleon, for it appealed strongly to English nature and tradition, it was rooted deeper in men's hearts than mere politics, and it held the middle classes loyal to the government through the long years of the war.

Since the revived Tory party had become enthusiastic for the House of Hanover and the Revolution Settlement, and since the Whigs had begun to demand civil rights for Roman Catholics, it may reasonably be asked along what line are we to trace the continuity of the two parties from the days of Titus Oates and Dr. Sacheverell to these very different times. The continuity was to be found mainly in the unbroken connection of the Tories with the Church interest and of the Whig aristocrats with the Non-conformist voters. Pitt in 1787 and again in 1789 opposed the abolition of the Test and Corporation Acts which debarred Protestant as well as Catholic Dissenters from civil office. Charles Fox, on the other hand, warmly espoused the cause of religious equality, and asserted the modern principle that 'religion is not a proper test for a political institution.'

The Dissenters, therefore, saw no chance of admission

to full civic rights except through the new Whig party under Fox, and through Parliamentary Reform. They believed that if once the rotten borough system were abolished, their electoral strength would compel Parliament to redress their grievances. For analogous reasons the clergy of the Established Church and their keenest supporters became determined opponents of Parliamentary Reform, which they feared might lead to disestablishment. The religious division on the great political issue of the new era continued to influence the course of politics until the Reform Bills of 1832, 1867 and 1884 laid the question to rest.

Just when English political parties were beginning thus to divide on the double issue of religious equality and Parliamentary Reform, came the great news from France. [1789–91.] France, not yet turned Jacobin, had replaced a despotism by a constitutional monarchy, and was framing a code of laws which put men of every creed on the same platform of civic rights. The attitude of English Churchmen and Dissenters towards the early stages of the French Revolution was naturally affected by the analogy of their own position at home. And the fortunes of Parliamentary Reform, hitherto a purely and indeed peculiarly English movement, became at once deeply implicated in the affairs of a country different in every social and political aspect from our own.

[1780–85.] The first agitation for Parliamentary Reform had arisen among the old-fashioned Yorkshire freeholders under the patronage of Whig landed gentry. It had no relation to the Industrial Revolution, or to any specifically modern conditions of society or of politics. It was not a movement to enfranchise the great towns or the new middle class. It proposed to abolish a few of the rotten boroughs and to increase the county representation. It advocated this mild measure of Parliamentary Reform, not on any theory of elevating the middle or the lower classes, or of enriching the poor, but simply to restore efficient government and to place the King and Parliament under some sort of control from public opinion. The agitation had been provoked by George III, and was intended to put an end to the personal rule which he exercised through the nominated and bribed majority of the Commons. It was as much a movement of occasion as of principle.

The wind was therefore taken out of its sails by the restoration of constitutional and efficient government under the younger Pitt. Burke's Economic Reform Bill of 1782, by reducing the power of corruption in Parliament, had acted in some measure as a substitute for electoral redistribution and reform. The rejection of Pitt's mild Reform Bill in 1785 marked the end of this first agitation, and Pitt himself soon became an anti-Reformer.

The second stage of the Reform agitation was the somewhat academic movement headed by the philosophic Dissenters, Price and Priestley. It aimed at religious equality through Parliamentary Reform, and adumbrated universal principles of democracy and the 'Rights of Man,' in general sympathy with the earlier and less extreme changes in France. As compared to the Reform agitation of the Yorkshire freeholders ten years before, the new movement was less uncompromisingly British; it scented of America, France and the brotherhood of mankind. The Tory upper classes were alarmed by its general and philosophic character which might carry it further than even the originators meant; Burke attacked Priestley and the French Revolution together in one of the greatest political pamphlets of all time; and the 'Church and King' mob of Birmingham, not discouraged by the local authorities, sacked the philosopher's house and burnt his scientific instruments. [1791.] Similar popular outrages in Manchester put an end to this movement for Reform led by the middle class philosophic Dissenters. The middle class as a whole had been indifferent and the working class had been adverse, at least in two great centres of working class life, which forty years later were prepared if necessary to fight for Grey's Reform Bill or for something yet more drastic.

The mob action at Birmingham and Manchester indicated that 'democratic' views would for another generation be those of a minority only, even among the poor. Nevertheless Tom Paine started the democratic movement proper among a section of the working classes, precisely at this critical moment. It is here first that we see a close connection between English politics and the new social conditions created by the Industrial Revolution. The drawing together of large numbers of workmen in factories and industrial districts throughout England and Scotland, created audiences and groups where Paine's doctrines could be disseminated and discussed; while the loss of independence and welfare suffered by many through economic changes, prompted the bewildered victims to look in sheer desperation to politics, in default of other remedy for their lot. Multitudes drifting up from the villages to the new manufacturing districts, heard there that Tom Paine declared all power to belong of right to the people, whereas in their own sharp personal experience it seemed to have been monopolized by capitalist employers, large farmers and landlord Justices of the Peace. Exploitation, resentment and mutual suspicion interrupted the harmony of classes which had so long been the mark of Eighteenth Century English life.

Perhaps it was all inevitable, but the extremism of Burke's *Thoughts on the French Revolution* and Paine's *Rights of Man* certainly did not make for mutual understanding. [1791–92.] These two works had enormous influence on two separate wings of the community for forty years to come. Burke's stately periods and profound though one-sided philosophy were eminently suited to convince and alarm the educated classes of that day, while Paine's crude and homely logic was like new wine to the unaccustomed brains of classes who had never yet thought about politics except as an occasion of riot and licence at election time. It is a pity that great thinkers can so seldom think of more than one side of a case. Burke and Paine stated in their most uncompromising form the Conservative and the Democratic position.

The Conservatism of that day, and of many a day to come, made no claim to be allied to Democracy. It stood for the 'balance of the constitution' between King, Lords and Commons on the basis of 1689. Pitt's Attorney-General

John Scott, afterwards Lord Eldon, demanded in 1794 the condemnation of the Radical shoemaker Thomas Hardy for High Treason, on the ground that he had advocated 'representative government, the direct opposite of the government which is established here.' That the light of Burke's wisdom should have served to darken yet further Eldon's obscurity is part of the irony of human fate.

Paine's *Rights of Man*, on the other hand, claimed that all hereditary government, whether by King or Lords, was 'an imposition on mankind,' that all power was derived from the people, and that government by a properly representative chamber should be at once established. Then, he prophesied, the pensions on the taxes granted to the rich would be diverted, and used, together with a graduated income-tax, to give education to the poor, old-age pensions and maternity benefit. These propositions,—some of them shrewd prophecies and valuable suggestions,—were prejudiced by his enormous folly in demanding the abolition of the Monarchy. Paine's easily excitable nature was full of the perfections of the new American constitution, mainly because it had no King and no House of Lords. His demand for the abolition of all the antiquarian 'lumber' of the British constitution deprived his propaganda of all chance of success, drove him into exile, and made the circulation of his writings a criminal offence,—though one that was very frequently committed.

For years to come, Paine's Republicanism stuck like a burr to everything liberal. It was in vain for Fox and Grey to repudiate him. When the war with the Jacobin Republic began, the last chance of people thinking reasonably on domestic politics disappeared. The man in the street, as he gazed through the latticed shop-windows at Gillray's cartoons, began to think of the aristocratic Whigs as people in red caps of liberty intent on beheading 'the good old King' and setting up a ragged republic of *sans-culottes*.

England was not at war with France until the beginning of 1793. The drama of 1792 was watched by the English as neuters, and the spectacle had reactions of permanent importance on opinion over here. The attempt of the European monarchs of the *ancien régime* to smother the French Revolution in blood, as proclaimed in the manifesto issued by their General, Brunswick; the desperate rising of the French people in reply; the unexpected victory of the new France in the Valmy campaign; [1792.] the simultaneous triumph in Paris of Jacobinism and Republicanism, massacre and the guillotine,—all these portentous events, which still attract the gaze of posterity, absorbed the attention of English politicians, recast our parties and determined the spirit of our government for forty years to come.

The Foxite Whigs in the fashionable purlieus of Brooks's, and the low-class Radicals of the Corresponding Society sympathized passionately with the French people against the German despotic invaders, whom Fox compared to the armies of Xerxes. In his warm-hearted, impulsive way, he wrote of the French, just before the news of the September massacres arrived, 'With all their faults and nonsense, I do interest myself for their success to the greatest degree.' Then came the first news of the massacres in the Paris prisons. 'I really consider,' he wrote, 'the horrors of that day and night as the most heart-breaking event that ever happened to those who, like me, are fundamentally and unalterably attached to the true cause. There is not, in my opinion, a shadow of excuse for this horrid massacre, not even the possibility of extenuating it in the smallest degree.'

But the sympathies of the great majority of the well-to-do classes had been all through on the side of Brunswick. And the September massacres and the regime of the guillotine aroused passions in our island akin to those aroused by the news of St. Bartholomew and the revocation of the Edict of Nantes. The democratic movement was effectively overpowered by public opinion that autumn and winter in every town and village in England. Loyalist Associations were formed all over the country, usually headed by Churchmen against their local enemies the Dissenting Reformers; these Associations organized opinion behind the government in the demand for the suppression of Reformers at home, and stern resistance, if necessary in arms, to French pretensions to 'liberate' Europe by the sword.

That same winter the French Republicans, intoxicated with the first draughts of victory and power, when they had expected the Prussian gallows, invaded Savoy, the Rhineland and the Austrian Netherlands, declared the Scheldt open to navigation all European Treaties notwithstanding, and prepared to invade Holland. [1792–93.] They offered armed assistance to all countries desirous of overthrowing their old governments. The pride and ambition of Louis XIV revived in the breasts of the men who were pulling down his statues, beheading his descendants and persecuting his religion. The occupation of the Rhine Delta by the Power with the greatest military and the second greatest naval force in Europe, challenged the English sense of self-preservation, as Philip of Spain and Louis and Kaiser William challenged it by like pretensions in the same quarter of the world. Resistance to the French hegemony in Europe, and particularly in the Netherlands, was pursued by Parliamentary England with a determination more steady than that of any of the despotic Courts, that had rashly provoked the Jacobin lion with their Brunswick blusterings and then run away.

The purpose of the old English nation not to allow the newborn French nation to annex the rotten States of Europe as her vassals, was nobly personified by Pitt, and was handed on by him to his followers, who in the days of Castlereagh won success at last for an effort sustained through the vicissitudes of twenty years. Unfortunately this determination was by circumstance identified with a policy of repression of Reform and of all discussion of Reform at home and with a hardness of heart towards the victims of the Industrial Revolution and to the poor generally, as potential 'Jacobins.'

By the same process of association of ideas, often so misleading to the political mind, moderatism in politics, the mildest proclivities to Reform, and sympathy with the victims either of economic oppression or of government persecution, usually went with a want of zeal for the war, and a slowness to acknowledge the intractable character of the nationalism and imperialism of the successive governments of the new France. Fox, Lord Holland, Sydney Smith, Romilly, Whitbread, Byron, and Cobbett in his Radical period, are striking examples of this law.

The Reformers, therefore, during the coming generation, laboured under a double stigma,—as lukewarm patriots in war time, and as supposed friends of Paine's republican doctrine, in spite of their protests to the contrary. This double unpopularity made it easy, as it also perhaps made it unnecessary, for Pitt to use the strong hand of power to prohibit all discussion of Parliamentary Reform outside the privileged walls of Parliament itself. In the first two years of the war, there were constant prosecutions of editors, Non-conformist preachers, and speculative persons of a propagandist disposition, who had ventured to argue for Parliamentary Reform, often indeed with unwise and provocative phraseology borrowed from France. [1793.] Muir and Palmer, tried before Braxfield, the Scottish Judge Jeffreys, were transported to Botany Bay by a most iniquitous sentence, which the ex-Reformer Pitt refused to mitigate. Sympathy with the fate of these two 'Reform martyrs' had its part in fostering the Radicalism for which Scotland became famous in the Nineteenth Century.

Finally, in 1794, the government was so far blinded by panic that it sought the lives of the Reformers. A charge of High Treason was instituted against Thomas Hardy the shoemaker, the founder of the Corresponding Society and the principal leader of the constitutional movement in politics among the working classes. Other innocuous and respectable persons, like Thelwall the lecturer and Horne Tooke the philologist, were tried on the same capital charge. But the good genius of England came to her rescue in her characteristic institution, the jury system. Pitt had outraged the English sense of fair play. Thanks to Erskine's persuasive eloquence, twelve Tory jurymen acquitted Hardy and his fellow prisoners on the capital charge, and reminded the government that the methods of Robespierre were not wanted over here. London, though strongly Anti-Jacobin, broke into loud rejoicings at the acquittal.

This timely check saved England from a reign of terror and perhaps ultimately from a retributive revolution. But the government proceeded, with more general approval, to silence further political discussion for many years to come. The Corresponding and other Societies were suppressed by Act of Parliament. *Habeas Corpus* was suspended and numbers of men against whom there was no evidence were kept in prison for years. Public meetings were prohibited that were not licenced by magistrates, and, in fact, none were any longer permitted. Except for the Anti-slave-trade movement, which also for a time declined, political life ceased in Britain. To make matters worse, the Foxite Whigs, in a mood of laziness and disgust, retired to their country houses in an aimless 'secession' from their duties in Parliament, where alone criticism of government was permitted. [1797–99.]

Pitt's Combination Acts were another manifestation of the repressive spirit of the times. These measures rendered Trade Unionism illegal, and punished all combinations of wage-earners. [1799–1800.] They were accompanied by no corresponding steps to enforce a fair wage, and simply put the employee into his master's hands. The policy represented not true *Laissez faire*, but State interference on the side of Capital against Labour. It was inspired not merely by a desire to keep down wages in accordance with the political economy of the day, but by Anti-Jacobin fears of all forms of combination by the 'labouring poor.' Two Whigs, Sheridan and Lord Holland, were the only important politicians who opposed the Acts in either House.

The new working class that the Industrial Revolution was bringing into existence and concentrating in the towns, had thus early shown an instinct towards self-education and self-help, along the parallel lines of political Associations and economic Trade Unionism. Pitt's government attempted to crush out both together, though with more success in the political field than in the economic.

When, after the war was over, the political life of the working classes and the Trade Union movement each made fresh headway in the era of Peterloo, they had to fight as outlaws for the right to exist. Then indeed popular opinion was being rapidly alienated from the Tory system, to which it had upon the whole adhered in the time of Pitt. But the habit of repression, begun by Pitt against a minority in time of war, had become custom of the country and was continued by Pitt's successors against the majority in time of peace. The partisanship of government against the poor and against those who attempted to plead their cause, however natural owing to the French Revolution and the French war, distorted and embittered the social processes of the Industrial Revolution and left marks which were never entirely healed in the remedial period that followed. It was in 1823 that the Combination Laws against Trade Unions were repealed, the first step in a great process of legislative evolution.

Between Anti-Jacobin Toryism and Painite Radicalism, the Parliamentary Whigs took up a half-way position, under the now middle-aged Charles Fox and his favourite young men, Lord Holland and Charles Grey. While repudiating the doctrines of Paine they continued, in the heat of the Anti-Jacobin reaction from 1793 to 1797, to move motions in Parliament for Reform based on abolition of the rotten boroughs. They were voted down by great majorities, who regarded them with horror as seditionists in sympathy with France; they were saved from worse consequences by the great respect felt by all Englishmen for the privileges of Parliament, and for the privileges of the well-connected and fashionable to be eccentric.

In these circumstances the quarrel of the Reforming Whigs with Burke and half the members of their own party was bitter and complete. But whereas the Whigs who followed Burke were merged among the other supporters of the Tory Ministry, the Whigs who followed Fox remained the nucleus of the party, and the keepers of its traditions. The continued opposition of the Foxites to Pitt and his Tory successors, prevented the whole machinery of Parliament from becoming a part of the Anti-Jacobin movement, and so left a bridge, however slender and insecure, still hanging across the gulf that divided classes in the new era. The adherence of the Whigs to Parliamentary Reform in days when it was impracticable, enabled them, when the wheel had come full circle, to avert civil war and social catastrophe by their Reform Bill of 1832.

Until that still distant era, the position of the Whigs was one of isolation, out of touch alike with the main stream of national enthusiasm for war against the French, yet equally far removed from sympathy with the lower class Radicalism of Tom Paine and of William Cobbett after him. Thirty years of unpopularity and exclusion from power failed to make an end of the Whigs. Their strong personal ties and party traditions held them together at gatherings in their large and pleasant country houses and at Brooks's Club. They were aristocrats, scholars and sportsmen, with much to make life delightful, in default of popularity or office. Their seats were safe, for they had a modest share of the rotten boroughs. They rather despised the Tory governors of the country as people less fashionable than themselves. They were so well-connected that they could afford to toy with democracy; they were so much in the mode that 'Jacobinism' seemed in them only a modish eccentricity. Their attachment to the person of Fox until his death in 1806, and to his memory afterwards, was one of the accidental circumstances which moulded the course of English politics. Fox was made to be loved by his friends. Where he was, there would the Whig party be. If he had gone over to Pitt and Anti-Jacobinism, there would never have been a Whig-Liberal party, and the process of British politics in the Nineteenth Century would very probably have been by armed revolution and reaction instead of by Parliamentary Reform.

When the youthful Pitt had first been called on by George III to govern the land, the Whig satirists had made merry over 'A Kingdom trusted to a schoolboy's care.' But Parliament and country soon found in Pitt not the schoolboy but a schoolmaster, austere, reserved, dignified, didactic. It was Fox who was the eternal schoolboy. Devoted to his friends; generous to his enemies but always up in arms against them for any reason or none; never out of scrapes; a lover of life and of mankind, he was born to be leader of opposition, and leader of opposition he was for almost all his long life in the House of Commons. Chatham was a greater orator, and his son perhaps a greater debater, than Fox, but for a union of oratorical and emotional with debating power, Fox has never been rivalled. His early extravagances as a gambler, his later extravagances as a politician, his coalition with North, his factious opposition to many of Pitt's best measures in the 'eighties,'–weigh heavy against him. But as advancing years and darkening public prospects sobered him, the fire of spirit of which he had wasted so much on faction, went more and more sincerely into the defence of the oppressed,–in England, Scotland and Ireland. But the cause of the Negro slave appealed to him most of all. Pitt, ever more preoccupied by the daily care of defending the British Empire and all Europe against Bonaparte, forgot all else, and would do nothing more to assist the Anti-slave-trade cause. But Wilberforce found in Fox an ever faithful ally. Owing to his zeal and to the chance that put the Whig chiefs in office, in a Coalition Ministry for a few months after Pitt's death, the slave trade was abolished in 1807 instead of many years later; that was Fox's bequest to the nation and to the world, made upon his death-bed.

The times were tragic, but the men England produced were great. With Pitt and Castlereagh, Nelson and Wellington to lead her through the most terrible ordeal she had ever till then endured, she had Fox and Wilberforce to keep her conscience alive even in time of war.

BOOKS FOR FURTHER READING: Rosebery and Holland Rose on *Pitt*; Edward Lascelles, *Life of Charles James Fox*, 1936; Russell, *Memorials of C. J. Fox* (4 vols.); Moncure Conway, *Life of Paine*; Coupland, *Wilberforce*; Veitch, *Genesis of Parliamentary Reform*; Morley, *Burke*; Graham Wallas, *Francis Place*.

CHAPTER FIVE

The Character of the French Revolutionary and Napoleonic Wars. Period of Pitt and Nelson, 1793–1805. Period of Wellington and Castlereagh, 1808–15. The Naval, Commercial and Military Struggle. The Final Settlement

Modern England has four times fought with success a great war to prevent the conquest of Europe by a single Power: the Spain of Philip and the Inquisition, the France of the Grand Monarch and the Jesuits, the France of the Jacobins and Napoleon, and the German military monarchy of our own day have each in turn been foiled. On each of these four occasions England had a double end in view,–the Balance of Power in Europe and the security of her own mercantile and colonial future beyond the ocean. And on each occasion European and maritime considerations alike required that England should prevent the Netherlands and the Rhine Delta from falling into the hands of the greatest military and naval State of the continent. It was no accidental coincidence, but danger to our shores and to our naval control of the Channel, that made the Netherlands the chief scene of English military interference on the continent, under Elizabeth, under William and Anne, and under George V. And for the same reason the wars conducted in the name of George III against Revolutionary France began with the defeat of our troops in the Netherlands in 1793–94, and ended with their victory in the same sector at Waterloo. But during the twenty years interval, the French hold on Belgium and Holland was strong enough to exclude our armies from that nerve-centre of contending interests, except for a few unsuccessful minor expeditions like those to Alkmaar and to Walcheren. [1799, 1809.]

The Napoleonic wars stand half-way between the Marlborough wars and the Great War of our own day, in time, in size and in character. The resemblance to the Marlborough wars is the most obvious, because the weapons employed by sea and land were very similar in the two periods, and the enemy was France. The geography and strategy, therefore, of the naval and military operations which quelled Napoleon resemble those which quelled Louis XIV. Again, in the days of Pitt and Castlereagh, as in the days of William and Marlborough, the two props of the alliance against France were British sea-power and British subsidies, applied along all the coasts and in half the Treasuries of Europe. The huge British sailing ships whose broadsides conquered at Trafalgar were of the same general character as those which had conquered at La Hogue, while the 'thin red line' and the British cavalry charge won Waterloo by tactics not so very different from those of Blenheim and Ramillies. Again a British General of genius, commanding a small but excellent British army, played a decisive part among the larger military establishments of the continent. Again British troops were landed in the Netherlands and in Spain, in Mediterranean islands and on American coasts. And again, in 1815 as in 1713, the war ended for England with the establishment in the Netherlands of a Power from which she had nothing to fear, and by great additions to her colonial Empire and her maritime prestige.

But the Napoleonic wars not only repeated the past but rehearsed the future. The issue of the campaigns against Louis had indeed been affected by the course of trade competition between England and France, but a hundred years later the commercial struggle was more formal and more decisive as a weapon of war. The British blockade of Napoleon's Europe, and his attempt to starve England by the Berlin and Milan Decrees, were warlike operations of the same general character as the British blockade of the Central Powers in our own day and the German submarine campaign; they disturbed the economy of the whole world and had serious consequences for the combatants in their relations with the United States and other would-be neutrals.

Furthermore there is a political element of a distinctively modern type in the wars that originated from the French

Revolution. The new regime in France, whatever its defects or crimes, filled the humblest French peasant and bourgeois with pride as a citizen and zeal as a patriot, opened military and civil careers to talent without distinction of birth, and, under the Consulate of Bonaparte, supplied the new nation with the administrative system of a wholly new type of efficiency. The other peoples of the continent were marched into the field as mercenaries or serfs, not as citizen soldiers. Britain alone could match the new spirit of France with a national patriotism of yet older date. But the Englishman's 'will to conquer' could be fully aroused only in defence of sea-power and commerce. After our expulsion from the Netherlands in 1794, it is true that we stayed in the war when others submitted to France, but we kept our armies out of Europe for a dozen years together, safe behind the shield of the Navy. We took no serious part, except naval and financial, in the wars of the two Coalitions that suffered defeat at Marengo and Austerlitz. Nor, until the Peninsular War in 1808, did we begin to fight on land as a principal, and even then with armies of not more than 30,000 British at a time.

Success only began to shine on the allies when the popular sense of nationhood was aroused in Spain, Russia and Germany, by indignation against French tyranny at length outweighing in Europe the sense of the benefits of French reform. Only in its last phase did the war become a contest between self-conscious nationalities, not altogether unlike those which fought the Great War of our own day. The horror and the slaughter increased in proportion as the peoples were aroused to fight willingly, to some extent on their own behalf and not merely as the obedient vassals of Emperors and Kings. The Moscow and Leipzig campaigns adumbrated the bloody future of nationalist Europe armed with the machinery of modern science and locomotion. [1812–13.]

During the greater part of twenty years of war, the immense superiority of the new French national spirit and organization over the lifeless and old-fashioned machinery

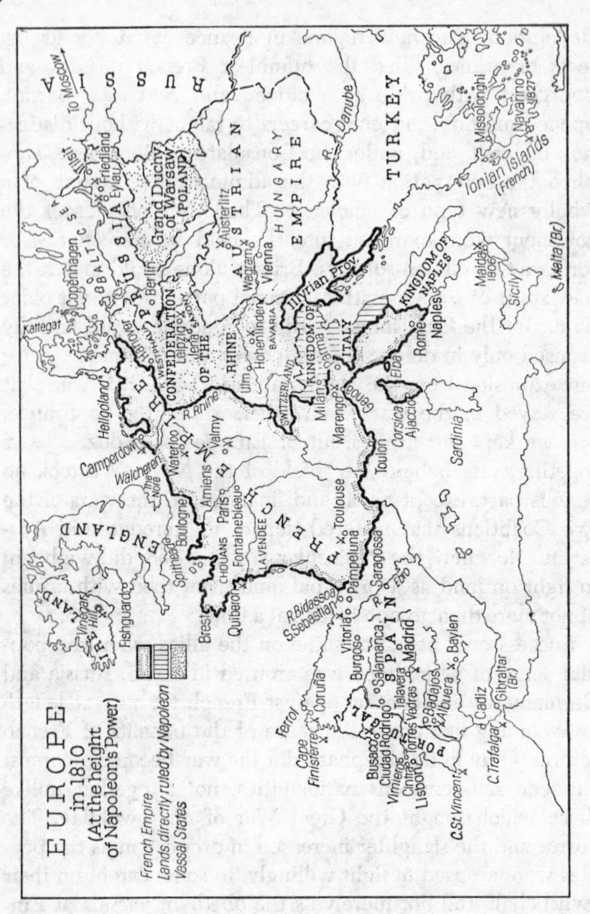

Map 3

of the continental States of the *ancien régime*, ensured the defeat of each successive Coalition that England encouraged and financed against France. [1793–1805.] Until the Peninsular War and the popular movements in Russia and Germany made possible the grand operations of Wellington and Castlereagh, England's effective action was limited to the sea. [1808–15.] It was much that she maintained her hold over all the waters of the world, when all the lands of Europe had passed into the orbit of French vassalage. Because the border of England's power reached to the enemy's coastline, she was able to refuse for years together to recognize the accomplished fact of the abrogation of Europe's independence. The double bent of the national purpose, successful naval enterprise and dogged resistance to French hegemony, were embodied in Nelson and in Pitt. The complete and hearty co-operation of the two men saved the British Empire.

Nelson, born in a fortunate hour for himself and for his country, was always in his element and always on his element. Pitt, on the other hand, was a great peace Minister, compelled against his will to take up the burden of war and bear it till he died under it. He had prepared the country and the Empire for this supreme test by ten years of sound government at home, and by his Canadian and Indian legislation.[1] But it was certainly not his expectation or his wish that Britain should be subjected to a fresh ordeal within so short a time of the loss of the American colonies. Pitt had refused to join in the original attack of the reactionary powers on revolutionary France in 1792; indeed, at the beginning of that year he had prophesied a long peace and reduced the numbers of our fighting forces. But the French attack on the Netherlands drew him into the war early in 1793.

By that time he had become a violent Anti-Jacobin, living in a state of panic about the activities of Reformers at home. But he never satisfied Burke by regarding the war as a crusade, nor did he consider it our business to dictate a form of government to France. His objects were to protect the State system of Europe from the aggression of France, in particular to prevent the annexation of the Austrian Netherlands and Holland, and incidentally to recoup the British tax-payer by seizing some French colonies in the West Indies.

[1] See pp. 122–25, below.

For good and for evil Pitt had not Burke's imagination. He regarded the world crisis as a repetition, under changed political conditions, of the Seven Years' War, and he accordingly hoped to fight, as his father had done before him, for naval supremacy and colonial conquest, while sending over a few British troops and much British money to enable our allies to maintain themselves in Europe. But he had not his father's genius for war; it was a very different France with which he had to deal; and there was no Frederic the Great—at least not upon our side. In 1793 a vigorous advance on Paris from the Netherlands might have changed the course of history, before Carnot had time to create the new democratic army of France out of the mutinous welter of the old royal army, deserted by its aristocratic officers. But the chance was let slip, and the Revolution had time to organize its latent energies. Neither the Austrian nor the British armies then in Flanders had the training or the leadership for such an enterprise, which Wellington or even Sir John Moore might have ventured upon with the reconstituted army that we afterwards sent to Spain.

Pitt, moreover, in 1793, sent a large part of the available British forces to the West Indies. He was imitating the war plans not of Marlborough but of Chatham: the French West Indian Islands should be his Canada, which he would win for the Empire. In his generation the wealth of the sugar islands, where great fortunes were made by English planters, caused them to be much more highly regarded than Canada, and the sacrifices which Pitt made to preserve and to acquire such islands for the Empire, though severely criticized by modern historians, seemed very natural at the time. But he had no knowledge of the local conditions of warfare in the West Indies comparable to the knowledge his father had acquired of how Canada and the Ohio valley were to be won. Disease swept off the British soldiers by thousands. The slaves in the French and English islands rose, adding fresh horror and difficulty to the undertaking, and rendering it impossible to withdraw the troops and allow the whole Archipelago to sink like Haiti into black savagery. The affair, which added little to the British Empire, was only liquidated after the death of 40,000 British soldiers in three years [1793–96.], a number roughly answering to that with which Wellington in six years drove Napoleon's troops out of Spain.

These fearful losses in the tropical world, and the inefficient army system of the day, crippled England's efforts in Europe. The selfish preoccupation of Prussia and Russia in sharing up the corpse of murdered Poland, prevented them from playing the part against France assigned to them in Pitt's scheme. The British and Austrian armies were driven out of the Low Countries to the sound of the Marseillaise. [1793–94.] Holland and the Rhine lands were revolutionized by the French, the inhabitants half sympathizing. Finally, Bonaparte's conquest of Italy [1796–97.], and his establishment there of vassal Republics, introduced a new era of French conquest and of world politics. In 1797 Austria, beaten to her knees by this astonishing young genius, crept out of the war, leaving England alone against France.

'The Grand Nation,' more formidable than even the 'Grand Monarch' whom William and Marlborough had tamed, was now in the hands of the Directorate, a set of energetic ruffians, the survivors of the guillotine, the fathers of modern war and conquest, who were determined to re-establish the finances of France by plundering the rest of Europe. And the ablest servant of these men, soon to be their master, was already learning from his Italian experience how a French European Empire might be founded, on the basis of uniting the social benefits of the Revolution to religious toleration and political order, which the Directorate were incapable of restoring.

[1797.] England meanwhile was in a sorry plight. Her ships were excluded from the Mediterranean waters, where the Spaniards had joined the war on her enemies' side; her home fleets at Spithead and the Nore were in mutiny against the neglect and harsh treatment which had always been the lot of the sailors who won her battles; on land her military reputation was at its lowest ebb; it seemed unlikely that she could, without an ally, hold out against all Western Europe united for her destruction.

In this evil hour she was saved by the high quality of Pitt's courage, and by his instinct for naval affairs. The mutinies were pacified and quelled, and somewhat better conditions of life on board were established. [1797.] The late mutineers sallied out under Duncan and destroyed the Dutch fleet at Camperdown. Pitt was clumsy and unsuccessful in diplomatic operations, which he conducted through Grenville, and in military operations, which he conducted through Dundas. But to call him a bad war Minister is to overlook the sea affair, which for English statesmen comprises half the conduct of war. He chose, in Spencer and Jervis, the right men through whom to act; he helped them to pick out Nelson, one of the youngest flag-officers on the list; and he insisted on sending him back to recover our hold of the Mediterranean, which had been a French lake for more than a year. The result was the battle of the Nile.

The battle of the Nile was indeed one of the cardinal events of the whole war. [AUG. 1, 1798.] It restored British naval power at the moment when it was wavering, and in the region whence it had been withdrawn; whereas Trafalgar only put the crown of glory on a campaign already decided and on a life whose work was done.

Bonaparte had been safely carried to Egypt by the French fleet, and had seized Malta on the way from the Knights of St. John. The path to Constantinople and India seemed open to the most ambitious spirit since Alexander the Great. But when Nelson annihilated his fleet, at anchor at the mouth of the Nile, these Oriental visions soon faded. [1799.] Next year Bonaparte was fain to leave his army locked up in Egypt, and slip back to France. There he rebuilt the structure of his ambitions on a Western basis, and only after many years attempted to cut a path back to the East by the route of Russian conquest. Nelson's cannonade that summer evening off the Egyptian shore secured the full establishment of British supremacy in the Indian Peninsula, in the difficult days of 'Tippoo Sahib' of

Mysore and of the Maratha Wars conducted by the Wellesley brothers.

Another consequence of the Nile was the restored dominance of Britain in Mediterranean waters. The power of our fleet was firmly based on Malta, which we took from the French in 1800 and never relinquished, and on Sicily, where the royal family, exiled from Naples, became Nelson's friends, and remained England's *protégés.*

But the Nile evoked other and more formidable allies than the South-Italian Bourbons. Austria and Russia felt encouraged to form the Second Coalition, which after a sudden and brief day of success in North Italy under Suvoroff [1799.], perished on the field of Marengo [1800.] at the hands of Bonaparte. As First Consul he now had at his command all the civil and military resources of France, which he reorganized in the four best years of his life as the resources of no nation had ever been organized before, giving to France the modern administrative institutions by which she has lived ever since.

Next followed the episode of the 'armed neutrality' formed by Russia and the Scandinavian Powers against England, partly on grounds of neutrals' complaints of the right of search as exercised by the lords of the sea, partly as admirers and would-be allies of Bonaparte, for whose friendship the Czar Paul had half-crazy yearnings. The assassination of the Czar [1801.] and Nelson's destruction of the Danish fleet under the guns of the Copenhagen forts, put an end to the peril in that quarter. In northern as in southern seas, the arm of Britain was omnipotent. French and Spanish, Dutch and Danish fleets had been shattered, and Britain helped herself at will to the colonies of the unhappy allies of France. The Cape of Good Hope and Ceylon were taken from the Dutch to secure the sea route to India.

But on land no one could make head against Bonaparte. The two victorious enemies recognized their respective limits by the Treaty of Amiens. [1802.] But though hailed with joy in England, the long-expected peace proved only a hollow truce. For it soon appeared that Bonaparte interpreted the Treaty of Amiens to mean the retirement of Britain behind the sea curtain, while he remained free to annex every State of Europe to which he had a mind. It was not so that British statesmen interpreted the peace they had signed, which in their eyes set an agreed limit to French expansion. So the two weary nations turned again to war. [1803.]

England was once more matched alone against France. For the moment, Bonaparte had no other use for his incomparable army than to threaten 'perfidious Albion' from the camp of Boulogne. [1804.] His vigorous but crude and unprofessional schemes for securing the mastery of the Channel, appointing an elaborate *rendez-vous* for the Brest and Toulon fleets in the West Indies, were baffled by the vigilance and energy of Nelson and his 'band of brothers.' Our ships hunted the French across the Atlantic and back, sometimes at fault, sometimes in full cry. The pursued ran breathless to earth in the ports of France and Spain, and no more was heard of the invasion of England. Then, when all seemed over, the anger of Napoleon against Villeneuve, his unfortunate Admiral, caused the main French and Spanish fleet to come out of harbour for the last time, to the final sacrifice off Cape Trafalgar. [OCT. 21, 1805.] It saved the British much rope and timber in blockading work during the remaining ten years of the war, and it stamped on the mind of Europe an indelible impression that England's naval power was invincible. That belief helped to make the Nineteenth Century a time of peace and security for the British, and stood them in good stead when that long period of prosperity and high civilization was at length broken by another great war on land and sea.

Nelson is the best loved name in English ears. There is more in our relation to him than can be accounted for by his genius and our obligation. For Marlborough was unpopular, and there was an element of fear in the respect and admiration felt for the Iron Duke. Indeed, Wellington's complete devotion to the public service was rooted in a noble but not very lovable aristocratic pride, which made him live reserved as a man apart, saving him indeed from mistakes and loss of dignity into which Nelson sometimes fell on shore. But Nelson entered straight into the common heart of humanity. As he lay expecting the Trafalgar fight, he chanced to discover that a coxswain, one of the best men on board the *Victory*, had been so busy preparing the mail bags that he had forgotten to drop into them his own letter to his wife, till after the despatch vessel was under full sail for England: 'Hoist a signal to bring her back,' said Nelson; 'who knows but that he may fall in action to-morrow? His letter shall go with the rest.' And the vessel was brought back for that alone.

[DEC. 1805.] Meanwhile Napoleon, now Emperor, had turned from the useless camp at Boulogne to conquer Eastern Europe at Austerlitz. His success matched Nelson's, and men could not then see that it would be more ephemeral than the dead man's empire over the waves. It was an hour of gloom and glory for England. Pitt, worn out with care and disappointment and illness, died at his post. [JAN. 1806.] His death and Nelson's, rather than the fruitless Treaty of Amiens, marked the close of the first half of the war of twenty years.

The great French war,—alike in its first phase in the time of Pitt and Nelson, and its last in the time of Castlereagh and Wellington,—was fought by the House of Commons. The comparison of the Roman Senate fighting Hannibal was in the mind of every educated man. The persons whom the House trusted could wield the nation's power and purse, on condition of explaining their plans to the benches of country gentlemen, and winning their approval. For this reason Parliamentary eloquence was at its zenith; popular oratory was not yet of importance, except at the hustings in the few open constituencies at election time. Public meetings there were none. So long as the war lasted, and longer, there was little freedom of press or speech for Reformers. When Cobbett denounced the flogging of British militiamen by German mercenaries, he got two years. The restrictions on popular liberty and propaganda were partly a measure of precaution in war time, but they did not end with the war, because they were also designed to prevent the revival of the movement for domestic Reform, which the Anti-Jacobin mind identified with sedition.

But though liberty was in partial abeyance, no one was tempted to abridge the power of Parliament, or to restore the rule of the King who had lost the American colonies. George III was not, indeed, entirely without power. Even in the intervals of the lunacy that closed gradually on his old age, he was able to prevent Pitt from emancipating the Irish Catholics [1801.], and he exerted a certain influence in the struggle for Cabinet office between the groups and personages of Parliament.

The temporary revival of the group system in place of the two-party system was indeed a feature of the period, which tended to a certain limited extent to revive the influence of the Crown as arbitrator. The two-party system was no longer in full working order, because the split in the Whig party over Reform and the French Revolution reduced the Foxites to about a hundred members, and left them for a generation without hope of power. The hibernation of the Whig party between 1793 and 1830 may be compared to the hibernation of the Tory party from 1714 to 1760, and it had the same result in the revival of a group system on the floor of the House of Commons. Just as the long weakness of the Tories caused the Whigs to divide into Walpole and anti-Walpole factions, so the Tories in the first year of the Nineteenth Century broke up into Pittites, Addingtonians and Whig-Tory followers of the Grenville family. These groups, personal rather than political in their differences, combined each in turn with the Foxite remnant to form the governments and oppositions of the remaining years of war.

[1811.] In these circumstances, a certain power of selection rested with the old King, and, when his insanity was pronounced incurable, with the Regent Prince George. They both used it heavily against any combination that included the Foxite Whigs. Immediately after Pitt's death George III was, indeed, compelled to submit for a year to the coalition Ministry of 'All the Talents,' including the dying Fox, with the result that the slave trade was at last abolished. [1806–7.] But the King managed speedily to rid himself of servants whom he so much disliked, and though the ground on which he dismissed them was indefensible, it was, perhaps, no real misfortune. For the Whig chiefs and their Grenvillite colleagues did not make good war Ministers. Ever since the camp at Boulogne the Foxites had, indeed, accepted the necessity of war with France, and their leader in his few months at the Foreign Office was converted on his death-bed to the view which he had so often denounced, that peace with Napoleon was impossible. Yet his successors in the Whig hierarchy, like Lords Holland and Grey, too easily despaired, and had neither the phlegm nor the *flair* necessary for those who conduct a long and doubtful war.[2]

The pure Tory groups combined after 1807 to govern the country and fight Napoleon through the agency of the House of Commons. The prestige of Waterloo and the final victory redounded most to the credit of the nation that had never submitted and always hoped. And, in the secure judgment of the world, the victory of the stubborn islanders was due, not to King or Regent, but to British Parliamentary institutions, to the British aristocracy, and to the steady character and rapidly increasing wealth of the British middle class.

Napoleon signalized his coronation as Emperor by conquering Eastern Europe up to the Russian border—a three years' task: each year there was

another deadly blow!
Another mighty Empire overthrown,

Austria at Austerlitz, Prussia at Jena, Russia at Friedland. [1805, 1806, 1807.] The work was crowned in the summer

[2] After a moment of first enthusiasm for the cause of the Spanish people risen against Napoleon, most of the Whigs took fright about the Peninsular War after Moore's retreat, and thought Wellington's campaigns there foredoomed to failure.

of 1807 by the Treaty of Tilsit, made on a raft in the Niemen, where Napoleon embraced the Czar Alexander, an impressionable young man, destined to play many different parts in Europe's tragedy, each with the same conscientious solemnity as the last. For four years it flattered him to be Napoleon's ally and half-sharer in the rule of the continent. From the Urals to the Pyrenees the civilized world was banded against England, and closed to her shipping and her goods. But in that vast hostile camp she had many secret friends, whom it was the chief task of her statesmanship to rouse into mutiny. The prospect of British subsidies if they should take up arms, was one inducement offered; while another and harsher was the deprivation of tea and coffee, sugar and cotton, so long as they remained French vassals.

England and France now organized the world-warfare of blockade and starvation, on a scale never before witnessed, because never in the history of war had there been sea-power like that of England after Trafalgar, or land-power like that of Napoleon after Tilsit. By Napoleon's Berlin and Milan Decrees, neutrals and French allies were forbidden to trade with Great Britain or her colonies. [1806, 1807.] Britain replied by the Orders in Council, a series of measures of ever-increasing stringency, of which the general drift was that all Napoleonic Europe was subjected to blockade. [1807, 1812.]

Of three sets of victims, which would rebel the first? Napoleon's German vassals and Muscovite allies, deprived of their luxuries and comforts for his sake? Or the United States, the one great neutral carrier, angry with England because her ships effectually barred the Yankee skippers from European ports, whereas Napoleon, having no submarines, could not by mere proclamation exclude them from trading with Britain? Or, finally, as Napoleon had in 1811 some reason to hope, would the strain prove too much for the English middle and lower orders, whose business, employment and real wages were subject during these terrible years to the vagaries of war prices and war markets?

In fact, by 1812, Russia had rebelled against Napoleon's decrees, and the United States against the British Orders in Council and the right of search as exercised by her captains. But the classes on the British 'home front' who suffered from the war, stood firm. The mercantile community refused to submit to Napoleon, but strongly urged the Perceval Ministry to relax the Orders in Council enough to prevent war with our largest remaining customer, the United States. But the middle classes were still for the most part unenfranchised, and stood outside the close ring of the Tory governing class. Their advice was heeded too late and war broke out between England and America, causing great momentary suffering to Britain by commercial stoppage. But neither that nor the distraction of naval and military bickering on the Canadian frontier and along the American coast, proved fatal to Britain's victory in Europe, because in the same years Russia and Germany rebelled against France. [1812–14.] The next generation of Englishmen forgot the American war as an unpleasant and unnecessary episode in the greater Napoleonic struggle; but Americans remembered it only too well, as a patriotic landmark in their early growth as a nation. From the point of view of future Anglo-American relations, it was most unfortunate that the first foreign war of the young Republic should have been waged with the motherland, against whom also her War of Independence had been fought.

The Napoleonic struggle, though as dangerous at times to Britain as the Great War of our own day, affected the life of the community at fewer points; above all it made a much smaller drain upon the manhood of the country. For a dozen years we had practically no troops on the continent, except for very small and very occasional raids. [1795–1807.] The total death-roll in the whole twenty-two years was probably about 100,000, nearly half lost in the West Indies in Pitt's time and 40,000 more in the six years' fighting in the Peninsula. It was in economic suffering that England paid. The course of the Industrial Revolution, during two critical decades, was warped and diverted by the exigencies of the war.

But the economic suffering was by no means evenly divided among the whole people. The upper class throve on enhanced rents, and paid too small a proportion of the war taxes; for revenue was raised largely by duties on articles of consumption, of which the effect was felt by the poor in the rise of prices. Pitt's useful new device of the income-tax, which was continued till the end of the war, did something, but not enough, to redress the balance. In 1815 twenty-five millions were raised by direct, and sixty-seven millions by indirect taxation. Those who enjoyed rent and tithe, composing a single governing class of the well-born, knew little of the hardships of war time.

It was, indeed, a notable period in the higher civilization of the island, where all through the war great landscape painters, poets and novelists were working for a large and eager class with the wealth and leisure to enjoy their works. Never was country-house life more thriving or jovial, with its fox-hunting, shooting, and leisure in spacious and well-stocked libraries. Never was sporting life more attractive, with its coaching on the newly improved roads, and its boxing matches patronized by the nobility. In the mirror that Miss Austen held up to nature in the drawing-room, it is hard to detect any trace of concern or trouble arising from the war.

The middle classes suffered more. Many merchants, like poor old Mr. Sedley in *Vanity Fair*, were broken by the sudden opening and shutting of markets, or the rise and fall of war prices. But many also made their fortunes in new factories, and in commerce with the black and brown peoples of the world, whom England was learning to clothe, wholesale, as yet without a rival in that profitable business.

The chief sufferers by the war were the working classes, for whom little was done except the general adoption of the policy originated by the Berkshire magistrates at Speenhamland, for granting rates in aid of wages to prevent families from positively dying of starvation. But the better policy of an enforced minimum wage, though discussed, was unfortunately rejected as old-fashioned and unscientific. Meanwhile, Pitt's Act made Trade Unions illegal, so that the workmen found it difficult, in the face of hostile authority, to keep up wages in their proper relation to prices.

That sense of the brotherhood of classes in the Great War which was so marked in our own more democratic day, had no place in the Anti-Jacobin mentality. Wellington's remarks about the soldiers who won his battles, as 'the scum of the earth,' enlisted 'for drink,'[3] represent the common limitations of upper-class sympathy at that period, though Nelson and his coxswain's letter strike another note. Harshness often appeared, not only in the treatment of the much flogged soldiers and sailors, but in the attitude to Luddites and the 'labouring poor' in general. While engaged in beating Napoleon, the authorities recognized a double duty in relation to starving men,—to keep them alive and to keep them in due subordination.

Napoleon's endeavour to enforce his 'continental system' for excluding British goods from Europe,—his only available means of chastising the insolent islanders,—drew him into the two most fatal errors of his career, the attempt to annex Spain against the will of its people [1808.], and the invasion of the vastness of Russia. [1812.] Those two acts let loose upon him the rising of the peoples, after he had dealt successfully with the Kings. The earlier and more criminal of these enterprises gave England the opportunity to commence the Peninsular War. [1808.] Our operations there began very humbly in an attempt to maintain according to precedent the independence of our ancient ally, Portugal. Throughout the next six years Portugal continued to be the base, and sea-power the condition of the whole affair, as in the less lucky operations of the British armies in Spain during the Marlborough wars.

The Portuguese consented to be drilled and commanded by British officers, with the result that in this war they made very respectable troops of the line. The Spaniards, on the other hand, seldom made even tolerable regulars,

[3] We must do the Duke the justice of remembering that he added words not always quoted: 'it really is wonderful that we should have made them the fine fellows they are.'

but seldom failed to act with amazing efficiency in guerrilla warfare. The more primitive nature of Spanish character and society rendered the land which Napoleon had despised, more formidable to the armies of French occupation than any of the more civilized nations of modern Europe, upon which they had so long trampled. For this reason the 300,000 French in Spain were mostly engaged in guarding communications, and could never concentrate enough force to destroy the persistent British army of some 30,000 men under Moore or Wellington. Issuing from Portugal in well-planned raids across Spain, Wellington year after year carried off the victory in an ascending scale of the decisive,—Talavera, Salamanca, Vitoria [1809, 1812, 1813.],—as Napoleon's increasing commitments in Russia and Germany gradually reduced the pressure of France upon the Peninsula. The military power and reputation of Britain, that had sunk so low at the beginning of the Revolutionary Wars, were raised to the height where they had stood under Cromwell and Marlborough. The Peninsular battles and sieges, recorded in such numbers on our flags, confirmed and perpetuated the regimental traditions which remained the true life of the British Army during the next hundred years.

The victories in Spain, though due largely to the previous work of the Duke of York and Sir John Moore in reforming the Army, and to Wellington's own strategical and tactical genius, were facilitated by the superiority of the British line over the French column. The history of that difference of formation is very curious. The dynastic wars of the Eighteenth Century, from Marlborough to Frederic the Great, had been fought in line,—three deep, reduced towards the end of the century to two. But this method of war, then universal in civilized armies, implied the perfect drill of highly professional troops. When, therefore, the first armies of the French Republic took the field with their high-spirited but ill-disciplined hosts straight from the counter and the plough, they could only be led into action in compact masses with a cloud of skirmishers flung out in front. But so great were their zeal and numbers, that in this crude formation they again and again chased off the field the well-ordered lines of the Austrian infantry. Thus defeated, the ancient monarchies of Europe imitated their conquerors by adopting their faulty tactics and formation, without the spirit that had been the true cause of the French successes. Only the British Army, guided by a combination of conservatism and good sense, continued to fight and manœuvre in line. On the rare occasions, therefore, when they had met the French in Egypt and in South Italy [1801, 1806.] they had an advantage over them shared by no other nation. And now, in the more continuous campaigns of the Peninsula, again and again the narrow head of the French column was mowed down by the concentrated fire of the long red line. It is indeed remarkable that the greatest military genius of modern times never attempted to reform the retrogressive tactics of his infantry.

The Peninsular War was finally won because the French disasters in Russia and Germany continually reduced the number of their troops in Spain. Similarly, the decisive victory of our allies over Napoleon in person at Leipzig, was rendered possible by the number of French engaged by Wellington in the South. [1813.] Early in 1814 France was entered by Wellington from across the Pyrenees, and by the Austrians, Prussians and Russians across the Rhine. The final success had been rendered possible by the wisdom and energy of Castlereagh's diplomacy in mid-Europe in 1813–14, which held together the alliance of jealous Princes until the common object was attained.

The first fall of Napoleon was followed by his return from Elba, the rally of the veterans of the army to his standard, while the French people looked on with divided feelings. His Hundred Days' adventure ended at Waterloo. [JUNE 18, 1815.] The fortunate brevity of this last war was due to the prompt and courageous action of the British Government in declaring war at once, and sending over Wellington to defend Holland and Belgium in alliance with Blucher and his Prussians, till the allied armies from the East could arrive in overwhelming numbers. The decisive character of the great battle put a sudden end to the war, because France was half-hearted in her desire that it should be renewed.

The reputation of Great Britain, as the most consistent and formidable antagonist of Napoleon, reached its height as a result of Waterloo. At the peace conference, Castlereagh and Wellington spoke with a voice of unrivalled authority among the Emperors and Kings. To the influence of these two Anglo-Irish aristocrats the merits of the Treaties of Vienna were largely due.

The most striking merit of the Settlement of 1815 lay in securing at the outset a long period of quiet for Europe by justice and even leniency to the conquered, a point on which Wellington and Castlereagh both insisted, with the aid of the Czar Alexander, against the very natural desire for vengeance on the part of Blucher and the Germans and a large part of the British public. France,—with the Bourbons restored but the social arrangements of the Revolution left intact,—was allowed her old boundaries of 1792, was not compelled to give up Alsace or Lorraine, and received back from England most of her possessions in Africa and the two Indies seized during the war. The indemnity which she had to pay was fixed from the first at a moderate sum, and in three years her territory was completely evacuated by the allied armies. Revenge was eschewed, but security was gained by an alliance to prevent, in arms, the return of Napoleon, whom meanwhile the English kept out of harm's way on remote St. Helena.

The defect of the Settlement was that nationality and popular liberty were both disregarded on the continent, outside the boundaries of France herself. Except England, the Great Powers who had triumphed were Powers of reaction and despotism, and even Castlereagh cared nothing for Parliaments outside England. The rulers of Russia, Prussia and Austria divided up Poland, Germany and Italy as if inhabitants were so many head of population to be bartered among royal hagglers. The Temporal Power of the Pope over Central Italy was restored. The hopes of national and popular self-expression, which in Spain and

Germany had partly inspired the late patriotic uprising against France, were crushed to the earth.

The merits of the Settlement of Vienna gave Europe forty years of peace. Its faults rendered war certain in the end,—war to assert national and popular aspirations which Metternich's system could not for ever keep in check.[4]

One of the points in the Treaties of 1815 in which Britain was specially interested was the restoration of the Anglophil House of Orange to Holland, and the addition of Belgium to their Kingdom of the Netherlands. The Delta of the Rhine was again in hands from which England had nothing to fear, but another sharp crisis was necessary fifteen years later, before a permanent settlement was reached by the separation of Belgium from Holland on a basis of two separate and independent States. [1830–31.]

But the greatest interests of Britain lay beyond the ocean, and there she was supreme arbiter. It was for her alone to decide how many she would give back of the colonies which she had seized in the war. On the whole she was not ungenerous in her restorations. While keeping Ceylon and the Cape of Good Hope and Singapore, and purchasing a part of Guiana for three million pounds, Britain gave back to the Dutch their old possessions of Java and the other East Indian islands which have ever since remained the

[4] Professor Webster, Castlereagh's distinguished biographer, writes: 'More worthy of reprobation is the discouragement of the idea of self-government, which had already come to a fuller consciousness than that of nationality. Alexander alone, with some of his advisers, showed any sympathy with it; and it was he who secured the "Charte" for the French with the assistance of Talleyrand, who was also aware of the fundamental importance of this aspect of the French Revolution. To almost all the other statesmen democracy meant nothing but anarchy and revolution; and among these must be included the Tory Ministers of Great Britain, who even secretly encouraged the attacks on the constitutions which had been set up with the direct connivance of British representatives. It was this policy that made the subsequent national movements take strange paths, instead of being an expression of the people's desires.'—*Congress of Vienna*, p. 147.

chief source of Holland's external wealth. France and Denmark got back their most valuable islands. But England kept Mauritius and Heligoland, and the Mediterranean vantage points of the Ionian Islands and Malta. The network of British naval, maritime and commercial posts, soon to be used also as coaling stations, had already begun to spread over the globe. Australia, peacefully acquired by Captain Cook's voyages (1769–1775), was in process of colonization. Upper Canada was filling with English and Scots. A Second Empire was arising to replace that which had been lost, based like the first on sea-power, commerce and liberty.

BOOKS FOR FURTHER READING: H. Rose, *Pitt and the Great War* and *Life of Napoleon* (2 vols.); Mahan, *Life of Nelson* (2 vols.); Corbett, *Campaign of Trafalgar*; Sir H. Maxwell, *Wellington*; Webster, *The Congress of Vienna* (No. 153, F. O. Handbook, H. M. Stationery Office); *Cam. Mod. Hist.*, Vols. VIII., IX.; Albert Sorel, *L'Europe et la révolution française* (6 vols.); Arthur Bryant, *The years of endurance* and *Years of Victory*.

CHAPTER SIX

The Empire in the Latter Years of George III. The Outward Expansion of the Island Life. England, Scotland and Ireland. Canada and Australia. India. The Anti-Slave-Trade Movement. Wilberforce and the Evangelicals

Nature had early decided that the inhabitants of Britain must be insular, but there are various kinds and degrees of insularity. After the Norman Conquest, the English had for several generations been to all appearance part of the feudal and Catholic world of French civilization. Then, by a gradual process in the later Middle Ages, culminating in the Tudor revolution, they had asserted an island individuality in law and government, religion and culture, character and habits of life. They had, in Elizabeth's words about herself, become 'mere English,' repelling the invading influences of the continent. But as their native strength and self-confidence increased they had become every year more active beyond the seas, in that new way ceasing to be 'insular.' They appeared in every quarter of the newly discovered globe, bringing with them English ideas and standards that had come to maturity at home.

In the era of Waterloo the life of the islanders was being constantly enriched and broadened by their activities as explorers, traders, warriors and rulers in all parts of the world, both in the lands of the ever-growing British Empire, and in countries like China and South America, where the British had become the characteristic representatives of European trade and influence. The Industrial Revolution had given fresh speed and vigour to the outward expansion of English life which had been going on ever since the days of Elizabeth. The reign of George III saw, in consequence, the emergence of a number of Imperial problems of a new order, connected with Ireland, Canada, Australia, India, and the relations of the white man to the African negro. In all these the younger Pitt played a leading part.

One source of anxiety, indeed, had been removed. The relations of England and Scotland no longer formed an Imperial problem of grave difficulty, but a domestic bond of singular felicity. The Union of the two States, after a period of uneasy working, had been adjusted by time and patience. The decease of Jacobitism, the measures taken after 1745 to abolish feudalism and tribalism in Scotland, and her ever-increasing wealth since that crisis had been adjusted, led to the better appreciation in England of the Scottish qualities. 'Sir Walter's' Scottish romances, and the kilted regiments who fought so well at Waterloo, seemed to Englishmen and to the whole civilized world to represent something new added to the island tradition and power. The mutual acceptance of each other by the two peoples has remained ever since one of the chief pillars of the British State.

The era of Burns and Scott was one of expansion, new prosperity and noble pride for their countrymen, upon the whole the happiest since first they were a nation. They had, indeed, internal difficulties, but since these were of the same general character as contemporary difficulties in England, they served to unite the two ends of the island in a common *malaise*. The social and economic problems attendant on the Industrial Revolution were aggravated by antiquated political institutions in both countries, by rotten boroughs and an absence of efficient municipal and local bodies suited to the new age. In Scotland, where even County elections were a farce, the political machinery was more out of touch with modern facts than even in England, and the spirit of Anti-Jacobin repression was more severe, while the democratic spirit was more fierce. The trouble bade fair some day to be worse in Scotland than in England. But in the coming era the process of political reform and social amelioration followed the same course in both countries, tending still further to unite their fortunes in one.

While Scotland was ceasing to be regarded at Downing Street as a problem, the Irish question, after a long period of quiescence, was entering upon a new phase of virulent activity, which continued to disturb the British Empire at frequent intervals until the great events of our own day.

During the early and middle Eighteenth Century, while Jacobite Scotland had been a source of trouble and danger, the native Irish had given no sign of lifting their heads. Ever since the days of Sarsfield, the active rebels, the 'wild geese' of Irish Jacobite tradition, were serving in French armies, and had the pleasure of shooting Englishmen only on occasions like Fontenoy. The island itself, twice conquered by Cromwell and by William, lay quiet under British and Protestant ascendancy, and under the iniquitous and partially enforced Penal Laws against Catholics.

In the last thirty years of the Century the old bones in that valley of desolation began to stir under the reviving winds of a new age. In the first instance the initiative was not Catholic and Celtic, but Protestant and Liberal. It was a movement partly of Ulster Presbyterians, partly of broad-minded statesmen like Grattan, against a system of tyranny that sacrificed Ireland as a whole to English trading interests, and all other Irish denominations to Anglican ascendancy. In this generous mood many Protestants forgot their grandfathers' fears of the native Catholics, who since the Century began had done nothing more dangerous than endure wrong.

During the War of American Independence, Ireland fell into the hands of the Volunteers, who were Protestants, but the movement was supported by Catholic opinion. [1778–82.] The Volunteers were prepared to defend the island against the French invader, but they dictated their terms to the government of England,—the abolition of Ireland's commercial disabilities, and the formal independence of her Parliament from British control. Ireland secured free markets for her goods, but her political autonomy during the next two decades was more apparent than real. [1782–1801.] For Catholics were still allowed no part or lot in the Dublin Parliament, and the oligarchy in Dublin Castle manipulated the rotten boroughs so that a Reform Bill would clearly be necessary before even Protestant Ireland could practise self-government.

But there was hope in the new era. The worst of the Penal Laws were repealed. Reform was in the air, under the leadership of Grattan, who hoped to reconcile races and creeds by a gradual process of evolution. Catholic and Protestant fanaticism were both dormant. The best spirit of Eighteenth Century toleration and latitudinarianism was still widely prevalent. If British statesmen had met Grattan half way in his own spirit, much might have been done. But the spirit of Jacobinism and Anti-Jacobinism, of neo-Catholicism and Orangeism, arrived too soon upon the scene and destroyed the generous opportunity created by the time-spirit of the Eighteenth Century. The Tories in England had taken over as their own electoral speciality the old Whig cry of No-Popery, while at the same time the French Revolution made them adamant against all change. The liberal-minded but incautious Viceroy, Lord Fitzwilliam, was recalled from Dublin, after he had kindled hopes that Pitt was unable to fulfil. [1795.] His recall put an end to any further attempt to gain Ireland's support for the war against France by a policy of conciliation to Catholics. When, therefore, the French military propagandists offered Republican liberty to Ireland, their aid was accepted by the leaders of the United Irishmen, Wolfe Tone and Lord Edward Fitzgerald, converts from the English garrison. These men hoped to unite the religions of Ireland in arms against England. But the actual effect of their reliance on French aid was to set Protestant and Catholic to kill each other in the old spirit of the Williamite wars. For, great as were the wrongs of the Ulster Scots and Presbyterians against the English Government, they could not join the French to set up a Celtic Republic, dominated by priests. The Rebellion of 1798 was put down by a combination of the hard-pressed British Government with the loyalists of Ireland, now reconverted to the anti-Catholic fears of their ancestors, and beginning to organize themselves in the new 'Orange' lodges. The military and political weakness of England at that critical moment made her dependent to a dangerous degree on the help of local partisans who in their panic treated the native Irish with cruel rigour. The memories of 'ninety-eight' became an heirloom of hatred, cherished in every cottage, and exploited by successive generations of patriots and agitators.

[JAN. 1, 1801.] In these circumstances Pitt decided that the Union of the two islands in one Parliament at Westminster was the only method of permanently restoring order and justice. But he was able to restore only order. He had not the political authority to pass Catholic Emancipation, which he had designed to accompany the Union and render it palatable to the Celtic Irish. That hope, and an orgy of Parliamentary corruption in Dublin, had just sufficed to carry the Union. But Pitt's royal master, many of his colleagues, his party and the majority of his countrymen feared the consequences of giving political rights to Roman Catholics either in Ireland or in England. The two most active forces of the day, Anti-Jacobinism and Evangelicalism, were at one on that score. For twenty-eight years Roman Catholics were prohibited from sitting in the United Parliament of Great Britain and Ireland. [1801–29.]

So the Catholic Celts were again thrust down, this time with the whole weight of England on the top of them, and with their fellow-Irish of the North waxing in Orange enthusiasm. The two Irelands were once more face to face, fighting the Boyne battle again daily with their mouths. Moreover, the land question was beginning to take a foremost place in politics, in that overpopulated, potato-fed island of oppressed tenant-farmers.[1] In these circumstances, a new and formidable amalgamation of clericalism, nationalism and uneducated democracy began to be organized by the popular oratory of the Catholic lawyer, Daniel O'Connell.

The last years of George II's reign had witnessed the conquest of French Canada in war. The long reign of George III saw the reconciliation of the French Canadians to their place within the British Empire. This was effected by complete toleration of their religion, rights and customs, in striking contrast to the policy of Protestant and English 'ascendancy' during the same years in Ireland. George III's reign also saw the settlement of English and Scottish colonists in Upper Canada on the shores of the Great Lakes, and to a less degree in the coast colonies of New Brunswick and Nova Scotia. The newcomers were many of them 'United Kingdom Loyalists,' that is to say, refugees from the intolerance and injustice of the victorious Republicans of the United States, who after the War of Independence made life impossible for their late political opponents. The other element in the British colonization of Canada was the economic exodus from the homeland. This movement reached vast proportions in the early years of the Nineteenth Century, owing to the rapid increase of population in Great Britain, which in spite of these emigrations rose from about seven and a half millions when George III

[1] By 1821 the Irish in Ireland had increased to the total of 6,803,000, and added yet another million in the next ten years. Great Britain held only about twice as many inhabitants at the corresponding dates.

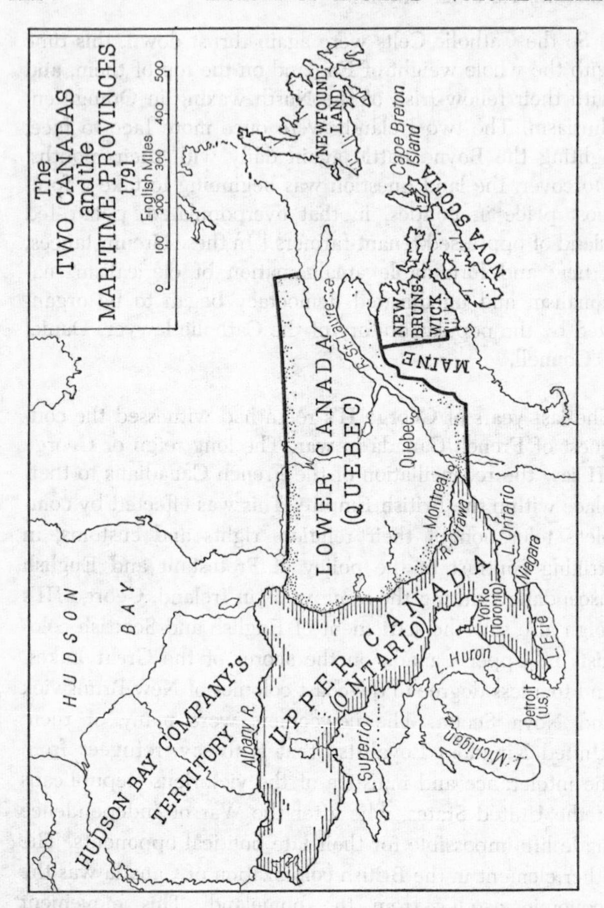

Map 4

ascended the throne, to over fourteen millions when he died.

The arrival of large numbers of men and women of British stock in Canada complicated the task of governing the French there in accordance with their own very different customs and ideals. The newcomers at once demanded self-government, to which they had been accustomed in the lost English colonies, and to a less degree in England herself. But the French peasants had no use for self-government. Their seigneurs had largely returned to France after the British conquest, but they trusted to their priests, and feared that the heretic strangers would make alterations in their laws. Fortunately, a good beginning had already been made by government in winning the confidence of the French before the arrival of the United Kingdom Loyalists. Lord North's Quebec Act of 1774 and Sir Guy Carleton's wise and liberal governorship of Canada had already given them a sense of security in their rights as they understood them.

The next stage was reached when Pitt boldly and successfully faced the complicated problem created by the juxtaposition of the two races in Canada. [1791.] He determined to solve it on geographic lines, separating Upper from Lower Canada, the older district to enjoy French law and custom, the newer settlements of the Lakes to be no less completely British in their institutions. Each of the two provinces was to have its own elected assembly, not indeed with full 'responsible' government or the right of naming Ministers, but with powers of taxation and law-making, and a fixed relation to the Governor and his executive not unlike that of an Elizabethan Parliament to the Crown. The arrangement met the needs of the time in Canada, as fully as the grant of 'responsible' government, made fifty years later on Durham's advice, met them for the later age. In the interval, the French were initiated into the mystery of representative assemblies, and the British population flourished and rose in the half century from 10,000 to 400,000 souls. [1790–1840.] English and Scottish immigration up the St. Lawrence largely accounted for this astonishing increase in a land where the backwoodsman had to prepare each step of the way.

The period that witnessed the plantation and early growth of British Canada, saw the same process in Australia. The occasion and method of the first settlements were different in the two cases, but the general character of the colonizing movement was much the same. Canada had been won by war, and the French were there before us to open the land to later immigrants. Australia, discovered but neglected by the Dutch in the Seventeenth Century, was still empty of men, save for a few Aborigines, when Captain Cook of the Royal Navy explored its coasts and brought it to the notice of British statesmen and public. [1769–75.] The first settlement [1786–87.] was made by order of Pitt and his Home Secretary, Lord Sydney, not with a view to founding a new Empire in the Antipodes, but merely to find a new place for the deportation of convicts, since the old American colonies were now closed for that purpose by their secession. But the convict settlements and the troops that guarded them afforded a convenient base and a method of communication with distant England, very necessary for the first stages of free colonization that speedily followed. Men went to Australia for the same economic reasons which sent them to Canada. By the time of Waterloo the capitalist sheep and cattle farmers, known as 'squatters,' had already begun to create the Australia that we know.

The reign of George II had witnessed the destruction of the French power in India by Clive, and his conquest of Bengal as the first great continental area of British rule in the peninsula. Its acquisition converted the East India Company from an armed trading corporation into an Asiatic Power. The logic of the change was worked out in the reign of George III by Warren Hastings, Cornwallis and Wellesley in India, and by Pitt at home.

The design of the French to erect an Empire of their own in Hindoostan had been thwarted by Clive, but for fifty years after Plassey Frenchmen continued to be a thorn in the British side [1757–1805.], stirring up Indian Courts and officering Indian armies, first against Hastings and then against Wellesley. In so doing, they hastened the pace at which the British power was forced to advance across the peninsula.

During the War of American Independence, Warren Hastings was left with very inadequate means to struggle against these external dangers [1772–85.], and at the same time to maintain his internal authority against the faction in his own Council led by his personal enemy, Philip Francis. He saved British rule in India in spite of all, but not without making the kind of mistakes which a strong man is likely to make in difficult emergencies. For these acts, much exaggerated and misconstrued by the malignity of Francis and the imagination of Burke, Fox and Sheridan, he was impeached in Westminster Hall. Those famous proceedings [1788–95.], substantially unjust to Hastings even though they resulted in his acquittal, had the advantage of bringing Indian problems and responsibilities forcibly to the notice of British statesmen and the British public. Burke preached the right ideal of our obligations to the Indians, but misunderstood the relation of Hastings' governorship to the problem.

Pitt, meanwhile, after denouncing and destroying a very similar but rather bolder Bill introduced by Fox, had by his own India Act established the practical control of the British Cabinet over the administrative work of the East India Company, while leaving its commercial monopoly intact. [1784.] At the same time Pitt's Bill relieved the Governor General at Calcutta from the tutelage of his Council, which became advisory only. Such scenes as those between Francis and Hastings were never to occur again at the Council Board. The Governor-General was made an autocrat in a land that only understood autocracy, but was himself subject to the ultimate control of the Home Government through the Board of Control under a President of Cabinet rank. Pitt's Indian legislation served India until the time of the Mutiny, as satisfactorily as his Canadian legislation served Canada until the time of Lord Durham.

Pitt had also the merit of sending out the right men to wield as Governor-General these tremendous powers. Lord Cornwallis completed [1786–93.] the internal work of Hastings, and fixed the taxation and government of Bengal on a system that became the model for all provinces subsequently administered by the British. Indians began to find that under the British flag, and there alone, was to be found security from warlike invasion, and from the grosser forms of domestic oppression. Upon that was based both the permanence and the justification of the British raj. The plunder and misrule that had accompanied our first conquest of Bengal in spite of Clive's efforts to stem the passions of his countrymen, could never be repeated under the new system and under the influence of the new spirit. The high traditions of the 'Anglo-Indian families' began to be formed; many of them were Scottish, for Pitt's friend, Henry Dundas, cannily combined his political jobbery beyond the Border with sending out excellent young Scots to India.

If Cornwallis did most to justify the British power internally, Lord Wellesley, the elder brother of Wellington, did most to expand it and to justify its expansion. [1798–1805.] He broke the power of the fighting Mohammedan ruler, 'Tippoo Sahib' of Mysore, and of the great Maratha Confederacy of Central India, whose horsemen had so long attacked and threatened all the neighbouring States. The Confederacy had recently, with the help of French officers, armed and trained its forces after the European manner. In effect it was the policy of Wellesley as Governor-General to extend the protection of Britain over a number of Indian States, such as Hyderabad, thereby stepping into the place of the deceased Mogul Empire as arbiter and keeper of the peace in the whole peninsula. The implications of this policy, which could in the end have no geographic boundary save the Himalayas and the sea, were little liked by the cautious East India Company at home and were only half liked by Pitt and his Cabinet. But all attempts to call a halt to the British advance, though seriously made after Wellesley's retirement, proved nugatory in the face of inexorable facts.

It was to be proved by repeated experience in the Punjab and elsewhere, that peace in India could only be maintained by the acknowledged suzerainty of a single Power. That, few will be inclined to dispute. But it is, perhaps, an

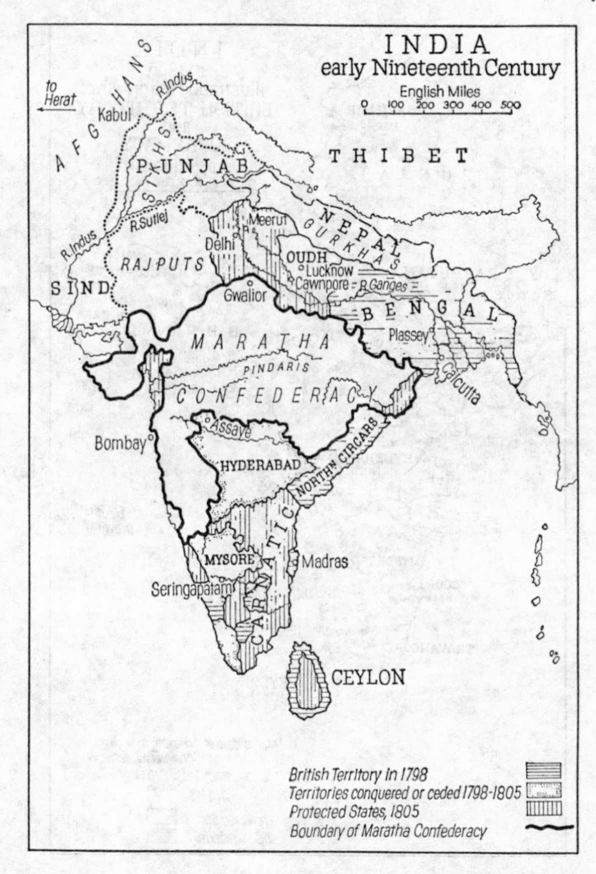

Map 5

open question whether the position might be easier to-day if a larger proportion of protected native States had, like Hyderabad, been left to Indian rulers, and if the actual area of direct British government had been more narrowly circumscribed. But the benevolent reforming zeal of rulers like Dalhousie made them favour the extension of direct British rule as the means of good administration. The politi-

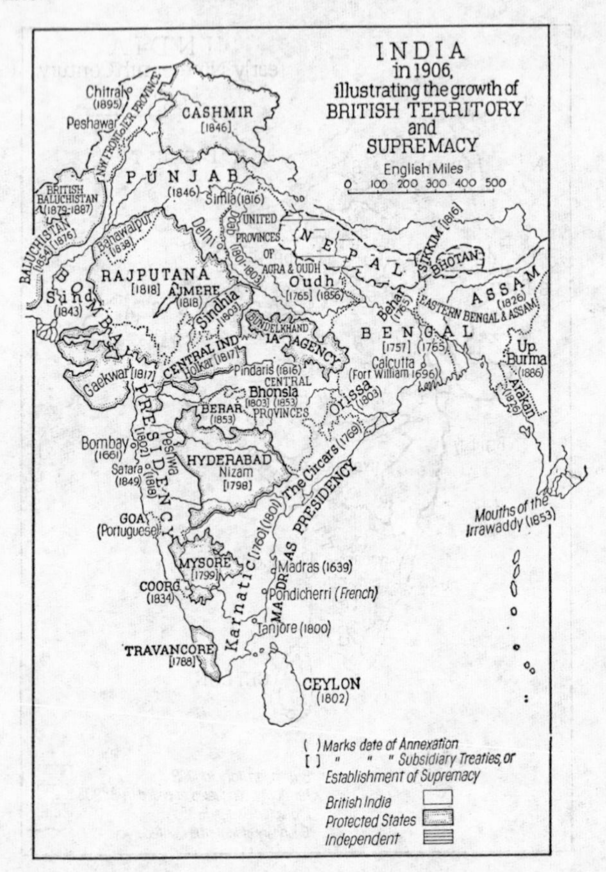

Map 6

cal, as distinct from the administrative aspect of Indian problems, was in the background during the fortunate Nineteenth Century, except for the lightning flash of the Mutiny year. [1857.]

During the Napoleonic war Britain's lead over the rest of Europe in colonization and trade was immensely increased.

She still enjoyed almost a monopoly of the advantages of the new mechanical era, and in the fight with Napoleonic Europe, her navy kept enemy merchant fleets off the ocean highways. When peace was re-established, her energies and her rapidly increasing population long maintained the initial advantage. In the early part of the Nineteenth Century there was nothing else comparable to the rapid expansion of the Second British Empire, except the advance of the English-speaking people of the United States beyond the Alleghanies, across the great plains and rivers of central North America. That advance turned America away from serious rivalry with Britain at sea or in the markets of the world.

Britain held, therefore, at this critical juncture, the destiny of the coloured races very largely in her own hand. She represented Europe in the contact with China, in the closer contact with India, and in the approaching development of Africa. If the ignorant, selfish and irresponsible ways of the white man with the 'native' were any longer to be continued, civilization was heading fast for disaster. Could either the conscience or the good sense of England be aroused in time? In India, as we have seen, the process had begun by the growth of the fine traditions of Anglo-Indian rule, among soldiers and civil servants devoted not to personal gain but to government as a means of peace and welfare for millions. In Africa the first business was to stop the slave trade and slavery, before the relation of white and black could be anything but a mutual curse.

It was a turning-point in the history of the world when William Wilberforce and his friends succeeded in arousing the conscience of the British people to stop the slave trade in 1807, and to abolish slavery in the Empire in 1833, just before the development of the interior of Africa by the European races began. If slavery and the slave trade had continued through the Nineteenth Century, armed with the new weapons of the Industrial Revolution and of modern science, the tropics would have become a vast slave farm for white exploitation, and the European races in their own homes would have been degraded by the diseases of slave-civilization of which the old Roman Empire had died.

Fortunately, when Wilberforce attacked the slave trade, it was still confined to a traffic carried on by British skippers crimping negroes along the African coast for the horrors of the Atlantic passage. The interior of the Dark Continent was still closed to Europeans. And the maritime predominance of England was such that no power would seriously dispute her determination that the slave trade should stop, if she once made up her own mind. If Wilberforce could convert England, she would soon persuade the world.

The method by which this conversion was effected, in itself constituted a new epoch in British public life. The anti-slave trade movement was the first successful propagandist agitation of the modern type, and its methods were afterwards imitated by the myriad societies and leagues —political, religious, philanthropic and cultural—which characterized Nineteenth Century England. Originally promoted by the Society of Friends, who never did a greater service to humanity, the slave trade question was taken up by philanthropists like Sharp and Clarkson, by Wilberforce the 'converted' man of fashion, and by Zachary Macaulay whose eminently Scottish qualities put a stiffening into the fibre of English Evangelicalism. Many of the workers in the cause were either Quakers or Evangelicals, inspired by the practical religious zeal of so many of the Protestant laity of that period. This gave them an easier route to the heart of many of their countrymen, especially the Dissenters, than if they had appealed on grounds solely of humanity or in furtherance of scientific plans for the future of the Empire. But they had a formidable ally in the non-religious humanitarianism of the new age, in veterans like Fox and young men like Brougham, whose zeal for the slaves waxed in opposition, while the cares of office sprang up and choked Pitt's first generous zeal.

The conversion of the country, begun just before the French Revolution, was carried on under difficulties during the Anti-Jacobin reaction, when the slave trade abolitionists were denounced as 'Reformers' tampering with the vested interests of Bristol and Liverpool merchants under the Leveller's plea—humanity. But after a period of depression the cause rallied, and by the Act of 1807 triumphantly put down the slave trade. The triumph was all the more remarkable for being won in the middle of the Great War, and in the middle of a period when no other agitation was permitted. In spite of much corruption in public institutions, the spirit of the British body politic was free, healthy and capable of response, as compared to any other public opinion then existing in the world. Wilberforce, the cross-bench member for Yorkshire, had found a new and nobler use for the political machinery of England.

[1815.] And so, at the time of the Treaties of Vienna, Castlereagh was both able and willing to induce the Powers of Europe to subscribe to the suppression of the slave trade as the rule of the sea in the new era. [1809–12.] The Union Jack had become, by a dramatic change, specially associated with the freedom of the black man.

By this time Evangelicalism had made a strong lodgement inside the Tory party. One Prime Minister, Perceval, had been an Evangelical. Many Tories of the old school disliked the 'Clapham sect' as they were called,—for their friendship with Dissenters, their too insistent interest in their own and other people's souls, their want of appreciation of the spirit of cakes and ale, their frequent unreadiness to play the party game owing to some scruple of humanity or conscience. This duality inside the Tory fold, and a corresponding rivalry in the religious world of the hearty or fox-hunting churchman and his more serious Evangelical brother, though they caused heartburning, were signs of life. Such differences of aim helped to keep the party and the Church in some touch with outside forces in the nation, during the years after the war when the limitations of the old Toryism and of the old Establishment began to be painfully visible. Evangelicalism and humanitarianism—often though not always allied—were forces of the new age that worked upon British affairs athwart the lines of party divisions, and gave a new reality to public and Parliamentary life.

BOOKS FOR FURTHER READING: Lecky, *Leaders of Public Opinion in Ireland,* and *History of Ireland in the Eighteenth Century* (5 vols.); Stephen Gwynn, *History of Ireland*; Lyall, *British Dominion in India*; Professor Coupland, *Wilberforce.*

For the Dominions and Colonies there are two excellent series, Wyatt Tilby's *The British People Overseas,* and the more detailed *Historical Geography of the British Empire,* edited by Sir Charles Lucas.

CHAPTER SEVEN

The Reign of George III in Its Economic Aspect. The Early Stages of the Industrial Revolution. Population. Canals. Machinery. Coal. The Movement of Industry from the Village to the Town. Enclosure. Housing. Administrative Defects. *Laissez-faire*

KING: George III, 1760–1820

The great changes in man's command over nature and consequent manner of life, which began in England in the reign of George III and have since spread with varying degrees of intensity over almost the whole inhabited globe, make bewildering work for the historian. Up to the Industrial Revolution, economic and social change, though continuous, has the pace of a slowly-moving stream; but in the days of Watt and Stephenson it has acquired the momentum of water over a mill-dam, distracting to the eye of the spectator. Nor, for all its hurry, does it ever reach any pool at the bottom and resume its former leisurely advance. It is a cataract still. The French Revolution occupied a dozen years at most, but the Industrial Revolution may yet continue for as many hundred, creating and obliterating one form of economic and social life after another, so that the historian can never say—'This or this is the normal state of modern England.' To speak, for example, in terms of traffic. Four successive civilizations of the riding track, the canal and coach road, the railway, and the motor have been superimposed one on the other in the course of a hundred and sixty years.

Want of statistical and economic information lightens the work of the historian of earlier times, while setting limits to the scope and certainty of his deductions. The age of Blue-books begins with the Nineteenth Century. The first census of Great Britain was taken in 1801. Our economic information, in fact, only becomes trustworthy in the middle of the first phase of the Industrial Revolution. We have, therefore, very slender means of estimating the material welfare of the majority of Englishmen before the latter years of George III. Then, indeed, the picture which economic historians present to us of England in the time of Cobbett, is in some important respects very unpleasant; but as it is the first 'close-up' in the cinema show of English social history, we are unable to say whether an equally hard and precise vision of any earlier period would be any less unpleasant to our modern susceptibilities. Candid persons will refrain from answering the question with any approach to dogmatism.

It is possible, of course, to prefer the rural to the city life, and to regret that the farmer and artificer have been so generally replaced by the minder of machines; it is possible also to hold exactly the opposite view. We must indeed all of us deplore the loss of beauty of shape and variety of surface in machine-made articles, and the landscape marred by industrialism, which have so largely deprived us of the purest æsthetic pleasures formerly common to rich and poor alike. But in no case must we imagine that Great Britain could, without modern machinery, have supported forty-two millions in 1921 at a standard of material comfort as high as that which then obtained; or even fourteen millions in 1821 at the miserably inadequate standard, as we now hold it, of that day. What precisely was the average standard of life among the six or seven millions in 1721, is a question on which experts differ in opinion, because statistical knowledge about that early date is fragmentary or non-existent. As to the extent of true happiness and moral welfare then as compared to now, we are still more in the dark. But the interest of the enquiry loses nothing by want of certainty and finality in the answer.

The most striking accompaniment of the revolution in machinery and organization was the rise in the number of inhabitants of Great Britain in the single reign of George III, from about seven and a half to above fourteen millions. But what precise relation as cause or effect this increase had to the industrial and agricultural changes of the time, is a question not easily answered. Certain explanations, till recently accepted, now appear doubtful. It must be remembered that a similarly unprecedented rise in population was taking place in Celtic Ireland during the same years, and in Celtic Ireland there was no Industrial Revolution at all. Neither is it safe to set down the rise in population to the 'Speenhamland' system of aiding wages out of rates, at so much per child; for that system only began in 1795, became fully operative a good deal later, and never obtained at all in Scotland, North England or Ireland, where the rise in population was just as rapid as in the 'Speenhamland' counties of the Midlands and South. Moreover from 1790 onwards the birth-rate slightly declined, although the population continued to multiply owing to the far more rapid fall in the death-rate.

The unexampled rise in population from 1760 onwards was due, not so much to earlier marriages and an increase in the crude birth-rate, though these had a considerable part in the affair before 1790, as to the saving of life by improvements in medical science and practice, and to an improved standard of living which may to some extent be attributed to cheap goods produced by the new mechanical inventions. The disappearance of the Plague so long endemic in the island; the control of the ravages of scurvy and ultimately of small-pox; the reduction of ague and fever by the draining of the land; the advance of habits of cleanliness and the use of cheap cotton shirts; improvements in sanitation in London and elsewhere as compared to the past, however appalling the age of Howard appears to our nice senses to-day; and above all else, more and better hospitals and better medical care of mothers and infants which greatly reduced mortality at child-birth or by 'convulsions,' rickets and other infantile diseases,—all these were features of the Eighteenth and early Nineteenth Centuries.[1]

It is not impossible that until the very eve of the Twentieth Century the crude birth-rate has varied very little down the ages, and that the modern increase of population was due to the more successful efforts of society 'officiously to keep alive.' At the end of George III's reign the French death-rate was twenty per cent. higher than the English. With all its faults, the later Eighteenth Century in England was a period of improved science, cleanliness and humanity. The patriotic pride of the historians of the Victorian era, like Macaulay, in the perpetual progress of the nation in its social life and comfort is perhaps after all no further removed from the whole truth than the more recent view that the Industrial Revolution was accompanied by a general throwback to harder conditions of life. Vital statistics are not everything, but so far as they go they are not unfavourable to the more optimistic doctrine of the older school.[2]

But if these causes, and others at present obscure, produced an increase in population wholly unexampled in history, it is certain that the additional millions could not have been maintained in the island, or even provided for

[1] See the important work just issued (1926) by the Cambridge Press, *Population Problems of the Age of Malthus*, by S. Talbot Griffith. See also Mrs. George's *London in the Eighteenth Century*, pp. 1–61.

[2] In Ireland improvement in health conditions was less operative than in England, though not totally wanting. The increase in Irish population was due largely to the absence of potato famine in the Eighteenth Century. The potato blight of 1846–47 initiated a rapid reduction of the population from over eight millions to under five millions by stimulating emigration to America. The potato is the easiest method of supporting life at a very low standard,—until a year comes when the crop completely fails.

in the colonies, had it not been for the agricultural and industrial changes of the new era. Indeed, if the old economic system had continued unchanged after 1760, it is doubtful whether the existing seven millions could have continued much longer to inhabit the island in the same degree of comfort as before. The depletion of British timber was already producing a fuel famine that left many domestic hearths cold, and was driving the iron industry across the sea to the still virgin forests of America and Scandinavia. At that moment the situation was saved by the new canal system, which brought coal to domestic hearths in inland regions of South England, and to the furnaces of the Black Country.

The way for the Industrial Revolution was prepared by the first rapid improvement in methods of transport since the Roman era.[3] From the beginning of the reign of George III, a network of canals was gradually extended over many districts, bringing to them benefits which London had always enjoyed from her maritime position and sea-borne coal. Canals were eventually made in all parts of the island, but those which paid dividends over ten per cent. were nearly all in the mining and industrial districts of the North and Midlands, or served to connect those districts with the Thames Valley. For the system of 'inland navigation,' as it was called,[4] no less than the modern merchant navy, throve by reason of the coal trade. Railways, when they came in their turn, were originally devised to serve the distribution of coal, and to link up the gaps in the canal system. But early in the days of George Stephenson [B. 1781, D. 1848.] it was clear to the foreseeing that the age of canals would be short in England.

Short, too, for the same reason was the glory of the hard 'Macadamized' road, with its Tally-ho coaches and post-chaise postillions speeding along at twelve miles an hour from the courtyards of the great London inns to Bath, or

[3] See Vol. I., pp. 69–70.

[4] Hence, the hosts of labourers who dug them were called 'navigators' or 'navvies.'

Holyhead, or York, or Gretna Green, and on over Sir Walter's Scotland. Like the contemporary canals, the hard roads were the work chiefly of capitalist companies, who recouped themselves from passengers at the toll-bars. But the movement was aided by the Post Office, one of the first Departments to conceive the modern idea of the duty of the Civil Service to the public. The gay and rapid life of the English road reached perfection only during the Napoleonic wars, and twenty years later the railways already clearly foreshadowed the end. Brief, but characteristically English while it lasted, was that age of the all-worshipped horse, with Horncastle Fair for its Mecca, with fox-hunters, stagecoachmen and jockeys as ministers to the national enthusiasm for the noblest of animals. Posterity still fondly regards that generation as the last of 'merrie England,'—except when it remembers that it was also the era of Peterloo and the very worst period of the 'evils' of the Industrial Revolution.

Indeed, when we picture the past to ourselves, it is not easy always to remember the great variety of things old and new that go on side by side in separate compartments in the life of a growing nation. We sometimes think of the factory system as the leading feature of the last years of George III. But though it was the new feature and had the future with it, it by no means as yet dominated the scene except in one or two districts. The cotton trade of Lancashire had indeed sprung into sudden being, first in small 'mills' planted beside the water power of the Pennine streams, then with more elaborate machinery and on a larger scale in the plain below. And there had been a corresponding development of Liverpool, as the port for this new industry which bought all its raw material in America and sold most of its finished goods overseas. But when Peterloo was fought [1819.], not a twentieth part of the families of England had a member in the cotton industry. Agriculture was by far the largest occupation, and next came the building trades and domestic service; the weaving of wool had not yet passed into the factory, though the spinning-jenny had already destroyed the cottage industry of many industrious wives and children of the peasant class; tailoring and shoemaking, that figured among the very largest trades in the country, were still conducted on the domestic basis; and the number of persons engaged in the service of horses must have been immense.

The Industrial Revolution was not an event but a process. It was the admixture of the old manner of life and the new that made the characteristic and vigorous Britain of the era of Wellington. Only as the Nineteenth Century wore on, an ever larger proportion of the population was harnessed to the new machinery and to big business, while the realm of the factory was extended every year at the expense of domestic and out-of-door occupations. Fortunately, as the factory had become the typical arena of work, its worst abuses were gradually remedied; from 1833 onward it became increasingly subjected to State inspection and regulation, which employees in the older type of domestic workshop had good reason to envy.

The greatest development of the reign of George III, greater even than the Lancashire cotton trade, was the revolution involved in the application of coal to iron-smelting, which created the Black Country in the West Midland shires. In forty years the production of iron in Britain increased ten-fold. The Black Country became the chief scene of this new development, and of a great number and variety of hardware, pottery and other industries more and more dependent upon iron or coal. All over the island new businesses sprang up, each helped by some adaptation of James Watt's [B. 1736, D. 1819.] steam engine to the various processes of mining and manufacture. With iron and machinery was born a new class—the modern mechanic. If the great economic changes as yet brought little good to the child in the factory or to man, woman or child in the coal-mine, it created a large class of well-paid, educated engineers, whose advice was sought with respect by their employers in innumerable industries scattered all over the island. To that class of wage-earners belonged the great Stephenson family of Tyneside. There was nothing 'bourgeois' about the origins of the man who invented the locomotive, after having taught himself to read at the age of seventeen. The motto of the coming age was 'self-help,' or individual opportunity, and its benefits were not entirely monopolized by the middle class. It was from the 'Mechanics' Institutes' that the adult education of the new age took a start.

For the first time since Anglo-Saxon days, the North-Western half of England, the ancient Northumbria and Mercia, became of importance in rivalry to the corn-bearing lands of South and East, and to London and its satellite counties.[5] Even the old textile industries of East Anglia, of Somerset and of the Cotswolds declined before the vigorous competition of the northern dales in the age of machinery. Moorlands which had formerly been the home of the moss-trooper, the feudal retainer and the shepherd, became centres of wealth and trained intelligence of the modern order. This shifting of the geographic balance of power in the island was to be a chief cause of the demand for political change and Parliamentary redistribution in the approaching era. But so long as the Napoleonic wars lasted, and for more than a decade after they had come to an end, the new middle class was content to accumulate wealth, and did not seriously challenge the political and social monopoly that excluded it from its natural weight in the new England. And although the proletariat assembled in the new industrial districts were driven by misery to Radical agitation under Cobbett and Hunt, it was still easy to keep them down so long as they had no middle-class support, and no legal Trade Union organization of their own.

With momentum ever increasing throughout the reign of George III, men and women were flooding into the industrial districts of Clydeside, the northern coalpits, Lancashire, the Black Country, South Wales, London, and any place where 'navvy' work was to be had on the new canals and roads. Round these centres of industry the miserably low agricultural wage was brought to a higher level than

[5] See Vol. I., p. 87.

in more remote rural regions where there was no competition of alternative employment. And yet the condition of the new industrial proletariat was very miserable, and was made more miserable by the vagaries of prices, wages and employment due to the violent fluctuations caused by the Napoleonic war.

The evils of this first period of the new economic system were great, but they were a concentration and multiplication of old evils rather than a creation of new. There had been coalmines for centuries and the miners had always been shockingly housed, paid and overworked, with little or no provision against accidents or enquiry when accidents took place.[6] Indeed, before 1815, it was not the custom to hold inquests on deaths in the mines of Northumberland and Durham. In Scotland the miners, incredible as it may appear, were bound serfs until nearly the close of the Eighteenth Century. And even in England women and children in the past had been literally harnessed to the work under unspeakable conditions in the damp darkness of the mine. The Industrial Revolution immensely increased the mining population without at first materially improving their condition, and their ill-treatment was revealed to a more humane and inquisitive generation by the epoch-making Mines Report of 1842. So, too, pauper children, who had previously been handed over individually to the domestic affections of Mrs. Brownrigg and Peter Grimes,[7] might in the new age be grouped together in a cotton mill run by a hard-bitten North country working man who had borrowed a couple of hundred pounds to start the business, and had no compunctions about making the lasses work. The 'free labour' of children who had parents to support was also passing from the home to the mill or factory, a change that must in many cases,—though not in all,—have been for the worse, before the era of Factory Inspection began in 1833. The relative misery of the poor at

[6] But no doubt the mines were getting deeper and the chance of accidents greater as the surface coal was exhausted.

[7] See Vol. I., p. 35.

this period as compared to that of their forebears is hard to estimate, for want of facts about earlier times. The absolute misery of many of them is a fact incontestable.

The immigration into the new industrial districts represented the overflow of population created by the continual rise in the number of inhabitants of Great Britain from 1760 onwards. They came to be the man-power for the new industrial world, 'bowing their heads for bread,' but glad to escape from rural England, Scotland, Wales and Ireland, where only starvation awaited them. Irish immigration had been a feature of London life and of English and Scottish harvesting since Stuart times at least, but in the Hanoverian epoch it became much more pronounced. Jews from Central and Eastern Europe also began to come over in great numbers, so that by the end of the Eighteenth Century there were 20,000 in London, mostly very poor. But for the attractions of America in the Nineteenth Century to these two races, the admixture of Irish and Jews in the English community would be much greater than it is. The Irish brought with them a low standard of life and wages, and helped to make the worst slums. The cellars they inhabited in London were as weather-proof as the hovels they had left in Connemara, and bread and cheese was at least better than potatoes. Partly because they tended to lower the English workman's pitiful wage, there were frequent riots against them in London and among the farm-hands. Indeed, the animosity against the Irish labourer was one of the causes of the feeling against Roman Catholics that distinguished the populace of Great Britain in the days of Lord George Gordon and for long afterwards. [1780.]

A large immigration of Englishmen from the rural districts must in any case have taken place, owing to the rise in population coinciding with new facilities for employment in industrial centres. But changes at the same time occurred in the economy of the rural village itself, which, in a variety of ways, affected the pace of the exodus to the towns. The change was twofold: the removal of industries from the villages to urban areas owing to the revolution in machinery and organization; and the enclosure of commons and open fields to grow more corn. The two movements combined to revolutionize English rural life, but they had no direct causal connection one with the other.

The Industrial Revolution, by introducing machinery and so favouring concentration in factories and urban districts, gradually made an end of two kinds of village industry. It destroyed first the spinning and other by-employments of the wives and children of agricultural families; and secondly the full-time employment of villagers in such various trades as clock-making, basket-weaving, carriage and waggon building, tanning, milling and brewing, saddlery, cobbling, tailoring, and the great national industry of cloth-weaving. Some of these arts and industries supplied the village itself, others supplied the national and the world market. In the course of a hundred and seventy years, starting from the accession of George III, British industries have been almost entirely removed to the towns.

The migration of industry and craftsmanship left the village once more almost purely agricultural, as in the time of Domesday. The rural outlook was narrowed, the villager's intelligence and independence lowered, except in so far as improved school education has applied a one-sided remedy of recent years. But there was no efficient school in the English village a hundred years ago. Apprenticeship and the craft were the old educational forces, and they were disappearing. With the flight of the industry by which they lived, many independent families had to obliterate themselves in the featureless streets of the modern city, forced, like Wordsworth's 'poor Susan,' to desert the cottage beside the stream,

The one only dwelling on earth that she loves.

Those who remained behind as hands employed by the farmer in his fields, no longer had any by-employment in their own homes to enable them to hold out for better wages, or to eke out what wages they got. The monotony of village life in the Nineteenth Century was due mainly to the migration of the industries to the urban districts, which eventually was more complete in England than in any other country of Europe.

When George III died, the migration of industry from the village was only half accomplished, but the enclosure of the land was more nearly finished. The period of private Acts of Parliament for the enclosing of open fields and of common wastes corresponds roughly to the years of George III's reign [1760–1820.], though it overlaps at both ends.

The survival in the best corn-growing area of the Midlands and East Anglia of the early mediæval system of open-field cultivation,[8] was an anomaly too gross to be any longer tolerated. The beneficial effects of enclosure in increasing production and ultimately population, had been demonstrated in many districts in Tudor and Stuart times.[9] And when, in the days of the elder Pitt, the population of the island began to grow by leaps and bounds, the enlargement of the corn supply became the first of national necessities. It was not till after the Napoleonic wars that Russia or any other land beyond the sea was able to supply any appreciable quantity of grain to Britain. In those days, the island must feed itself or starve.

It was, therefore, in the reign of George III that the Midlands and East Anglia and much of the North English and Scottish landscape took on their present appearance of a chess-board pattern, made up of innumerable fields 'enclosed' by hedges or stone walls. The extreme south-east corner of the island, and many western counties, had displayed those familiar features for centuries past.[10]

[8] Described, Vol. I., pp. 203–6.

[9] Vol. II., pp. 33–35.

[10] See the maps at the end of Gonner's *Common Land and Enclosure* for a rapid view of the geographic area of the enclosure in the Eighteenth and Nineteenth Centuries. In the North-Western corner of England the enclosures were of common of waste; the open-field system of agriculture had never had a great part in the life of the North, where scattered farms had been the rule.

The wholesale enclosures of the reign of George III, like the partial enclosures of Tudor and Stuart times, opened the way for better agriculture by farmers with a compact holding in place of scattered strips in the open village field. These opportunities were not neglected, for the Eighteenth Century was the age of 'improving landlords,' who put their capital into the land, and who studied, practised and preached scientific agriculture and stock-breeding. Sheep and cattle, as well as horses, were developed to the point of perfection in England during 'the century of improvement.' Artificial grasses, root crops and proper methods of growing grain, all alike impossible in the open-field system, became the usual instead of the exceptional practice of English farmers. The prophet of the new agriculture was Arthur Young, and its typical man was 'Coke of Norfolk,' that sturdy Whig and enemy of George III, who reigned at Holkham from the American Revolution to the premiership of Peel, increased his rent-roll from £2200 to £20,000, made the fortunes and won the affections of all classes in his neighbourhood, turning a sandy rabbit-warren into a model estate which agriculturists came from all over Britain and Europe to visit.

Scotland, when George III began to reign, was hedgeless and treeless. It was not, like central England, a land of large villages, but, like northern England, a land of hamlets and scattered farms, set in the surrounding wilderness. The power of the Scottish landlords was very great, and the tenants often held their farms on precarious leases of one year. But the spirit of scientific improvement became even more prominent in Scotland than in England. The lairds used their power to have the land enclosed and tilled on modern methods, while the new practice of giving long leases encouraged the enterprise and independence of the farmer. The solid farm buildings, field-walls and plantations of Scotland date from the beginning of George III's reign onwards.

Rural Wales changed less than Scotland and England in this period, because in the Celtic mountain-land enclosure had been co-eval with agriculture. But Wales was acquiring a 'Black Country' of its own, where on its southern coast the coal measures ran down to the sea.

The enclosure movement was a necessary step to feed the increasing population. And it increased not only the wealth of the landlords who put money into their estates, but that of the large tenant farmers who were their principal agents in the movement. The spleen of Cobbett was moved by the number of farmers who at the end of George III's reign lived in a smart new brick house—often entitled 'Waterloo farm,'—who drove in a gig to market, had wine on their tables and a piano in the parlour for their daughters; yet these things were a sign of increasing wealth, comfort and education. Nor had the old-fashioned small 'husbandman' by any means disappeared, although he had been long declining. The census of 1831 showed that the agriculturists who neither employed labour nor were themselves employed, were still as one to six in comparison with employing farmers and their hands. And as late as 1851 two-thirds of the farms of Great Britain were still under one hundred acres in size.

Enclosure had been a necessity, but the enclosures had not brought equal benefits to all. The share of the poor had been inadequate. The loss of their village industries has been already referred to, and accounts for half their distress or more. But the method of the enclosures had not taken enough consideration of the small man, and too little had been done to fix the lesser peasantry on the soil as part of the new scheme of things. When similar changes took place in contemporary Denmark, a land ruled by a monarch dependent on his general popularity, the interest of all classes down to the poorest was carefully considered, with excellent consequences in the agricultural Denmark of to-day. But the England of George III was completely aristocratic in the sympathies and constitution of its governing class, whether Whigs, Tories or 'King's Friends' bore rule. The Houses of Parliament which passed the Enclosure Acts were closed by law to anyone who was not a considerable owner of land. The Justices of the Peace were autocrats of the countryside and represented one class alone. The proprietorship of most of the land of England was in the hands of a comparatively small group of 'great landed families.' Under these social and political conditions it was inevitable that the enclosures should be carried through according to the ideas of the big landlord class alone. Those ideas rightly envisaged the national necessity of more food production, but not the national necessity of maintaining and increasing small properties or small holdings.

In the redivision of the open fields and common wastes among individual proprietors and farmers, there was no intention to defraud the small man, but no desire to give him more than his apparent legal claim. Often he could not prove a legal claim to the rights he exercised on the common. Oftener his legal rights to keep cows or geese there, or his personal right in one or two strips in the village field, were compensated with a sum of money which was not enough to enable him to set up as a capitalist farmer or pay for the hedging of the plot allotted to him; the compensation might, however, pay for a month's heavy drinking in the ale-house. And so he became a landless labourer. Arthur Young himself was horrified at some of the results of the movement of which he had been the chief apostle. In 1801 he wrote 'By nineteen out of twenty Enclosure Bills the poor are injured and most grossly.'[11]

The condition of the agricultural labourer, deprived of the industries previously conducted by his wife and children, was, indeed, most unhappy. The enforcement of a living wage was not opposed to old English theory and practice; and it was the labourer's due in common justice, because Pitt's Acts made Trade Union action illegal. But the landlord class, represented by the Justices of the Peace, decided not to compel the farmers to pay a living wage. They adopted instead a policy elaborated by the Berkshire Magistrates at Speenhamland in 1795, namely,

[11] It is not true, however, that the enclosure movement sweepingly deprived the cottagers of their gardens. Cottage gardens and potato patches were quite common when George III died.

to give rates in aid of insufficient wages. To keep the poor alive, it was decided to tax the rate-payers, instead of forcing farmers and employers of labour to shoulder their proper burden. It was a fatal policy, for it encouraged farmers to keep down wages. The system, which lasted till the New Poor Law of 1834, made the rural labourer a pauper, and discouraged his thrift and self-respect. It paid better to cringe to the authorities for the dole, than to attempt any form of self-help. The 'Speenhamland system' spread over the Southern and Midland Counties, but was not adopted in Scotland and North England, where the agricultural labourer suffered no such moral and social degradation, though there too times were often very hard.

Wealth was increasing so fast in town and country that the contrasts between the life of the rich and the life of the poor were more dramatic and more widely observable than of old. In the industrial world, members of the new middle class ceased to live over the workshop, and built themselves separate villas and mansions in imitation of the life of the gentry. They no longer formed one household with their apprentices and journeymen. The landed gentry, for their part, were enlarging the manor-house for the heir and the parsonage for the younger son, and too often replacing a tumble of gabled roofs that had grown up piecemeal in the last three hundred years, by a gorgeous 'gentleman's seat' in the neo-Palladian style. Game-preserving in the midst of a hungry population, with mantraps and spring guns lurking in the brambles to guard the pheasant at the expense of man's life or limb, led to a poaching war with armed skirmishes, and several thousand convictions a year. It was these contrasts that made the Radicalism of the new era, a spirit unknown in early Hanoverian England, even though the poor may have been materially as ill off in the one period as in the other.

Coal and iron in the Northern and Midland Shires were creating industrial cities not so immeasurably smaller than London, as Norwich and Bristol had been in the Stuart epoch. Yet London though it distanced its rivals less, was still growing with a rapidity that astounded and alarmed the world. Its prosperity continued to be based, as before the Industrial Revolution, on its unique place in commerce and distribution, and on highly skilled finishing trades still conducted on the domestic system. It still, therefore, attracted two classes of immigrants—the roughest kind of labour for porterage at the docks and in distribution, and the most skilled and intelligent workmen for the finishing trades. It had also a much larger proportion of clerks, organizers, civil servants and men of education than any other city in the world.

All round London, bricks and mortar were on the march across the green fields. When George III died, the city was linked up by an almost continuous line of houses with Hammersmith, Deptford, Highgate and Paddington. For London, like other English cities, had always grown outwards, not upwards. Paris and many foreign cities, where houses used to be forbidden outside the fortifications, being unable to expand sideways, grew towards heaven, with tenements for the poor and flats for the middle classes. But the Englishman traditionally lived in his own house, however low and small and however distant from his work. On the whole, the English system was the best, though not the cheapest.[12]

Jerrybuilding was perhaps the gravest evil of the Industrial Revolution. It was much, no doubt, that the immensely increased population was housed at all. Nor is it clear that on the average men were, in the strictly material sense, worse 'housed' in the new urban areas than in the old country cottages whence they or their fathers had come. But cellar and one-room tenements for families were dreadfully common for the lower class of labour, whether in London, Glasgow, Manchester or the mining

[12] The tall 'wynds' of Edinburgh, many storeys high, recalled the days when life outside the High Street region was unsafe. But in Sir Walter Scott's day, Princes Street and the new modern town down below were growing apace. Scottish housing in town and country then, as now, was behind English. One-room hovels of turf or unmortared stone could still be found in the poorer farming districts.

districts. A large proportion of the wage-earners and all the large class of commercial 'clerks' were better housed. But even their dwellings were monotonous and sordid in appearance; town-planning and any effort to brighten or embellish the face of the street were alien to the ideas of the age. The enterprising employer wanted dwellings where the new hands he wished to employ could live. The builder looked to make money on the transaction. No one else gave the matter a thought. Thus was the new England built.

Laissez-faire, or the objection to interference by government, became a theory, but it was first a fact. The whole framework of Eighteenth Century England was incompatible with efficient administration. A modern nation was being governed by Tudor machinery, or rather by what was still left of that machinery after the passage of two hundred years. In these circumstances, what little taste men had of State or Municipal control, did not encourage them to ask for more. Till the machinery of local and central government was modernized, as it only began to be after 1832, opinion based on experience said that the less government did the better. Among the few things it had actually done in recent times was the attempt to suppress Trade Unions by law, the supplementing of wages out of the rates, and the Corn Law of 1815. As to town-planning, factory-inspecting, sanitation and public education, much had to happen before either State or Municipality could dream of undertaking such tasks. Whole new generations of men and ideas had first to be born.

The political spirit of the English Eighteenth Century,—aristocratic power tempered by Parliamentary control and individual rights,—had little in common either with continental despotism or with the bureaucratic democracy of our own time. When the Reformers, inspired by Bentham, Cobbett and Brougham, took in hand the problem of the relation of this old governmental system to the new facts of the Industrial Revolution, their first belief was that the remedy lay in reduced taxation and less State interference.

Such, it was expected by many, would be the result of Parliamentary Reform. The exact opposite proved to be the case. In the event, Liberalism meant not less government, but more. But the government had first to be made the instrument of the general will. The gradual creation of social services by public action and at the public expense was to be the chief contribution of the Nineteenth Century to social welfare. But this was not foreseen by anyone in 1816, when Brougham compelled the government to drop the Income Tax on the return of peace, as a sop to democratic opinion.

BOOKS FOR FURTHER READING: J. H. Clapham, *Economic History of Modern Britain,* Vol. I. *Early Railway Age*; Halévy, *History of the English People in the Nineteenth Century,* Vol. I. (*England in* 1815); Hammond, *Rise of Modern History,* and series of *Agricultural, Skilled,* and *Town Labourer*; Mrs. George, *London Life in the Eighteenth Century*; Lord Ernle, *English Farming* and *The Land and The People*; Meredith, *Economic History of England*; Stirling, *Coke of Norfolk*; Griffith, *Population Problems of the Age of Malthus*.

BOOK SIX

The Later Hanoverians. Sea-Power in the Age of Machinery. The Transition to Democracy.

INTRODUCTION

The Parliamentary aristocracy under the first three Georges had developed British maritime power to the point where Nelson left it; had lost one overseas empire and acquired another; had completed the reconciliation of Scotland and perpetuated the alienation of Ireland; and had guarded the arena for the early stages of the Industrial Revolution, but without any attempt to control its social effects, or any foresight of its political implications. In the course of their long hegemony the Whig and Tory aristocracies had perfected a new form of governmental machinery, hinging on the Cabinet and Prime Minister, which lent efficiency to the rule of Parliament. By the help of this system the English House of Commons had risen triumphant from a succession of wars with despotic monarchies, and under Pitt and Castlereagh had defeated Napoleon himself, given peace to Europe, and won a hundred years of security for Great Britain.

The task awaiting their successors, under the later monarchs of the House of Hanover, was to adapt this system of Parliamentary Cabinet government to the new social facts created by the Industrial Revolution. [1832.] This was found to involve the admission first of the middle and then of the working class as partners in the control of the political machine. [1867.] A failure to make these adjustments would have led to a breakdown of the Parliamentary system and a war of classes, such as seemed adumbrated for the future at the time of Peterloo and the Six Acts. [1819.]

But the good genius of English politics has often retrieved apparently hopeless situations. The last British Revolution is still that of 1688. By a gradual transition towards democracy, seldom hastening and never turning back, political rights were extended to all without a catastrophe. This great manœuvre was safely accomplished because all classes and all parties showed, upon the whole, sound political sense and good humour, because the Victorian age was a period of peace and external security for Britain, and because its middle years were years of unexampled prosperity. Finally, the extension of the political franchise to all compelled the nation to elaborate a system of national education out of the fragmentary efforts of private and denominational enterprise. [1870 *et seq.*]

In the main the transition was effected through the revival and strengthening of the old two-party system. The peculiarly English tradition of the two perennial parties had been to some extent replaced by a group system of politics during the unchallenged Tory predominance with which the Century opened. But at the time of the Reform Bill of 1830–32, the Whigs furbished up their old traditions with new war-cries and programmes, and both parties thenceforth moved forward, forming as they went a kaleidoscopic succession of new social alliances in the rapidly changing world.

The underlying principle connecting the Liberals and Conservatives of Victoria's reign in an actually traceable succession with the Whigs and Tories of Charles II, was the continuous antagonism of Church and Dissent. That lasting dualism of English religious life was bound to reflect itself in a political dualism, so long as certain monopolies of the Church were maintained. For two hundred years it gave a reality to the otherwise artificial permanence of the traditions of the two parties from one changing period to another. The working-class movement at the beginning of the Nineteenth Century was in part connected with Dissent and was at that time almost altogether outside the influence of the established Church. The denominational aspect of politics therefore served to connect the Radicalism of the working classes to some extent with the Whig-Liberal party; through that party they sought political enfranchisement, while seeking economic and social amelioration by their own methods of Trade Unionism, Co-operative Societies, and incipient Socialism. The fact that the majority of Englishmen in the middle of the Nineteenth Century were religious but not of the same religion, was a steadying influence in the strife of parties and classes, although it was in itself an additional cause of controversy.

But the gradual adaptation of Parliamentary government, and with it of local government, to the democratic character of the new age, was only a small part of the adaptations necessary if the new society was to be saved. To render life increasingly tolerable to forty millions in an island where seven millions had found it hard to live before, new organizations of the most various kinds had to be created. The Eighteenth Century had been prolific of men and great in individual energies, but its corporate and institutional life had been lethargic. The Nineteenth Century, on the other hand, not only put fresh democratic vigour into Parliament, municipalities, Church, Universities, Schools and Civil Service, but created a wealth of new organisms, public and private, dealing with every department of life. It was the age of Trade Unions, Co-operative and Benefit Societies, Leagues, Boards, Commissions, Committees for every conceivable purpose of philanthropy and culture. Not even the dumb animals were left without organized protection. The Nineteenth Century rivalled the Middle Ages in its power to create fresh forms of corporate and institutional life, while yielding little to the Eighteenth Century in the spirit of self-help and personal initiative. The list of great men whom the Nineteenth Century produced is often repeated; the list of new organizations that it created would be yet longer and no less significant.

The new forms of government and of human activity which were evolved are indeed too complex for brief description in this book, but many of them are familiar to us as matters of our own everyday life. A characteristic of the new national machinery, fully apparent towards the end of Queen Victoria's reign, was the close inter-relation that had grown up on the one hand between private philanthropic effort and State control, and on the other between local and central government. As Parliament and local government began to respond to the needs of the community as a whole, and as the State became more and more intelligently interested in the work of private effort in education, medicine, sanitation and a hundred other sides of life,—an elaborate system of State aid, enforcement and control came into being, through Treasury Grants in Aid to local bodies, State inspection of conditions of labour and of life, industrial insurance and the modern educational system. Voluntary and private effort aided by the State did many things that in other countries of Europe were done solely by the State or were not done at all.

The complicated and constantly shifting relationship between central and local government, between private enterprise and State undertaking, was rendered possible by the evolution of the permanent, non-political Civil Service of Great Britain with its accumulated stores of knowledge, experience and sound tradition. In the third quarter of the century, the Civil Service was removed from the field of political jobbery by the adoption of open competitive examination as the method of entrance, a device that seemed as strange as it has proved successful.

British methods of coping with the problems of the new era showed great practical inventiveness, and were all in the line of a strong native tradition. Relatively little was copied from continental movements. The Parliamentary system was our own; local government was reformed and elaborated on British lines; factory inspection, Trade Unionism, the Co-operative movement, were of British origin; the Civil Service was native in its traditions, and in the peculiar method of its selection by examination.

The advance in humanity, democracy and education, and the changes in industrial method bringing large crowds of wage-earners of both sexes together in offices and factories, led to a new conception of the place of woman in society. The education of women, from being almost totally neglected, became in a couple of generations comparable to that of men. The position of women in the family was altered in law, and was yet more altered in practice and opinion. Finally the movement for their political enfranchisement ceased to seem absurd.

All these great changes would never have been carried through without disaster but for the peace, prosperity and security that marked the Nineteenth Century in Britain. Except in the episode of the Crimean War, the general policy of Britain was to abstain from taking part in the strife of continental nations, when it renewed itself forty years after Waterloo. Since the Balance of Power was for the time safely adjusted, there was no call for us to fight in order to prevent the conquest of Europe by a single nation and its vassals.[1]

So, too, relations with the United States, though of growing importance, remained peaceful from the Treaty of Ghent [XMAS EVE, 1814.] onwards, in spite of some ugly crises. This happy result was due in no small degree to the work of Castlereagh and Monroe in agreeing to a permanent disarmament along both sides of the Canadian frontier [1817.]; it followed that while that frontier was being prolonged further and further to the west, the grave disputes that necessarily accompanied the process were never submitted to the decision of war. Another great step forward was taken when Gladstone consented to submit the *Alabama* claims to the arbitration of a third party. So too, in the division of Asiatic and African territories, the dis-

[1] Speaking of our friendly relations after 1886 with the Triple Alliance of Germany, Austria and Italy, then the strongest group in Europe, Lord Grey of Falloden writes in his memoirs:—'Great Britain has not in theory been adverse to the predominance of a strong group in Europe when it seemed to make for stability and peace. To support such a combination has generally been her first choice. It is only when the dominant Power becomes aggressive and she feels her own interests to be threatened that she, by an instinct of self-defence, if not by deliberate policy, gravitates to anything that can fairly be described as a Balance of Power.'

putes with France and Germany, though sometimes acute in the later years of the century, were settled by peaceful arbitration or agreement, largely through the action of Lord Salisbury, who held that Britain's 'greatest interest' was peace.

Peace, then, and the amazing prosperity which the state of the world in Queen Victoria's reign brought to the door of Britain's commerce and industry, formed conditions highly favourable to the solution of the grave political and social problems of the new order within the island. The chief external interests of Britain were not war or preparation for war, but her ever increasing foreign trade, more fabulous every decade, and the development of her new colonial empire bequeathed by the victors of Trafalgar and Waterloo. The over-population and unemployment in Britain after the Napoleonic wars, unrelieved in those days by any form of industrial insurance, drove English and Scots to the Colonies by hundreds of thousands. In the first half of the Nineteenth Century, many of these emigrants were agricultural or semi-agricultural labourers, glad to get hold of land and work it for themselves. Only towards the end of the period did the decay of rural life in England and the attraction of the modern town life create a danger that the English race should become a race of city-dwellers, unwilling to settle or to remain on the land.

By the beginning of the Twentieth Century, the Colonies had become Dominions, new nations in effect. After enjoying complete self-government as regards their internal affairs for fifty years or more, they began to look out upon the world, each with its own national point of view, —Canadian, Australian, South African. In these circumstances, the hopes entertained by British statesmen during the Imperialist movement at the close of the Nineteenth Century that it would be possible to unite the Empire more closely in some kind of Federal Constitution, were not destined to mature. A looser bond of common interest and affection held the Empire together when it was plunged into its next great crisis by the outbreak of the War with Germany in August 1914.

CHAPTER ONE

Repression and Reform, 1815–35. Corn Law and Income Tax. Cobbett, Peterloo and the Six Acts. Tory Reform. Peel and Huskisson. Castlereagh and Canning. The Wellington Ministry. The Whigs and the Reform Bill. The Municipal Corporations Act and Slavery Abolition. Belgium

KINGS: George III, died 1820; George IV, 1820–30; William IV, 1830–37.

The sudden fall in prices after the peace ruined many farmers and business men, and threw multitudes out of employment, though it momentarily increased the purchasing power of wages. Now, for the first time in English history, prices were seriously affected by the importation of foreign foodstuffs, not yet indeed from America but from Europe. The Corn Law of 1815, designed to prevent this entry of cheap grain, seemed insult and injury not only to the poor but to the manufacturing middle class, who had no wish that the poor should have to spend all their wages in buying bread alone. Industrial employers and working men for the first time found themselves combined in angry opposition to the use made by the landlord class of its monopoly of political power.

This first united movement of the middle and lower orders soon died down, though not for ever. The poor, indeed, were kept by sheer misery in a state of unrest, and went on with the agitation inspired by Cobbett and Hunt that culminated four years later in Peterloo and the Six Acts. But the middle classes retired for a while from the political arena, contenting themselves with a victory won by their champion Henry Brougham and the Parliamentary Whig leaders, who wrested from the Government the abolition of the Income Tax. [1816.] The agitation had been carried on by Petitions to Parliament from 'the most respectable' inhabitants of town and country in all parts of the island against the continuance of Income Tax in time of peace, and especially against 'the compelling the petitioners to lay open their concerns by a train of inspectors and spies.' The Government was forced to bow to the storm. It was the first step made by popular control of policy, and unfortunately it was clean in the wrong direction. It increased the already excessive proportion of indirect taxation, which fell on the poor as heavily as on the rich, and this state of things lasted till Peel revived the Income Tax in 1842.

Because indirect taxation was employed to pay for the sinecures, pensions and places secured by aristocratic political jobbers, as well as to pay the interest on the National Debt to prosperous fund-holders, the National Debt and political jobbery were confounded together in Cobbett's sweeping censures. The poor, it was said with some justification, were being taxed to keep the rich. To the Radical of those days, the 'tax-eater' seemed to belong to a separate, half-human species, with interests wholly opposed to those of the 'tax-payer.' Whigs and Radicals in opposition hoped to relieve distress mainly by retrenchment and cutting down of taxation, instead of by redistribution of its burdens. But when they came into power after the Reform Bill they soon found that 'retrenchment' was not a royal road to 'the greatest happiness of the greatest number.'

Though William Cobbett wrote a vast deal of angry nonsense about finance and many other subjects,[1] he played a great and beneficent part in English history. He revived the political movement in the working class which Paine had begun and Pitt suppressed, and he revived it not as a Republican or Jacobin movement but as a Parliamentary

[1] Speaking of Hyde Park Corner in 1826, Cobbett wrote 'The *Great Captain of the age*, as that nasty palaverer, Brougham, called him, lives close to this spot, where also the "English ladies'" naked Achilles stands, having, on the base of it, the word *Wellington* in great staring letters, while all the others are very, very small; so that base tax-eaters and fund-gamblers from the country, when they go to crouch before this image, think it is the image of the Great Captain himself!'

movement, demanding the vote for the working classes and teaching them to look that way for relief of their distress. At the height of his influence in 1816 it stands on record that he turned many of his readers from rioting and rick-burning to political discussion and organization. They would have paid little attention to his advice if he had not been a journalist of genius in the early youth of journalism, and if he had not given expression, as no one else then did, to the insufferable position in which the poor found themselves. In town and country every person in authority in Church or State seemed to them in league with their employers against them; they had no tribunes to speak for them; they had no franchise in central or in local government; they had no legal means of trade organization to make their numbers felt in the labour market. Cobbett was the first who gave effective voice to their case.

William Cobbett was the old-fashioned John Bull, a lover of the past and of the sweet-smelling countryside, of the yeoman and the plough and the thatched cottage. A despiser of foreigners, a hater of theory, he had begun his journalistic career as an Anti-Jacobin, opposed to Paine and the 'rights of man.' But when he saw, or thought that he saw, the ancient rights of Englishmen being stolen from them, he rushed noisily to the rescue, to the no small wrath and consternation of his former allies. His *Political Register* [1802–35.] was read aloud to illiterate audiences under the hedgerow and in the workshop; and even the 'respectable' sometimes read the rascal for his shrewd hitting, laughed and cursed his impudence, and rode off thinking on what they had read. In this way the upper world first got a glimpse of the life and sufferings of the poor. Judge, then, how the poor loved him, when everyone else seemed to them to have entered into conspiracy to rob, oppress and vilify them. A bully was needed to stand up against that host of conscious and unconscious bullies. Old England, the passing England of the yeoman and the alehouse on the heath, produced as a last effort this glorious, unchallengeable bully, with no touch of cowardice in all his vast bulk, and, when out of the ring, no malice.

Cobbett became the father of the very unphilosophic Radicalism which effected so much in Nineteenth Century Britain. It was not a doctrine but a spirit—indignation at the wrongs of the poor. It was not tied to Liberalism, though often in alliance with it; still less was it tied to *laissez faire*. Working on and through many different politicians and parties, it passed Factory Acts, abolished Corn Laws, forced on the franchise, education, freedom of speech and press, and in the end altered the whole attitude of the upper to the lower class. Bentham and Mill were wiser men than Cobbett, but they would not without his aid have so transformed England from their study-chairs.

The history of the working-class movement, ever since the Industrial Revolution gave it self-consciousness, has moved in a perpetual alternation between political and economic action. Immediately after Waterloo its action was political. It was not yet highly organized in Trade Unions, and was not yet identified with any economic gospel or programme except an ungratified desire for better wages.[2] The Corn Law of 1815 seemed a challenge to political action; Parliamentary Reform was demanded as the first step to economic betterment of any kind.

[1817–19.] As yet the middle class stood aside as neuters, leaving the battle of Reform to be fought by unorganized labour led by Cobbett and Hunt, against the upper class and the full force of Government. The Whig, or aristocratic liberal, party also remained an impotent spectator, because it was still divided on the question of Parliamentary Reform. The Whigs, while denouncing the repressive measures of the Tories, disliked no less the tone

[2] Robert Owen, who always decried political action, was still at this period a philanthropist employer, not yet a democratic leader. In the first years of the peace he was still engaged in trying to persuade his brother employers, the Cabinet and Parliament that improved conditions of life and education in the factories would pay the employers and the nation, as he had demonstrated in his own New Lanark Mills. If he had been listened to then, we should live in a different world to-day.

of Radical propaganda, and could suggest no positive remedy of their own. The game therefore remained in the hands of the Tory Government of Liverpool, Wellington and Castlereagh.

Unfortunately the victors of Waterloo and of the Peace Conference were less happily inspired in dealing with the crisis that now confronted them at home. They had no economic or political remedy to propose except the severest forms of repression. Pitt's Anti-Jacobin repression had succeeded against a small minority, in time of war; it was now applied in time of peace against a majority, perhaps, of the nation. Rioters were tried for high treason, and printers and authors for sedition, but not always with success before middle-class juries. Spies and *agents provocateurs,* like the notorious Oliver, were let loose by Government among the Radicals. The Habeas Corpus Act was suspended. A tax of fourpence a copy on all periodical publications put not only Radical propaganda but knowledge of all sorts as far as possible out of the reach of the poor. Till 1836 fivepence was the minimum price for a newspaper worth a penny—so had the wisdom of Parliament decreed.

Public meetings, too, were generally prohibited. It would have been better if none had been allowed at all, for when a vast but orderly concourse of working men and women assembled on St. Peter's Fields, Manchester, to demand Parliamentary Reform, the magistrates, seized by sudden panic, let loose a charge of yeomanry which killed a dozen and seriously injured hundreds of both sexes. [AUG. 16, 1819.]

The Ministry approved of this tragic blunder without waiting to make enquiry. The bulk of the nation thought otherwise. Not only Radicals and working men, but Whigs in their high country-seats and merchants in their cosy parlours were horrified at the callous slaughter of their fellow-citizens. It was called 'Peterloo,' because it seemed to cancel the debt of the nation's gratitude for Waterloo. It had a great effect on the mind of the rising generation of all classes and of all parties, for it showed the end of the blind alley up which the old Anti-Jacobin Toryism of mere negation had long been leading the country. But for the moment there was no alternative to that policy. Since there was to be no conciliation, order must be rigorously maintained, as it was by the 'Six Acts,' passed in that winter.

There followed, next February, the Cato Street Conspiracy of physical-force Radicals, under Thistlewood, to murder the whole Cabinet as it sat at dinner. [1820.] The reaction in favour of Government was considerable, but, considering the horrid nature of the conspiracy, curiously evanescent. The unsavoury episode of the divorce proceedings against Queen Caroline, instituted that summer by Ministers to gratify their royal master, George IV, at the time of his accession, plunged them into deeper unpopularity than ever before. The subjects of the land were in some doubt as to the Queen's character, but in none at all about the King's. The fact that he was actually married to two women at once was not then generally known, though much suspected. But the English sense of fair play was outraged by the low type of Italian witness brought over by the King's agents to swear away his wife's good name before the Peers of the land, while the King himself was openly living with other women. The 'Bill of Pains and Penalties' had to be withdrawn before ever it reached the Commons' House. The rising generation of caricaturists, headed by George Cruikshank, were depicting George IV's no longer elegant shape, and the yeomanry charging over the bodies of shrieking women, with the same brutal force with which their predecessors in the time of Gillray had attacked Fox and the 'Jacobins.'

After the fiasco of the 'Queen's Trial' had a little cleared the air and improved the humour of the nation by inflicting a severe defeat on Government, the Tory Ministry began a recovery which gave their party another decade of power. Three circumstances gave them this opportunity to make good: first, better times in trade; secondly, the atrophy of the Whig party, their only rivals in Parliament; and thirdly, the death of Castlereagh [1822.], whose genius lay in foreign not in domestic affairs, and whose presence in the Cabinet stood effectively in the way of the rise of Canning, the powerful representative of the new and more liberal brand of Toryism.

During the eight years that followed, not only the rigid Anti-Jacobin structure of recent times, but the British Constitution as men had known it since 1689, began to crack and give way in unexpected places. [1822–29.] Although the electoral system gave little direct representation to any large section of the public, Parliament did not altogether fail to reflect the new spirit of the age. The old two-party system could not revive till the abolition of the rotten boroughs gave the Whigs a fair chance, but the group system did some service in representing varieties of national opinion. There were two groups inside the Tory Cabinet itself: Canning and Huskisson stood for the more liberal[3] view of things, and Wellington and old Lord Eldon for the rigid past, with the Prime Minister Liverpool and the judicious Peel striving to keep the peace. Yet when, under Wellington as Premier, the Old Guard drove out their rivals, they were compelled by the stream of events to pass measures yet more liberal than any which Canning himself had found it possible to introduce. [1828–29.]

The outcome of the last eight years of Tory rule was a number of important reforms and the dissolution of the Anti-Jacobin Tory party, that had borne rule for more than a generation. In its place there arose, during the crisis of the Parliamentary Reform question [1830–32.], a new Whig-Liberal party and a new Conservative party, which governed the country in alternation in the coming epoch. Thus, after a period of peculiar confusion, Parliamentary life reverted to the two-party system in spite of greater complication of issues and the increasing number of classes and interests involved in the larger life of the reformed Parliament.

[3] 'Liberal' was not the name of a party till after the middle of the century. It denoted only a man of progressive views, whether Radical, Whig or Canningite Tory.

Of the liberal measures that signalized the last years of Tory rule, one of the most important, the repeal of Pitt's Combination Acts making Trade Union action illegal, can be ascribed not to any section of the Ministers, but to a change of public opinion, and to the shrewd activities of a remarkable individual outside Parliament—the Radical tailor Francis Place—acting through the Radical member of Parliament Joseph Hume. Place organized petitions and witnesses in the factory districts of the North, and brought them up to Westminster to impress and persuade members of Parliament. [1824–25.]

To Peel's initiative as Home Secretary belongs the credit of a series of important reforms. The son of a great Lancashire manufacturer of the modern type, Robert Peel junior had been introduced into the governing Tory group through Harrow and Christ Church, and had in early youth become the favourite political agent and spokesman of the squires and clergy of England and of the ascendancy party in Ireland. His life-long connections had thus been formed in the most prosperous period of the old-fashioned Toryism, while the Peninsular War was still raging. If he had entered public life ten years later, he would probably have found out the truth that he was a Liberal-Conservative like Canning or Huskisson. Actually, the position of trust that he held among the defenders of the last ditch made that line less tenable in time of trouble than it would have been if he had fought among the recognized assailants. The Duke, it is reported, once complained of Peel that he never foresaw the end of the campaigns that he began. Though even more true of the Duke himself as a politician, the criticism of Peel is not unjust, provided we add, in Cromwell's words: 'None goes so far as he who knows not whither he is going.' It is characteristic of the England of that period of rapid transition, that her greatest statesmen could never see four years ahead.

The substitution of Peel for Lord Sidmouth at the Home Office in 1822 soon brought an end to the system of espionage and repression exercised by Government against the Radical working men, and established fairer dealing with classes and parties. Peel also put into legislative effect the principles of the crusade carried on for many years past by Bentham, Romilly and Sir James Mackintosh for reform of the criminal law; he abolished the death penalty for a hundred different crimes. And finally in 1829 he established for the first time in our history an efficient civilian Police, whom the populace endearingly called by either of his two names. Their social value in dealing with common crime was equalled by their political value in dealing with Radical mobs: for at last the place of the soldiers had been taken by a civic force armed only with batons, who were none the less capable of looking a crowd in the face, and who, unlike the soldiers, could be used to quell the first signs of disturbance. There would be no more Lord George Gordon riots, and no more Peterloos, in towns where 'the force' exercised its functions. The Reform Bill riots that set Bristol on fire two years later, could have been easily stopped by a hundred of the 'new Police' acting in good time. Set up first in London alone, they were in the course of a generation adopted all over the country, in answer to a universal demand. From the first they were dressed in civilian blue, and in their early years they wore not helmets but stout top-hats.

In the same period, the finances of the country were taken in hand by Huskisson. The tariff, whether aiming at revenue or protection, was a jungle of unscientific growths and unrelated experiments, hampering trade at every turn. Huskisson did not desire to introduce complete Free Trade, and his operations were limited by the popular objection to a revival of the Income Tax as a source of revenue. Nevertheless he greatly reduced the tariff list, and put order and purpose into what was left. One article only was sacred: 'Corn was King' in English politics, so long as a section of the country gentry held the monopoly of power through the rotten boroughs.

Huskisson also made the first great inroad [1823.] on the old system of Navigation Acts, which had for a century and a half given to British shipping monopolistic privileges in British ports.[4] The time had come when this artificial support, which had been praised in its day by Adam Smith, could be dispensed with by the full-grown strength of the British mercantile marine. The process of abolishing the Navigation Acts was completed during the later period when Free Trade was the accepted national policy, and when the remainder of the protective tariffs were abolished [1849.]. The removal of the monopoly right conferred by the Navigation Acts forced British ship-owners and ship-builders to bestir themselves and improve their methods. Owing to the industrial supremacy of Victorian Britain, the coming of the age of steam and iron at sea was all to her advantage, especially as she now had difficulty in obtaining timber. And the outward cargo of coal, which was saleable in most ports all over the globe, was a great stimulus to British shipping. Throughout the remainder of the century our mercantile marine continued to grow without a serious rival.

The substitution of Canning's influence for Castlereagh's as the strongest personal force in the Cabinet, gave a stimulus to the forces of change in domestic affairs. [1822.] At the Foreign Office, the special sphere of these two great men in succession, Canning did not reverse Castlereagh's policy. But, in contrast to his reserved and aristocratic predecessor, he loved to appeal not only to the House of Commons but to the people at large. Foreign affairs ceased to be a mystery of Elder Statesmen, as under Grenville and Castlereagh. Canning's new methods of publicity were destined to grow under the hands of Palmerston, Gladstone and Disraeli, until general elections were lost and won on questions of foreign policy. At the end of the century, Lord Salisbury reverted somewhat to the more quiet methods of Castlereagh.

The advent of Canning meant therefore an important change of method, consonant with the more democratic and inquisitive spirit of the age. But the direction, in which

[4] See Vol. II., pp. 211–12 and note.

British foreign policy was moving, was not altered, though the pace of the movement was accelerated, and its liberal and British standpoint were both more clearly emphasized.

[1815–22.] Castlereagh, eminently a 'good European,' favoured periodical Congresses of the Powers to arrange international disputes. But as the Powers did not then represent the peoples, and as the States did not represent the races, there was no chance that these Congresses could develop into anything approaching the League of Nations of our own day. On the contrary, under the influence of Austria's Metternich and of the Czar Alexander, now in the final reactionary phase of his life, the Congresses were perverted into clearing-houses for the obscurantist policy of the governments of the Holy Alliance, leagued to suppress the first stirrings of liberty and of nationalism. Castlereagh, who had no wish to involve England in the internal police questions of foreign countries, was tending reluctantly to a less close participation in the congressional politics of the continent, when the strain of overwork caused him to commit suicide. [1822.] But his strongly expressed dislike of the movements for Greek and Italian independence, may lead us to suppose that he would never have taken the actively liberal line pursued by his successor.[5]

Canning, in one sense the continuator of Castlereagh's work, introduced an element of more active opposition to the reactionary parties on the continent. He was more acutely aware than Castlereagh that the English State stood for something midway between Jacobinism and Despotism. The same British feeling that had inspired the brilliant Anti-Jacobinism of his youth, made him, as a middle-aged Foreign Minister, the dread of the despots and the hope of the Liberals of the continent. He sympathized with the indignation felt by his countrymen, that the powers which British arms and subsidies had helped to restore to the 'legitimate' monarchs of Europe, were used everywhere, from Poland to Portugal, to trample out political, racial and cultural liberty. When the France of the Royalists and

[5] For Castlereagh and the settlement of Europe in 1815, see pp. 114–16, above.

Clericals was commissioned by the Holy Alliance to put down the constitutional movement in Spain by force of arms [1823.], all England was furious, without distinction of class or party. But Canning, whilst protesting against the French invasion of Spain, wisely refrained from threats which would have involved this country either in a new Peninsular War or in an ignominious diplomatic retreat.

But the other sphere of the Spanish question, the revolt of the Central and South American Colonies against the old monarchy, was more fully in Canning's control, because no crusaders of France or the Holy Alliance could cross the Atlantic to suppress the rebels under Bolivar, without the acquiescence of the British fleet. Moreover, the independence of South America was a direct material interest of Great Britain. The restrictions set by Spain on English commerce with her American Colonies had been a burning question for nearly three hundred years. There was now a golden opportunity for its happy solution, if the Colonies themselves should become independent States, friendly to Britain and anxious to trade with her merchants. The heart-burnings that had caused the wars of Drake, of the buccaneers, and of 'Jenkins' ear' in the time of Walpole, would at last and for ever be laid at rest.

In these circumstances the anxiety of British merchants and industrialists to open new markets for the congested produce of the new English factories, was blended with a sincere enthusiasm for the cause of liberty all the world over; with joy in Cochrane's gallant exploits off the coast of Chili and Peru as Admiral for the rebel governments; and with the satisfaction felt by all true Englishmen at paying out the French and their perjured and bigoted protégé Ferdinand VII of Spain for their recent military triumphs in the Peninsula. It was to these popular sentiments that Canning successfully appealed when he pronounced in the House of Commons that he had called a New World into existence to redress the balance of the Old. Eldon and Wellington, who preferred old worlds to new at any time, were disgusted beyond measure at their colleague turned demagogue, and the rift in the Tory party became deep and wide.

In proclaiming and defending the independence of South America, the statesmen and people of England were at one with those of the United States. President Monroe had seized the occasion to lay down his 'doctrine,' so famous and important in years to come, denying to European States the right to acquire new territories or political influence in the American continent beyond what they already held. [DEC. 1823.] This was meant as a warning to the powers of the Holy Alliance at the moment, but it was meant also as a warning to Great Britain with regard to the future. Canning did not like it. Neither he nor his pupil, Palmerston, after him, was so friendly to the United States in feeling as Castlereagh had shown himself over the Canadian boundary disarmament.[6] But in Canning's day the questions in dispute with the United States were dormant, and on the question of the hour the two branches of the English-speaking race were at one. It was not, however, President Monroe's 'doctrine,' but the British fleet, that prevented France or the Holy Alliance from suppressing the independence of the Spanish Colonies. [1823–26.]

Besides the vast regions of South and Central America, a smaller spot upon the political map of the world still bears the mark of Canning's handiwork. The independence of Greece was largely due to him. In the Levant, Canning could not override the will of all the Powers of Europe, as he could on the open Atlantic. But on the question of the Greek revolt against the Turk, the governments of the Holy Alliance were at variance with one another. Austria indeed consistently supported the Turk as representing the 'anti-revolutionary' side. Russia, for her own ends, and from traditional sympathy, was the champion of the Eastern Christians. France, partly from religious and cultural inclination, inclined the same way. Much depended therefore on England's attitude. Wellington, following the example of Castlereagh, was pro-Turk. But the British public, moved by Byron's self-sacrifice and death, and at that time

[6] See pp. 211–12, below.

profoundly 'classical' in its culture, idealized the Greek 'Klephts' as heroes of Thermopylae. Canning was happily inspired to put up a barrier to Russian aggression in the Levant by erecting an independent Greek nation, rather than by supporting the continued abominations of Turkish misrule. His policy of trusting to nationalism to keep Russian ambition in check, succeeded in the case of Greece, but was abandoned by later British statesmen when Palmerston, Russell and Gladstone, at the time of the Crimean War, and twenty years later, Disraeli, sacrificed the interests of the Balkan Christians to British fears of Russia.

[OCT. 1827.] The success of Canning's policy was secured, as regards Greece, when, a few weeks after his death, the British, French, and Russian fleets under Admiral Codrington blew the Turkish fleet out of the water in Navarino Bay. In that conflagration the Holy Alliance was dissolved as a force in European politics. Wellington, when he came to the Premiership, regretted Navarino as an 'untoward event,' but he was unable seriously to limit the extent of its consequences.

Canning, as Foreign Secretary in Lord Liverpool's Cabinet, had so stirred the romantic liberalism of the new England and the new Europe, that in the absence of effective Whig leadership he had become the principal hero in the eyes of the forward-looking party in Britain. When, therefore, on Liverpool's illness and retirement, the Tory Cabinet split, and Canning formed a government which the Old Guard under Wellington, Peel and Eldon refused to join, the new Premier obtained the co-operation of more than half the Whigs in Parliament and the good wishes of liberal-minded men in the country. [FEB. 1827.] His own death a few months later [AUG. 1827.] brought his Ministry to an end before it had accomplished anything remarkable, but the fact that it had been formed was an important step in the break-up and reshuffling of parties. Most of the 'Canningite' Tories who served in it, like Palmerston and Melbourne, soon afterward joined the revivified and enlarged Whig Party that passed the Reform Bill.

It is remarkable, however, that Canning himself to the last opposed Parliamentary Reform. Probably, therefore, his removal from the scene actually precipitated the speed of political change which he had done so much to set moving. He was the one man in England who might have preserved the rotten boroughs for many years. But after his death everything played into the hands of the Reformers. The hope that the unreformed Parliament and the Tory Party would lead the country forward in the new age, which had burned brightly under Canning and Huskisson, was effectively quenched by the High Tory Ministry under Wellington. [1828–30.]

But before the final reconstitution of parties on the Reform Bill issue, important concessions to the new principle of the civic equality of religions were wrung by events from the unwilling Cabinet of Wellington and Peel. The tide of change was indeed coming in with an elemental rapidity, overthrowing in turn every position taken up by embarrassed statesmen from day to day. Whereas Canning in 1827 had thought it necessary to pledge his Cabinet to prevent the repeal of the Test Act and to leave Catholic Emancipation alone, in spite of his own views on Emancipation, fifteen months after Wellington took office on the basis of 'no-surrender,' both these relieving Bills had become law of the land under the ægis of an ultra-Tory Ministry.

The Test Act, which prevented Catholic and Protestant Non-conformists from holding State or Municipal office, had been regarded by the Church as the very ark of the Covenant ever since the reign of Charles II, and had been the condition of her accepting the Revolution settlement and the Hanoverian succession. Its repeal [1828.], on the motion of Lord John Russell, was of symbolic importance, but was not of great immediate effect. For until the Parliamentary and Municipal elections had been democratized, Dissenters had little chance of holding office. It was only in conjunction with the Municipal Corporations Act of 1835 and the Second Reform Bill of 1867, that the Repeal of the Test Act effected the full political emancipation of Non-conformists.

In 1829 a still more remarkable surrender was made. For half a dozen years past the Irish people had been organized in the Catholic Association, under the priests as officers and under Daniel O'Connell as Commander-in-Chief. Though everyone in authority was hostile to the movement, the unanimity of the population was terrible. No great body of men moves so completely to order, as a nation consisting of a single class of ill-educated peasants, in whom the instincts of herd-morality have been fortified by centuries of oppression. O'Connell demanded Catholic Emancipation, that is to say, that Roman Catholics should not be debarred from sitting in either House of Parliament. The victor of Waterloo shrank from the contest with the Catholic Association of Ireland. The British Army had been reduced to its lowest point in pursuit of retrenchment and lower taxes, and scarcely sufficed to protect property in Britain from starving operatives and rick-burning peasants. Moreover, Wellington always abhorred the idea of civil bloodshed, though he so frequently refused until the very last moment to make concessions which were the only alternative. The surrender of Peel and Wellington to O'Connell infuriated the High Tories, who had put their trust in them. [1829.] Indeed Wellington had purged his administration of the Canningites, and of nearly every man who believed in Catholic Emancipation, only a year before he emancipated the Catholics. The fabric of the Tory party was split into three mutually enraged sections—Canningites, High Tories, and embarrassed supporters of government. The strategical and tactical errors of Wellington's political campaign had cleared the way for what he most dreaded—a real Parliamentary Reform Bill and a real Reform Ministry.

Charles, Lord Grey, the nominal chief of the Whig Party since the death of Fox, had for many years played a very inadequate part as leader of opposition—at least by our modern ideas of political leadership. The rural leisure of his home on the Northumbrian shore, with its library and his fifteen children, grew to have many more attractions for him than Westminster. But in his hot youth he had been the principal agent in leading Fox to pronounce for Parliamentary Reform in 1792, and so to break with Portland and the Whig seceders who followed Burke into the Anti-Jacobin camp. Grey had never given up his belief that a redistribution of seats, based on the abolition of a large number of the rotten boroughs, would ultimately be necessary to save Parliamentary government in Britain. He had for many years ceased to preach the doctrine, regarding it as untimely, so long as only the working-class Radicals would move in the matter. But he still maintained that it would be necessary to wait only until the time when the question should be taken up 'seriously and affectionately' by the people themselves, meaning more particularly the 'solid and respectable' middle class. That time had at length come, and greatly to the surprise of friends and the consternation of foes, the old nobleman proved as good as his word, and for three years left his rural seclusion to give Britain the reformed Parliament of which he had dreamed in his youth.

In 1830 the movement for Parliamentary Reform seemed to be generated by a natural process out of the circumstances of the hour—the return of bad times, the violence of working-class despair in town and country, the gravity of middle-class fear of a social uprising beneath their feet, and the belief that it could no longer be averted by mere repression; to all these causes were added disillusionment with the Tory party resulting from the Duke's blunders, and the example of the July revolution in Paris that put an end to Charles X's reactionary government, without, as in 1789, causing social overturn. From squire to postillion, from cotton-lord to mill-hand, everyone was talking of the need for Reform, though with great varieties of meaning and emphasis. On the extent and character of the proposed new franchise there was wide divergence, but all were united in a detestation of the rotten boroughs. Their owners, hitherto regarded with obsequious deference, were now held up to general execration as 'borough-mongers' who had stolen the nation's birthright. There was also general agreement that the new industrial and the old rural districts ought to obtain a representation more in proportion to their wealth and the numbers of their inhabitants. The alliance of all classes against the rotten boroughs found expression in the Birmingham Political Union, ably led by Thomas Attwood. In the Birmingham of forty years before, the mob had sacked the Reformers' houses, but the citizens were now agreed that the Midland capital had a right to representation in Parliament.

Grey and his more advanced lieutenants of the younger generation, Lord John Russell and Lord Durham, saw that the moment had come to place the Whig Parliamentary party at the head of this movement. On the basis of a sweeping redistribution of seats and a level ten-pound household franchise in all boroughs, the aristocratic Whig leaders in Parliament placed themselves at the head of middle-class opinion in the country. Owing to the Industrial Revolution, the middle class counted for much more than in the Eighteenth Century; and owing to the growth of Wesleyanism, Dissent was reckoned at nearly half the religious world. Therefore the renewed leadership of the middle classes by the Whig aristocracy, on the basis of a reformed electoral system, was destined to remain the most stable element in the government of Great Britain for a generation to come. The man who represented the alliance was the plebeian Henry Brougham, the agitator and leader of the 'intelligent middle classes,' who with his hard but mobile features was the very incarnation of the new age of 'machinery and the march of mind.' He was closely connected also with the Whig leaders and with the *Edinburgh Review*. No Whig Cabinet in 1830 could be formed without him. If his wisdom and reliability as a colleague in office had been on a level with his activity and genius as a free lance in opposition, he would have been the leading statesman of the new era; but he declined, instead, into its most magnificent oddity.

The political alliance of Whigs and middle classes was joined by other recruits. Canningites like Melbourne and

Palmerston,[7] and independents like young Stanley and Sir James Graham representing the 'respectable' classes of Northern England, had recently come to believe that the country could only be saved by a moderate measure of Parliamentary Reform. In the autumn of 1830 they still looked to Wellington to supply what the country demanded, but he alienated all moderates by declaring that 'the system of representation possesses the full and entire confidence of the country,' and that to improve it was beyond the range of human wisdom. As a result of this famous pronouncement, Stanley and Graham at once entered into a temporary alliance with the Whigs to secure a Reform of Parliament, and the Canningites, Palmerston and Melbourne, became recognized as Whig leaders and remained so during the rest of their lives. Wellington's Ministry tottered, and the High Tories seized the opportunity to take their revenge on him and Peel for passing Catholic Emancipation, by voting against them in the critical division. In November 1830 the Duke fell from power, and Lord Grey was called on by the new and popular 'sailor King,' William IV, to form a Ministry based on the programme of 'peace, retrenchment and reform.'

The Cabinet formed by Lord Grey was aristocratic in *personnel*, but the aristocrats in the Whig Ministry included some of the ablest and most advanced men in Parliament. The measure of Reform which Lord Durham and Lord John Russell framed under Grey's general direction, and which Lord Althorp piloted through the House of Commons, though criticized ever since for not going far enough, in its own day astounded friends and foes by the distance that it went. It was indeed, as the Tories complained, 'a new constitution,' in the sense that it extended political power to new social classes and to new districts of the island.

[MARCH, 1831.] A Bill abolishing all the rotten boroughs

[7] The other leading Canningite, Huskisson, was killed by an engine at the opening of the Manchester-Liverpool railway in Sept. 1830. He was in negotiation with Grey at the time.

at a stroke had never been expected, and its announcement aroused a shout of surprise and enthusiasm from Land's End to John o' Groat's, while throwing the Tories, who had looked for a much milder proposal, into angry opposition. The most influential working-class leaders and organizers, like Place and Cobbett, actively supported 'The Bill, the whole Bill, and nothing but the Bill,' because they knew that to pass working-class enfranchisement was impossible in the existing House and, indeed, in the existing state of public opinion. But they foresaw that it must follow some day, whatever the Whigs might say about 'finality,' if once the time-honoured system of vested interests in nomination boroughs were overset. To get that done would require the union of all classes, for the House of Lords had by the law of the constitution the power to veto the Bill, and was determined at all risks to use it.

The upper middle-class and the shopkeepers in the newly enfranchised boroughs saw in the ten-pound household franchise all that they could ask for themselves. The half of the middle class that was still excluded from the vote, looked to find indirect representation of their interests in the enfranchisement of the new industrial areas: that Manchester should have two members instead of Old Sarum, and Sheffield instead of some Cornish hamlet, would before long secure the disappearance of the Corn Laws. But the squires and tenant-farmers overlooked that danger, for they themselves were gratified by the increase of County representation under the Bill, and by the concession of a tenant-farmer franchise that rather increased than diminished landlord power in the rural constituencies.[8]

[8] Before 1832 there were only two members for each county in England, while there were 400 borough members, most of them sitting for more or less rotten boroughs. The Whigs in 1830 were reckoned to hold 60 out of the 200 rotten borough seats which they destroyed by the Bill. About 140 of these 200 were abolished altogether, and about 60 more had their electoral character restored by the new ten pound franchise. In a very few cases, like Preston and Westminster, the franchise was limited by the application of the uniform ten pound line, to the disadvantage of the working class in those few localities.

It may seem strange to-day that a proposal to divide political power between half the middle class and all the landlords should have aroused so much popular enthusiasm. But the cry of 'Down with the rotten boroughs' united almost everyone except the numerous beneficiaries, direct and indirect, of the old distribution of power, and the Church clergy, who mistakenly believed that the Reform Bill would lead to disestablishment and disendowment. It did not even lead to the abolition of compulsory Church rates, nor to the admission of Dissenters to the Universities, till yet another extension of the franchise had been granted, so imperfectly were even the middle classes admitted to power under the Bill of 1832.

[MARCH 1831–MAY 1832.] After fifteen months of political agitation unparalleled in the history of Great Britain, the Reform Bill was carried in the teeth of the resistance of the Peers. The first crisis was a general election which produced a sure majority of 136 for the Bill, in place of an unreliable and evanescent majority of one. [MAY 1831.] The second crisis was the throwing out of the Bill by forty-one votes in the Lords, chiefly by the Peers of recent Tory creation and by the Bench of Bishops. [OCT. 1831.] That winter there was great economic distress in the industrial and agricultural districts,[9] cholera was raging, and the popular anger at the Lords' action threatened society with chaos. But the Bristol riots served as a warning to all sensible men, and the movement of violence was controlled by the Political Unions that had sprung up all over the country in imitation of Birmingham. The existence of the Unions implied, however, a more serious threat of real civil war if the Bill were finally rejected.

[9] On first taking office the year before, in November, 1830, the Whigs had been faced with 'the last peasants' rising' in some of the southern counties, to obtain the wage of half-a-crown a day. The starving agricultural labourers rioted, but shed no blood, and destroyed little property; they were most cruelly punished by the panic-stricken Whigs, who allowed several of them to be hanged and 450 of them to be transported to Australia from all knowledge of their families.

The danger to the Bill was lest its working-class supporters should break off and begin a revolutionary movement of their own. Reaction might then ensue in the struggle to maintain order. But the middle classes had thrown off their long political apathy, and were determined to have the Bill passed before society was destroyed by a clash of the Radical with the Tory forces. The peace of the country depended, indeed, on the passage of the Bill. At length King William, a perturbed and honest sailor in such a gale as no State skipper had seen before, promised Grey to use his prerogative of creating Peers to carry the Bill. There was the useful precedent of Queen Anne's creation of Peers to carry the Peace of Utrecht for the Tory Ministry of that day. Then at the last moment William hesitated, and endeavoured to get the Tories to take office and pass the Bill in their own way. This occasioned the last crisis, the famous 'Days of May.' [MAY 1832.] Lord Grey gave in his resignation, and for a week the country believed that Wellington was coming back to rule by the sword. The big towns prepared resistance. But Peel saw that the game was played out, and Grey was brought back triumphantly, on the condition of the surrender of Peers and King.

This final crisis, that secured the actual passage of the Reform Act, gave dramatic emphasis to the popular element in the 'new constitution.' The people, as a whole, had wrenched the modern Magna Carta from the governing class. The nation was thenceforth master in its own house. But the political extent of the 'nation' would yet need to be defined by a succession of franchise struggles, each less violent indeed than the great original. [1867, 1884, 1918.] Ten-pound householders and tenant-farmers were not likely to constitute 'the nation' for ever. They had no such prescriptive right to govern the land as the borough-owners, whose vested interest had been swept away by the pacific revolt of a nation.

In Scotland the old representative system had been worse than in England, for not even the county elections had any reality north of the Tweed. Politically Scotland was one vast rotten borough. The violence of the northern democracy at the crisis had been proportionately great. In 1832 the Scots obtained for the first time popular institutions, other than the Kirk, through which to express themselves. The immediate consequence of the Reform Bill was the Burgh Act of 1833, which created the first popularly elected Municipalities that Scotland had possessed since the Fifteenth Century.

England waited till 1835 for her Municipal Corporations Act. The fall of the Parliamentary rotten boroughs involved the fall of the Municipal rotten boroughs, analogous sister bodies in the field of local government, which would never have been disturbed under the old regime. The Act of 1835 was more democratic than the Reform Bill, for it gave all ratepayers the right to vote for the new Municipalities. At last the ice-age of English institutional and corporate life had come to an end, and the life of the community began to be remodelled according to the actual needs of the new economic society. The spirit of Jeremy Bentham was abroad in the land, though the old man himself was on his death-bed. His test question—'What is the use of it?'—was being applied to one venerable absurdity after another. The age of Royal Commissions and their Reports had begun with the Whig Reform Ministry. The Municipal Corporations Act was among its first-fruits.

The Act only applied to the larger towns. The rural districts were still left under the administrative control of the Justices of the Peace until the establishment of elected County Councils by Lord Salisbury's Ministry in 1888. This difference in types of local government corresponded to the fact that rural England was still mentally subordinate to the squires, while the new urban England was already in spirit a democracy.

Inadequate as it was in its geographical scope, the Municipal Corporations Act of 1835 established in the chief urban areas a powerful form of authority, subject to popular control, and able to levy a local rate. From this beginning there grew up a concentration of new functions; throughout the coming century powers were perpetually being added to the Municipal Corporations. Finally they dealt with almost all aspects of local government except public-house licensing and judicial power, which were regarded as unfit functions for an elective body. In 1835 very few foresaw that the new Municipalities would end in educating the children of the people, and in supplying the public with trams, light, water, and even houses, or that they would become traders and employers of labour on a large scale.

Starting from 1835 there also grew up the connection between the governmental departments of Whitehall and the popularly elected local bodies, based on State supervision and Treasury grants of the taxpayers' money in aid of local rates. All this, though not foreseen, was rendered possible by the bold and uniform Whig legislation of 1835. In this way was begun the tardy process of catching up the uncontrolled social consequences of the Industrial Revolution. But where, in all this, was the place for 'retrenchment'? That panacea faded into thin air.

In 1833 Lord Althorp passed the first effective Factory Act, fixing legal limits for the working hours of children and young persons respectively. The great merit of the Bill, little recognized at the time, was the institution of government inspectors to enforce the law. It was the beginning of a whole new development in social welfare.

Another immediate consequence of the Reform Bill was the abolition of slavery in the British Empire by the Act of 1833. Wilberforce died the same year, his work marvellously completed. During the later years of his life the active leadership of the Anti-Slavery cause had been carried on by Sir Thomas Fowell Buxton, with Brougham as trumpeter. In Wilberforce's original campaign the defenders of the slave-trade had been important British shipping interests in Bristol and Liverpool.[10] But after the slave-trade had been stopped, the defenders of slavery were found less in England herself than in the colonies. If slaves could no longer be imported, they could still be bred from the existing stock. The planters of the West Indies and

[10] See pp. 129–31, above.

other tropical colonies saw ruin in the proposal to emancipate their slaves on any terms. But they did not conduct their case wisely, or treat either their negroes or the negrophil missionaries well; their violence aroused the indignation of the British public, more particularly the religious world of Evangelicalism and Non-conformity, then very influential. The Slavery Abolition Act of 1833 gave the slave-owners twenty millions in compensation for their slaves, willingly paid by the mother country.

The other great successful action of the Whig Ministry was the settlement of the Belgian question. In 1830 the Paris revolution had been followed by the revolt of Belgium from the partnership with Holland to which the Treaties of 1815 had assigned her. The revolt was partly liberal, partly clerical, and was promoted by French influences, clerical and liberal alike. The reactionary Powers of Eastern Europe regarded a breach made in the Treaties of 1815 by a popular revolt, as a thing to be suppressed after the fashion of the Holy Alliance. That was not the view of Great Britain, especially under the liberal Ministry of which Grey was Premier and Palmerston Foreign Secretary. But Britain, for her part, objected strongly to the establishment of French influence over Belgium either by annexation or by the reign of a French Prince at Brussels. The Chauvinist party in Paris was with difficulty kept in check by Louis Philippe, 'the Citizen King,' and his Ministers, anxious on the whole for the friendship of the new liberal England in face of the hostile Powers of Russia, Austria and Prussia. It was a situation of delicacy and danger, but was satisfactorily solved, after a number of crises, on the basis of the adoption of Prince Leopold of Saxe-Coburg Gotha as King of the Belgians; [1831.] he was a personal friend of the British Ministers and the favourite uncle of the future Queen Victoria. In 1839 Palmerston crowned the work by a treaty which settled the vexed question of Dutch-Belgian boundaries, and guaranteed Belgian neutrality. The treaty was signed by Belgium, Great Britain, France, Russia, Austria and Prussia. In this way the perennial British interest of securing a

Power in the Netherlands from which we had nothing to fear, was again made safe for a long period of years.

BOOKS FOR FURTHER READING: Spencer Walpole, *History of England from* 1815, Vols. I.–III.; Webster, *Foreign Policy of Castlereagh,* and Temperley, ditto, *Canning*; Graham Wallas, *Francis Place*; Cole, *William Cobbett* and *Short History of the British Working Class Movement*; Dicey, *Law and Opinion in England* (on Bentham); Trevelyan, *Lord Grey of the Reform Bill*; Butler, *The Passing of the Great Reform Bill*; Porritt, *The Unreformed House of Commons* (2 vols.) for details of the old system; Sir D. Le Marchant, *Lord Althorp*; Redlich and Hirst, *Local Government in England,* Vol. I.; Sir Herbert Maxwell, *Wellington*; Atlay, *The Victorian Chancellors,* Vol. I., for Brougham; Bagehot, *Biographical Sketches.*

CHAPTER TWO

Whig Financial Failure. Peel and the New Conservative Party. The New Poor Law. Chartism. The Repeal of the Corn Laws, 1846. Disraeli and Peel. The Whig-Palmerston Regime. The Civil Service. Queen Victoria. The Crimea and Italy. Prosperity and Social Assuagement. The Franchise Agitation and the Second Reform Bill, 1867

QUEEN VICTORIA, 1837

In the reign of William IV, the Whigs, under Benthamite inspiration and Radical pressure, had introduced into the organs of government elements of modern efficiency and popular representation, through the Reform Bill and the Municipal Corporations Act. It was only a beginning, but the first step counts. If the Whigs had produced among them a great statesman who understood the social problems of the day, or if they had even produced an able finance Minister, they might at once have led the nation far along the path of progress which they had opened out to the eager hopes of their suffering and impatient fellow-countrymen. But the party which in old times had benefited by the services of Charles Montagu, Godolphin and Walpole, was stricken with financial paralysis, and left it to Peel to discover in the Income Tax and Free Trade the key to the financial and economic enigma of that day. At the time of Queen Victoria's accession the Whig Chancellor of the Exchequer appeared 'seated on an empty chest by the side of bottomless deficiencies, fishing for a budget,' as Peel said in one of his rare, deliberate lapses into humour.[1]

And so, within half a dozen years of the passage of the Reform Bill, it was clear to all that the Whigs had shot their bolt, and had no further programme for the relief of the still acute economic and industrial distress of the country. It was well for the fortunes of Parliamentary government under the new regime that an alternative Ministry could be formed from the opposition at Westminster. Peel had reconstituted a 'Conservative' party out of the wreckage of the 'Tory' party destroyed by the Reform Bill, and he was attracting back many who, like Stanley and Graham, had supported the Whigs in order to get the rotten boroughs abolished. It was characteristic of England in the Nineteenth Century, as distinct from several foreign lands, that when the various sections of the upper class lost their special privileges they did not on that account retire to private life, but accommodated themselves to the new conditions. The very limits of the Reform effected in 1832, with which modern criticism is often impatient, had the advantage of keeping unbroken the tradition of upper-class connection with political life, and avoiding the development of a class of 'professional politicians.' There may be no logic in a process of bit-by-bit enfranchisement, but there may be great practical advantages to the life of the

[1] O'Connell, who disliked Peel not without personal cause, said 'His smile was like a silver plate on a coffin.' His shy manners, taken for coldness and hauteur, isolated him personally from the ordinary members of his party, and go some way to account for their repudiation of him in 1846; his Cabinet colleagues who knew him better stood by him and became 'Peelites.' Queen Victoria also disliked him till she knew him well—not afterwards.

nation in the very graduality of an uninterrupted movement towards democratic control.

Peel's 'Tamworth manifesto' in 1834 had accepted the Reform Bill as a *fait accompli*, with all its implications, and Peel at least understood what those implications were. His 'bourgeois' origin and natural affinity to the trading and manufacturing classes enabled him to understand the economic and financial needs of the country better than most Tories and most Whigs. Indeed, he understood the middle-class mind, on its economic side, and sympathized with the sufferings of the poor better than he understood or sympathized with the mentality of the landlord party which he led. He came to regard that party as an instrument of government given into his hands for whatever wise purpose he wished.

The majority of the new Conservative party had, however, interests and feelings of their own. They disliked Peel's favourites, the manufacturers; they were deeply interested in the defence of the Corn Laws, and equally in the defence of the Church. They believed the Church to be in danger from the Whig proposals to admit Dissenters to Oxford and Cambridge, and to apply a part of the superfluous wealth of the Irish Establishment to secular purposes, although the House of Lords was there to prevent the actual perpetration of these outrages. Such questions, it is true, interested Peel as well as his followers, but the leader's heart and mind were moving more and more into the study of the financial aspects of the relief of trade, and the 'condition of the people problem,' which Carlyle and others were beginning to regard as the principal business of Parliaments and Cabinets. What Peel lacked was the gifts of personality and popular persuasiveness to draw his party after him in these thoughts, as he succeeded in drawing many of his intimates and colleagues, the future 'Peelites,'—Graham, Aberdeen, Cardwell and Gladstone. He had had his political training in days before the Reform Bill and before Canning, when the decision of the Cabinet was law. After the Reform Bill, he understood the new relation of the Cabinet to the people at large, better than he understood its new relation to its own partisans.

Before the Whigs finally handed over the government of the land to Peel as a result of the General Election of 1841, they had taken, with the full concurrence of Peel and Wellington, an important step in social reorganization, by passing the New Poor Law. [1834.] On the advice of Nassau Senior and his fellow Commissioners, they had abolished the Speenhamland system of giving rates in aid of wages.[2] In that way they had begun the depauperization of the labourer in South England, and the restoration of his qualities of self-respect and self-dependence. Unfortunately, this necessary operation was carried through with a ruthless and doctrinaire disregard of the human side of the problem. When out-door relief was the means of livelihood to many thousands in town and country, it was terrible to cut it all off at one stroke, without at the same time enforcing a living wage, or supplying any shelter for the unemployed and their dependents except the workhouse. Moreover, in their just alarm at the pauperizing effect of the system which they abolished, the Commissioners made it a principle that the workhouse life should be more unpleasant than the life of free labour beyond its walls. The economic theories of the day did not permit of setting to work at the problem from the other end, and trying by statute to raise the condition of free labour to one of greater attractiveness than the workhouse. Even the aged and the sick, for whom in those days there were no pensions or industrial insurance, had not the means to live at home, and yet received no better treatment in the workhouse than if they had come there through their own fault. It was in these circumstances that the youthful author of *Oliver Twist*, [1838.] by describing what workhouses meant for those who inhabited them, appealed from the Benthamite abstractions in which the Commissioners dealt, to the flesh and blood realities which interested the more sensitive rising generation of the new Victorian era.

[2] See p. 147, above.

By these all too drastic measures the rot of pauperism was stopped. Too great local variation and parochial independence had been faults of the old Poor Law. The national and centralized character of the New Poor Law, though far too harshly used in the first generation, made it easier to carry out the alleviations and improvements on which later public opinion insisted. The workhouses gradually ceased to be penal settlements for the unfortunate, and in our own day of Old Age Pensions and national insurance, they have been to a very large extent emptied of their folk even in bad times.

The anger of the wage-earning classes at the New Poor Law, and the political impotence of that anger, sharply reminded them that another Reform Bill was needed before they could make their wishes directly operative at Westminster. So, too, their agitation for the Ten Hours Bill, to limit by statute the hours of work in factories, led by Lord Shaftesbury and by Fielden, the great master cotton-spinner, divided both the Liberal and Conservative parties so that the Bill was not passed till 1847.[3] These continued agitations in the manufacturing districts, and the continued distress caused the rise of Chartism. [1838.] Chartism demanded in effect only what was granted in 1867 and 1884, that is to say the enfranchisement of the classes left out by the Bill of 1832. The six points of the 'People's Charter' were purely political. But the motive and character of the agitation were social. It repelled middle-class aid. It was a cry of rage and class-consciousness on the part of the suffering wage-earner. It had its influence on Parliament, now a more sensitive barometer to outside opinion than of old. The ominous shadow of Chartism in the background accelerated the passage of Factory Acts, Corn Law Repeal, Acts against truck payments, Shaftesbury's Mines Act and the first belated Public Health Act of 1848 when Chadwick's Reports had at last persuaded Parliament that Sanitation was a public question.

In this way Chartism indirectly improved the lot of the

[3] See p. 192, note, below.

working classes, and so attained some of its real objective. But its political programme of Universal Suffrage had no chance of success so long as it was demanded as a class measure, to be won not by the help of middle-class organization and leadership, but as an attack on employers. The Chartist leaders themselves were of little use as practical politicians. Success crowned the movement in the 'sixties, because then the middle classes, half of whom were still excluded from the franchise, joined with the wage-earners under the leadership of Bright and Gladstone to demand the further extension of the franchise.

The better terms on which the middle and working classes stood to one another in that later decade as compared to the earlier period of Chartism proper, are to be accounted for in part by the increased prosperity that had come to all ranks of society in the interval, abating much of the bitterness engendered by want. Other causes of class reconciliation were the beneficent finance of Peel's Ministry, and the remarkable circumstances under which the Corn Laws were abolished. [1846.] Cobden's Anti-Corn-Law League skilfully combined and mobilized working and middle-class opinion on a subject where there was no difference of interest between them. Their common victory, won, after half a dozen years of constant agitation, over the determined resistance of the landlord class, did much to prevent the line of political demarcation from being drawn between the wage-earners and the rest of society. It opened the way for the gradual transformation of Melbourne's and Palmerston's Whig party,—an alliance of part of the aristocracy with the middle class,—into Gladstone's Liberal party,—an alliance of part of the middle class with the wage-earners.

By these complicated movements of classes and parties, involved in an endless network of cross divisions and double allegiances—yet always with the two-party system functioning in the Parliamentary world,—the Victorian era succeeded in avoiding the sharp battle of classes which had seemed to threaten in the days of Chartism [1838.] and of

Robert Owen's Grand National Trade Union.[4] [1833.] Class war in some form would not have been avoided if steady improvement had not been going on in conditions of life, at any rate outside the purely rural districts. The salvation of society was due not only to the efforts and the good sense of various sections of the community, but to the improved trade and prosperity that set in during the 'forties. In the mid-Victorian era Britain was the manufacturing centre of the world. Other nations largely depended upon her for coal and for manufactured goods in return for food and raw material.

In such a world the middle class saw its interest in a policy of complete Free Trade. In that matter it asserted itself against the landlord class, whose political leadership it otherwise accepted with gratitude. It was the old custom of England for the townsfolk to be led by the gentry, provided the followers had a say as to the direction. The ten-pound householders enfranchised in 1832 often chose country gentlemen to represent them. Until the Second Reform Bill of 1867, the presence on the benches of the House of Commons of persons of middle-class origin and standards like Cobden and Bright, was tolerated as a curiosity or resented as an impertinence by the Whig and Tory squires around them. For in those days the distinction between the well-to-do middle class and the gentry still existed: they had not yet been merged in one grade of society by passing through the standardising process of Public School education. There was very frequently a difference of religious observance, which counted for much in those days because it represented social facts, such as the exclusion of Dissenters from Oxford and Cambridge. The culture of the one class was based mainly on

[4] Robert Owen wanted to draw the wage-earners away from political agitation to economic action of a semi-revolutionary kind, and to socialism. He never cared about a democratic franchise, being by origin an autocratically minded employer who organized the lives of his employees for their own good. But, like Bentham, he was compelled, by facts, to realize that society would never be reformed from the top.

the Classics, of the other mainly on the Bible. The one was interested in sport, government and landowning; the other stuck close to its ledgers and had fewer amusements and shorter 'week-ends' than the business man of to-day.

Even after 1832, the middle class put up with a good deal of exclusiveness and patronage on the part of those above them, but in the matter of Free Trade in Corn they made up their minds and on that issue they had the formidable masses of the unenfranchised behind them. The Parliamentary Conservative party was opposed to Corn Law abolition and the Whig party was divided on the question. Peel, in the early days of his great Ministry, revived the Income Tax, and with its help reduced and abolished import duties on many articles with excellent results to the trade of the country. [1842–45.] But he was in no position to abolish the duties on foreign corn. Corn remained the outstanding question. The Anti-Corn-Law League was almost as formidable in industrial England as O'Connell's Catholic League had been in rural Ireland. Peel, who had surrendered to the one in 1829, surrendered to the other in 1846, partly from a sense that government must be carried on by consent of the governed, partly because Cobden's speeches on the floor of the House had persuaded him on the economic issue, and partly because the potato-blight in Ireland in 1845–46 left him no other choice than either to suspend the Corn Laws or to allow the Irish to die by tens of thousands. And the duties on foreign corn, if once suspended, could scarcely be put on again without causing a revolutionary movement in Great Britain. The 'total and immediate' repeal of the Corn Laws was an unforeseen consequence of Pitt's Act of Union.[5]

The Repeal of the Corn Laws was for a number of reasons the most important political event between the First and Second Reform Bills. In the first place, it broke up the

[5] Wellington characteristically supported Peel's *volte-face*, not because he agreed, but because he believed in Peel as a Minister. 'Rotten potatoes have done it,' he said resignedly; 'they put Peel in his d—d fright.'

Conservative party and so put the Whigs into power, with short intervals, for twenty years, with the occasional addition to their counsels and their voting strength of Peelite statesmen like Aberdeen, Cardwell and Graham, and the much needed financial ability of Gladstone.

[1846.] The revolt of the Conservative private members against Peel had not been generally expected. It was the force and quality of Disraeli's philippics against the traitor in command that compelled the back benches to rise and mutiny, as gunpowder must needs blaze up if fire is applied. It does not appear that Disraeli had deep convictions on the Corn Laws as an economic policy, and he was soon afterwards speaking unconcernedly of Protection as 'dead and damned.' But he had, like Bolingbroke before him, attached himself in a professional capacity to the gentlemen of the 'country party' and felt bound to show them sport. The 'great historic Houses' of England appealed strongly to his imagination as a foreign observer of our institutions, though he was obliged to except the Whig Houses which belonged to the other side. Peel had maltreated and betrayed 'the gentlemen of England' in abandoning the Corn Laws, and as they found it difficult adequately to express their own feelings on the matter, Disraeli became their champion against the man who stood also in his own way. His conduct in overthrowing Peel kept the Conservative party out of power for twenty years, but raised him from the back benches to the direct succession of the leadership after Stanley. It thereby enabled him, twenty-one years later, [1867.] to 'educate his party' to the performance of a *volte-face* just as complete and just as unpalatable as that on account of which he had put a sudden end to the career of Peel, at the height of the great Premier's popularity with the mass of his countrymen.

Genius has its privileges, which no one need grudge it, for genius alone can make Parliamentary proceedings as attractive to contemporary observers and historical students as the more dangerous annals of war and revolution. It seemed as if Palmerston, Disraeli and Gladstone were raised up at this time to captivate, each in a totally different way, the imagination of the new democracy, and give to it that personal interest in Parliamentary government, for lack of which Parliamentary institutions in some countries have withered like waterless plants.

The victory of the Anti-Corn-Law League was the first signal victory of the middle classes over the gentry, and of the industrial over the agricultural interest. But the agricultural interest, in the wider sense of the term, had in fact been divided on the issue. If there had been a numerous peasantry owning or occupying the land in small portions, the landlords and big farmers would not have been left isolated in the struggle. The landless agricultural labourer, so far as his almost negligible opinion was asked by politicians, on the whole inclined to the policy of the cheap loaf.

But even the 'agricultural interest' of landlords and large farmers soon found that they had not been ruined by Repeal. Free importation prevented corn prices from soaring even when the value of money fell with the gold discoveries in California and Australia, but corn prices remained fairly steady for another generation, and with better times there was a greatly increased consumption of bread. The country-houses and farmsteads of England were never more wealthy, populous and happy than during the mid-Victorian age,—the age of Trollope's novels and John Leech's pictures. Indeed, the removal of all serious cause of bitterness between town and country left the 'great houses' in a most enviable social position for another thirty years. Then, indeed, the development of trans-continental railways and great steamships enabled America to pour forth such quantities of food that, during Disraeli's Ministry in the late 'seventies, British corn-growing was at last very seriously affected. The world-wide organization of British commerce drew food to the island from every quarter, and the agricultural situation which we know to-day began to develop itself.

The victory of the Anti-Corn-Law League in 1846 had been a victory of new methods of political education and advertisement, which were another step along the road of democracy. These methods were to some extent left in abeyance in the two following decades of prosperity and social peace, but they became the common stock-in-trade of both political parties after the enfranchisement of fresh millions in 1867 and 1884.

The sharp tussle between landlords and millowners, which had resulted from the Corn Law controversy, had caused each party to champion the victims of its opponent. The miserable wages and housing of the rural labourer were proclaimed on League platforms; the wrongs of the factory hands were the most popular argument in reply. In this way the unenfranchised had their wrongs advertised, and in some cases remedied. The years of mutual recrimination between landlord and millowner saw the passage of Shaftesbury's Mines Act [1842.] and the famous Ten Hours Bill for factories.[6] [1847.] Less was done for the agricultural labourers, because they were more widely scattered than the workmen organized in Trade Unions and congregated in factories, and they were therefore less feared and less easy to help.

With the laying to rest of the Corn Law controversy there set in at the same time the great period of mid-Victorian commercial and industrial expansion, which submerged beneath a tidal wave of prosperity the social problem and the mutiny of the underworld. Politics reflected the relaxed tension. From 1846 to 1866 we have the period of quiet Whig-Peelite rule, dominated by the figure of the popular

[6] The Bill limited the hours of *young persons* and *women* in factories to ten hours a day: in effect this meant a similar limitation of the hours of male adults, on account of working arrangements in factories. This was the Bill that was opposed by Bright, who never opposed factory bills to protect *children*, as is often erroneously stated. The ten Hours Bill divided both the Whig and Conservative parties. The effective Bill for the protection of *children under thirteen* had been the Whig government's Bill of 1833, which introduced the all-important principle of Factory Inspection to put the law in force. See on the whole subject Hutchins and Harrison, *History of Factory Legislation*, and Hammond's *Shaftesbury*.

favourite, Lord Palmerston. His performances were eminently suited for a period when everything was safe, when nothing seemed to matter very much either at home or abroad, and when even to provoke a war with Russia involved only a limited liability.

Gladstone, meanwhile, at this stage of his long passage from old-world Tory to advanced Liberal, saw the duty of a statesman to the community chiefly in sound finance, and in the creation of the Treasury traditions with which he was closely associated in these years, implying strict economy and probity in the expenditure of public money. It was a great period for the growth of system and tradition in many Departments of the permanent Civil Service, preparatory to the much greater weight of administration which the next more active age would throw upon the offices of Whitehall. At the same time experiments were made in competitive examination, instead of jobbery, in making selections for the Civil Service. The idea of the value of examination as a test of men was derived from Oxford and Cambridge, where examinations had come greatly into fashion since the beginning of the Century. Palmerston, with his Regency standards of public life, scornfully opposed the wholesale abandonment of government patronage to a board of examiners. But the tone of the new age was all against favouritism and aristocratic inefficiency, and shortly after Palmerston's death Gladstone, who was much in earnest in the matter, imposed the system of open competition on almost all the avenues leading into Whitehall. [1870.]

No doubt a more far-seeing generation would have used the fat years of mid-Victorian prosperity to make provision against the return of the lean, by more social legislation, and by the establishment of a national system of primary and secondary Education. Something indeed was done in the way of Public Health provision. [1847–65.] But, on the whole, while the voice of complaint was no longer loud in the land, statesmen of all parties were glad to rest and be thankful, hoping that the ugly facts and passions which the wave of prosperity had covered from observation, would never again obtrude themselves on the notice of Parliament.

As to Education, Prince Albert, it was remembered, was a German, and popular education a fad,—fit perhaps for industrious foreigners in Central Europe who had not our other advantages of character and world-position. At any rate it would be the height of political unwisdom to touch the Education question, because nothing could be done that would not make either Church or Dissent spring up in angry protest. The new Whig policy, like Walpole's of old, was not to rouse the sleeping ecclesiastical Cerberus, chained at present at the entrance of the House of Lords. The Whigs, allied as they were to the Peelite Conservatives, could not even remedy the Non-conformist grievances of compulsory Church Rates and exclusion from the Universities. And, indeed, in a world so comfortable and prosperous, it was difficult for any set of men to feel grievances very acutely, though Bright kept up a bulldog growl of his own, that might some day swell into a chorus.

In these circumstances at home, the main political interests of the period were those of Foreign Affairs. Here Palmerston was born to shine, and he shone with a lustre that no one can deny, though the amount of gold that went to make the glitter was then, and always will be, a subject of agreeable controversy.

Palmerston, who like Peel had begun public life as a Tory Minister in Peninsular days, had later been a follower of Canning, and in his strong old age may be defined as a cross between a Canningite Tory and a Whig aristocrat. He voiced the popular feeling of Britons against foreign despots, in the manner common to Canning and the Whigs. He was Whig aristocrat in his attitude of Gallio towards religion and the Church, and in his resistance to the influence of the Court. Opposed as he was in home politics to an increase of democracy and especially to an extension of the franchise, he was not opposed to a certain degree of popular control over Foreign Policy, for he regarded himself, when Foreign Minister, as responsible rather to public opinion than to his Sovereign or even to his colleagues. Like Canning before him, he appealed to the middle classes to defend his foreign policy against the hostility of Court and Cabinet, sometimes, it must be confessed, with less good cause than his master had been able to show.

Palmerston's popularity was great in the country, considerable in the House, small in the Cabinet, less than nothing at Court. His influence with his countrymen arose in part from a personal impression that 'Old Pam' was a 'sportsman,' and in part from the nature of his policy. It had a double appeal. He combined the Liberals' dislike of the despotisms of Austria and Russia, Naples and Rome, with a tone in asserting purely British rights which a later generation would have called 'Jingoism.' In Palmerston's spirited language, a British subject was '*civis Romanus*,' and even if he were only a Maltese Jew swindling at Athens, had the British fleet at his back. The same nonchalant spirit was more happily shown in the sympathy extended to the victims of Austrian and Russian tyranny in Hungary, Italy and elsewhere after the collapse of the Liberal movement of 1848 upon the Continent. The attitude then adopted by Palmerston on behalf of Britain, in defiance of the wishes of the Queen and Prince Albert, was neither ignoble nor entirely useless, for it signified that constitutional liberty had still one hearty well-wisher among the Great Powers.

The strife between Palmerston and the Court was a constant source to him of amusement and joy in adventurous living, and to the Queen of grave annoyance. The Court had under her auspices become the reverse of what it had been under George IV as Regent and King. Probably Palmerston preferred what he recollected of the Regency—though scarcely of the Regent. In those days no one had expected Monarchs, Peers or Ministers to pay their debts to tradesmen or otherwise to conduct themselves as school-models to the unprivileged. In politics the change was equally marked. George III and George IV had been identified with High Tory resistance to reform. But Queen

Victoria, in her impressionable youth, had learnt from her mentor, old Lord Melbourne, what she never forgot, that the strength of the British monarchy did not lie in intriguing against Ministers or fighting against popular aspirations. At that time she had, it is true, shown too great a partiality to the Whigs, but she learnt on closer acquaintance to rate Peel at his true value. Under Prince Albert's teaching, her personal affection for foreign dynasties, particularly German, was emphasized; but her non-partisan liberality of outlook on home affairs was perhaps increased, and was certainly rendered more intelligent, by her student Consort.

The Crown had not yet reached the full position which it held by the end of the century in the popular imagination and in the new fabric of Empire. But already it was released from the unfortunate traditions of recent reigns. All through her long life as Queen, Victoria made a habit of following the actions of her Ministers with close attention, expostulating strongly when she disagreed, often obtaining thereby modifications, but never attempting to reverse or alter policy on which her Ministers remained determined after they had fully heard her views. She also exerted an occasional influence on opposition, particularly in the House of Lords, and was singularly successful in averting conflict between the Houses on several important occasions [1869, 1884.] in the last half of her reign, after the revival of a more militant Liberalism under Gladstone.

The two mid-Victorian decades of quiet politics and roaring prosperity were broken in the middle by the Crimean War. [1854–56.] Forty years had elapsed since Waterloo, and the new generation of Britons were therefore easily stirred to a fighting mood. The modern press, especially that part of it subject to Palmerston's influence, fed the war-spirit with selected news and incitements to hatred of Russia. The choice of Russia as the adversary appears at first sight somewhat arbitrary. But the dread of Russian power had of recent years been growing both in India and in Europe. It was not, indeed, Russia's nearest neighbours, Austria and Prussia, who considered that the Balance of Power needed redressing at the Czar's expense; it was France and England who felt called upon to champion against him, among other things, the 'independence of Germany.' The reason of this was in part political. Austria, Prussia and Russia stood together for the old principle of the Holy Alliance that had recently effected the repression of the risings of 1848. The Britain of Queen Victoria and the France of Napoleon III stood, each in a different way, for something more liberal. In England, Liberal sentiment had been outraged by the treatment of Poland, and by the aid lent by the reactionary Czar Nicholas to Austria to put down Hungary in 1849.

But the actual occasion of the quarrel of Palmerston and Russell with Russia was their defence of Turkey. Russia, it is true, accepted our proposed terms of settlement, embodied in the Vienna Note of July 1853, and Turkey refused them. Nevertheless we fought for Turkey against Russia. Such an exhibition of diplomatic incompetence left Ministers with very little answer to some of Bright's censures in the House of Commons, but no answer was needed in the enthusiasm of war. The condition, or even the existence, of the submerged Christian nationalities in the Balkans, was little surmised in the Britain of that day. There was therefore no proposal made to check the advance of Russia by establishing a free Bulgaria and Servia, as Canning had for that purpose established the independence of Greece. The old Turkish system was regarded as the only possible barrier to Russia's ambition.

The Czar Nicholas was considered, not without reason, to be the mainstay of reaction in Europe outside the Balkans. The enthusiasm for the Crimean War was a mixture of Liberalism and Jingoism arising out of the circumstances of the period, and incarnate in Palmerston. But the war was not fought as a war of liberation, for Austria was invited to join the Anglo-French alliance. Only when Austria refused, was the proffered help of Cavour's little Piedmont accepted instead. The substitution of Piedmont for Austria in the Crimean undertaking afterwards hastened the liberation of Italy, but such was not the original intention of the makers of the war.

Among the good results of the Crimean War should be set down British friendship with France and Napoleon III, in an age when France was inclining to take the war-path once more and when British sensibilities were preparing to resist the beginnings of a new era of Napoleonic conquest. The extraordinary man who had so ably manœuvred himself onto the throne of France had not studied his uncle's career in vain. He saw that it would always be fatal to a French Empire to antagonize the Eastern despotic Powers and England at the same time. He ardently desired the friendship of Britain. Palmerston was the first to believe in his good faith, but the British in general were incredulous. The anti-Russian alliance was for a while good security against the danger of war with France.

The course of the war exhibited the soundness of the British regimental drill and tradition, and the utter incompetence of the higher command, the lack of organization and staff work, the deficiency of commissariat and medical provision. Half a dozen miles from our fleet in Balaclava harbour, our soldiers starved and died because supplies were not brought up to them. The raw recruits, sent out to replace the splendid troops who had thus unnecessarily perished, [1855.] failed in the assault on the Redan, and thereby to some extent lowered in the eyes of Europe the respect for British arms won by the victories of Alma and Inkerman the year before. [SEPT., NOV. 1854.]

The shortcomings of our military organization formed indeed at that time a remarkable contrast to our commercial and industrial efficiency. They were the result of the obscurantist spirit of the Horse Guards and the War Office, undisturbed hitherto by any popular demand for Army Reform. Rotten Boroughs, Municipalities, Universities, Church, Civil Service had all in various degrees felt the breath of criticism and change. But the nation had since Waterloo been so pacific that it had never enquired into the state of its Army, so long as War Office estimates were kept well down. Then, in a sudden fit of warlike zeal,

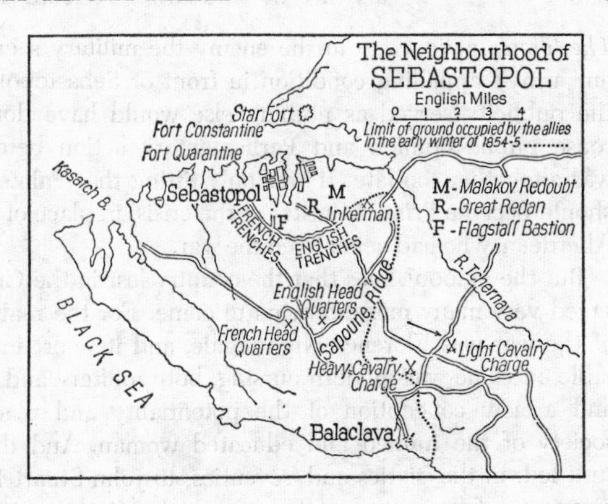

Map 7 Crimea

John Bull remembered that he had 'a thin red line of heroes,' and sent them out to fight the Russians, expecting results of the old Peninsular kind. But nothing was left of Wellington's army except the spirit of the regiments and the old Brown-Bess muskets with which many of them were still armed. At the time there was a great outcry against the Generals and the War Office; yet as soon as the war was over the old indifference to things military returned. Army Reform was put off for yet another dozen years, till Cardwell came to the War Office in the first Ministry of Gladstone. [1868.]

The reaction of the Crimean War on the national life was not remarkable in the political sphere. There was a temporary reaction against Cobden and Bright as critics of the war policy. But many Radicals had been strong for the war. And on the whole the aristocratic system of government lost rather than gained prestige by the inefficiency with which operations had been conducted. William Russell, of *The Times,* created the new profession of war-correspondent, and subjected the Generals in the field to direct civilian criticism such as no British commanders ever had to undergo before or since. His communications to

The Times gave away to the enemy the military secret of our army's appalling condition in front of Sebastopol; but the publicity served as nothing else would have done to rouse public opinion and Parliamentary action before it was altogether too late. It was only fitting that Palmerston should become Prime Minister at the crisis, in place of Lord Aberdeen, who had never liked the war.

But the 25,000[7] lives that the country lost in the Crimea saved very many more in years to come. For the real hero of the war was Florence Nightingale, and its most indubitable outcome was modern nursing, both military and civil, and a new conception of the potentiality and place in society of the trained and educated woman. And this in turn led, in the 'sixties and 'seventies, to John Stuart Mill's movement for woman's suffrage, which Miss Nightingale supported, and to the founding of women's colleges and the improvement of girls' schools, when at length some provision was made for the neglected higher education of one-half of the Queen's subjects. From the frozen and blood-stained trenches before Sebastopol, and from the horrors of the first Scutari hospitals, have sprung not only a juster national conception of the character and claims of the private soldier, but many things in our modern life that at first sight seem far removed from scenes of war and the sufferings of our bearded heroes on the winter-bound plateau.

In the Victorian era, the field of action where British foreign policy was most obviously successful was the Italian. Without war or serious danger of war, by legitimate diplomatic action in unison with strongly expressed popular sympathy, Britain helped the creation of a new independent Power in the Mediterranean and in the counsels of Europe, contrary to the wishes of the other Great Powers. This event removed a running sore in the body politic of Europe, and

[7] According to Miss Nightingale 16,000 of these lives were lost by bad administration. She brought down the death rate in the Scutari hospitals from 42 per cent. to 22 per thousand.

started a tradition of Italian friendship for England which continued to be an important element in affairs down to Italy's participation in the Great War of our own day.

In 1848 Palmerston was at the Foreign Office. British opinion was then divided about Italy, more or less on party lines. Palmerston was favourable to Italian autonomy, and hoped to negotiate Austria out of the Lombard plain by appealing to her enlightened self-interest. But in that year of revolutions, Palmerston did not hold the key to the Italian question. For as British Minister he felt it his first duty to prevent a general European War, particularly one in which France might attack Austria, and so launch out on a new era of conquest and militarism. Yet without a war between France and Austria it proved impossible for Italy to make any advance towards freedom.

When next the Italian question became acute in the summer of 1859, Palmerston formed his second Ministry, which lasted till his death half a dozen years later. [1859–65.] Russell was his Foreign Minister, and Gladstone as Chancellor of the Exchequer was the third of the controlling members of the Cabinet. Much as these three differed on other subjects, they agreed about Italy; and by a remarkable chance each of the 'Triumvirate' had an intimate knowledge of things Italian, in contrast to the ignorance from which all three then suffered as regards America, Germany and the Near East. The result was that they acted with wisdom and vigour in the decisive Italian crisis of 1859–60 with very happy results.

England held the key to the Italian situation, as she had not done in 1848. In spite of the efforts of Lord Derby's late government, Napoleon III in alliance with Cavour's Piedmont had gone to war with the Austrians. [1859.] His object was to expel Austrian influence from the Italian Peninsula and substitute French influence, in forms less galling and injurious to the Italians, for whom he had a real sympathy. But he wished to erect, not an independent Italian State, but a number of Italian States dependent on himself. Cavour, on the other hand, used Napoleon to expel Austria, but hoped then to effect a liberation of all Italy on such terms as would render her truly independent. Cavour was the cleverer man of the two, and won the game: but he could scarcely have done so without British help.

Russia and Prussia supported Austria in opposition to Italian liberation of any sort or kind, though since the Crimean War Russia was neither so powerful nor so friendly to Austria as before. In this complicated situation England, by taking up the cause of Italian independence and unity more thoroughly and more sympathetically than France, helped Cavour to force the pace. After Garibaldi's liberation of Sicily [1860.], the fall of the reactionary Neapolitan kingdom and of the Papal government in most of Central Italy followed, with Napoleon's enforced consent; for, since he could not permit Austrian reconquest, he was in no position to oppose the full flood-tide of Italian national movement sweeping on to unity under the Crown of Piedmont, when that movement received the diplomatic countenance of British Ministers and the enthusiastic encouragement of the British people.

A less fortunate episode in European affairs closed the epoch of Russell and Palmerston. A dispute lay between Denmark and her German neighbours, over the Schleswig-Holstein provinces, whence fourteen hundred years before a large part of the English people had migrated to Britain.[8] The merits of the case were divided, and there was room for the good offices of a judicious third party, friendly to all concerned. But Palmerston and Russell took up a position of bravado in encouraging 'little Denmark,' which they could not make good when Bismarck called their bluff. Palmerston had declared that 'it would not be Denmark alone' with whom her assailants would have to contend. Yet when war came, she found no ally, for our still unreformed army was in no condition to take the field against the united forces of Prussia, Austria, and indeed of all Germany. And the famous Volunteer movement of the mid-

[8] See Vol. I., pp. 51, 63.

Victorian epoch was as yet for home defence alone. Nor could we expect the help of France and Russia, whom our diplomacy on other questions had recently offended.

The Palmerstonian era ended therefore with a humiliating rebuff. The importance of the case was even greater than men knew at the time, for the full meaning of the modern military monarchy of Prussia had yet to be revealed by the victories over Austria in 1866 and France in 1870. Palmerston's popular and jaunty diplomatic performances had had their day. If longer continued, they would have become a serious danger in the terrible new world that was coming into existence, as nationality learnt to prepare for war with all the prodigious powers of modern science and modern locomotion.

The fact that of 'the two old ringleaders' Palmerston died the first [1865.], had important consequences in political history. Russell, now become an Earl, was left as chief of the Whig-Liberal party, and, in spite of the fact that he had once been called 'finality John,' he had long favoured a further extension of the franchise, and a development of the party out of aristocratic Whiggism into democratic Liberalism. If Palmerston had survived Russell, he would have opposed any such growth and would probably have broken with Gladstone, who was his opposite both in temperament and in policy. Russell, too old to take a leading part in the new age of transition, became Prime Minister, but permitted Gladstone, now at the zenith of his powers, to take over the virtual headship of the party.

[1866.] Gladstone, thus become the leading man in the State, formed an alliance with John Bright, who stood at the head of the movement for the enfranchisement of the town artisans and of the lower middle class. The strength of the working-class movement on its political side lay, during this decade, in its alliance with the middle-class Radicals, on the ground of their common exclusion from the franchise. The class-consciousness that had inspired the older Chartist movement had died away, largely owing to better times.[9] Bright was the leader in the country and the spokesman in the House of this combined movement. Both he and the cause he advocated had recently gained prestige by the correctness of his judgment on the American Civil War, in which he had been a strong and well-informed advocate of the Northern cause. Most Whig and Conservative statesmen had in various degrees inclined to favour the cause of the South. While the war was raging [1861–65.], opinion in Britain had been largely divided on the issue according as men wished for democracy or aristocracy, a wide or a narrow franchise, in their own country. The ordeal by battle had gone in favour of Abraham Lincoln and the Northern Democracy, and the effect upon internal English affairs, though not clearly measurable, was certainly very great. Gladstone, an exception to many rules, had indeed been a hot 'Southerner,' although he was moving fast to democracy in home affairs. His alliance with Bright after the end of the American War and the death of Palmerston, brought the franchise question straight to the forefront of British politics.[10]

The manner in which the Second Reform Bill was carried was very different from the passage of the First. And the difference indicated how much in the last thirty-five years the governing and conservative classes had grown accustomed to change as a normal condition of political life, instead of regarding it as the end of all things. One might almost say that Darwin's then much contested doctrine of 'evolution' had already won its place in political consciousness.

There was, however, a sharp struggle. A very moderate measure of working-class enfranchisement was introduced by Gladstone. [1866.] But the Whig-Liberal majority had been elected the year before to support Palmerston, not to enfranchise the working classes. Under Robert Lowe's eloquent but imprudent leadership, a group of discontented

[9] See pp. 186–87, above.

[10] See pp. 213–16, below, on Britain and the American Civil War.

Whig members, nicknamed by Bright 'the cave of Adullam,' joined with Disraeli and the Conservatives to defeat this very moderate instalment of Reform. It was bad tactics from their own point of view, more particularly since Lowe openly based his objections to Reform on the moral and intellectual inferiority of wage-earners as compared to the *bourgeoisie*. His incautious eloquence on this interesting theme roused the working classes to fury, and the agitation for enfranchisement became formidable and threatening. The Trade Unions in the great industrial centres joined with the middle classes to organize monster out-door demonstrations, addressed by Bright, in an age when political meetings were still a rarity.

After the defeat of Gladstone's Reform Bill, the Liberal Government had resigned; there was no dissolution, but the Conservatives took office. Disraeli, as Chancellor of the Exchequer in Lord Derby's new Ministry, led the Commons and dominated the Cabinet, just as his rival Gladstone had done in Earl Russell's government a few weeks before. Now Disraeli, when he was not consciously allowing his oriental fantasy to roam upon some useful errand, had a shrewd eye for facts. He understood the situation of the country and saw that it required settlement by concession. Moreover, he had more real sympathy than Lowe with the working class, and in theory he had sometimes spoken well of the working man with no vote, as against his employer who wasted his franchise upon Whig candidates. It is true that Disraeli had recently denounced Gladstone's argument for an extended franchise as 'the doctrine of Tom Paine,' but, Tom Paine's or another's, he now saw that the time had come to put it into force.

Moreover, Disraeli could not keep control of the Parliamentary situation on any other terms, for the Conservative Government had no majority of its own, and the bulk of the Liberal party was no longer willing to be put off with a mere instalment of Reform. Outside, the country was in a ferment. The advice of Queen Victoria was all in favour of a 'settlement' of the question. Lord Derby, who as young Stanley, 'the Rupert of Debate,' had taken a leading part in passing the First Reform Bill, was now quite prepared to 'dish the Whigs' and to 'take a leap in the dark.' So Disraeli very ably settled the question and pacified the country by carrying a measure which, as finally amended, was much stronger than the Bill which the Adullamites and Conservatives had thrown out the year before as being too strong. The agricultural labourer and the miner in county constituencies were indeed still left unenfranchised, but household suffrage in the boroughs was in effect the principle of the Second Reform Act. [1867.] Being the measure of a Conservative government it easily passed the Lords.

Lord Cranborne, afterwards the famous Lord Salisbury, was not alone in considering the transaction as a dishonest betrayal of principle. Perhaps it was rather the growth of political good sense. But in any case there was no one capable of treating Disraeli as Disraeli had treated Peel on a like occasion. By accepting the great change without undergoing internal schism, the Conservative party prepared a future for itself in the new democratic world. But the immediate advantage accrued, at the General Election of 1868, to Gladstone and the Liberal party, which had a programme of overdue reforms to carry through before a real age of Conservatism could set in.

BOOKS FOR FURTHER READING: *Queen Victoria's Letters* (5 vols.); Spencer Walpole, *History of England,* Vols. IV.–VI.; Thursfield, *Peel*; Kitson Clark, *Peel*; Disraeli, *Lord George Bentinck*; Strachey, *Queen Victoria*; Buckle, *Disraeli* (6 vols.); Morley, *Gladstone* (2 vols.) and *Cobden* (2 vols.); Cook, *Florence Nightingale* (2 vols.); Trevelyan, *Bright*; Hammond, *Shaftesbury*; Cole, *Robert Owen* and *Working Class Movement*; Halévy, *Histoire du Peuple Anglais,* Vol. III. (1830–41); Arthur Bryant, *English Saga.*

CHAPTER THREE

External Development in the Latest Era. Character of the Second British Empire. Growth of Canada. Relations with the United States. Australasia. South Africa. India

The Second British Empire, as we have already seen, was a flourishing child when the Napoleonic Wars came to an end.[1] In the following century its growth was enormous in area, wealth and population, owing to the developments of commerce, communication and transport due to steam and iron, electricity and petrol, and applied medical science in the Tropics. Conditions at home favoured emigration. Little check was placed on the increase of population in Great Britain until the last decades of the Nineteenth Century, and for long there was no other provision for unemployment save the workhouse. A constant stream of emigrants, therefore, poured out of the island; part flowed into the United States then engaged in peopling the vast plains beyond the Alleghany mountains, but a large part went to Canada, Australasia and South Africa. The Colonial Office in the 'thirties was lethargic and stupid as regards emigration, but Lord Durham and Gibbon Wakefield, helped by the Churches and by private organizations, set going a movement for scientific care and encouragement of British settlement in British Colonies, which eventually made a convert and ally of Downing Street.

Until the end of the Victorian era there were still large numbers of persons in Great Britain born and bred as agriculturists, and desiring no better than to obtain land of their own beyond the ocean. It is only of recent years that a fear has arisen lest the English race, at home and in the Dominions, may by choice and custom eschew the rural life and crowd too exclusively into the cities.

[1] See pp. 116–17, above.

The other aspect of the Second British Empire has been the development of vast portions of Asia and Africa by commercial intercourse and by political rule. The political rule has been conducted in Africa and in the East and West Indies, according to the benevolent ideals that have been generally prevalent in Downing Street since the days of Wilberforce and since the reorganization of Indian Government by Pitt and his Governors General. Great benefits have been conferred on a very large proportion of mankind: in Africa, inter-tribal war and slave-raiding have been stopped; in India, Egypt and elsewhere the material benefits of modern science and organization have been applied for the advantage of all, not least of the humblest cultivators of the soil.

But two difficulties have beset the path of executive rule over the non-European races. First, the counter-claims of white farmers and traders, especially where, as formerly in the West Indies and permanently in South Africa, they are numerous enough to practise self-government. And, secondly, the class of difficulties which inevitably arise, particularly in India, when a long period of peace, good government and contact with Western civilization has caused the ruled to desire to become self-rulers. The questions how best, how fast and how far this demand can be met without disaster, form perhaps the most difficult problem that good government has ever created for itself.

The new conditions of the Industrial Revolution for some time only increased the advantages of Britain as the clearinghouse for the world's trade and finance, and as the manufacturing centre for less developed countries. These circumstances led to the adoption of Free Trade and the abolition of tariffs and Navigation Acts. The change of policy put an end to the old 'mercantile' theory, which had regarded the commercial interests of the Colonies as involved in but subordinate to those of Britain. It was no longer desired to control British Colonial trade as a British monopoly. The end of the mercantile system led, by the inevitable logic of liberty and equality, to the grant to the self-governing Colonies of permission to decide each for itself whether it wished to protect its own manufactures by tariffs, even by tariffs against the mother country. In our own day this principle is being applied even in the case of India.

But taken in its largest aspect, the Free Trade policy of Britain, and the refusal any longer to keep trade with our colonies and possessions as a reserve of our own, removed many sources of friction with other nations, which could not have willingly seen themselves shut out from trade with so large a portion of the world as came to be included in the Second British Empire.

The principle of self-rule for the communities oversea was only an extension of the methods of government which had formerly prevailed in the lost Thirteen Colonies, and which had been initiated by Pitt in the two Canadas.[2] But the logical and complete application of the principle of responsible Parliamentary government for the Dominions, owes its timely triumph to the wisdom and energy of Lord Durham. [1838–39.] He had the peculiar merit of regarding freedom as the means of preserving the Imperial connection, and not as a step towards separation, which most Whig and Conservative statesmen in that era believed to be inevitable.

Towards the close of the century a full consciousness of the meaning of the Empire swept over Great Britain and the Dominions in the days of Joseph Chamberlain. But the hope of the later Victorian age that this consciousness could be expressed in some form of Imperial Federation and a more unified constitution has not been fulfilled. Rather the Colonies, which had already developed into Dominions, are now developing into separate Nations. The Second British Empire is becoming an English-speaking League of Nations, officially united by the Crown. How strong the indefinable bonds of that Imperial unity may prove, was shown by the events of the Great War, an ordeal that no merely paper constitution could have survived.

[2] See Vol. II., p. 230 and p. 123, above.

The North American policy of British statesmen in the Nineteenth Century had two fields,—Canadian problems and British relations to the United States: they reacted closely on each other. The Canadian problem, thanks to Lord Durham and Lord Elgin after him, received wise attention and treatment at an early date. But the full significance of our relations to the United States was not recognised by Whig and Conservative statesmen or by British public opinion in general, until after the American Civil War. [1861–65.]

[SEE MAP 4.] In 1837 two easily suppressed rebellions flared up in Canada,—one in the Lower Province among the French *habitans,* the other in the Upper Province among the English-speaking settlers. Fortunately for the British connection, the two sections were mutually antagonistic and neither had any desire to join the United States. But both had grievances against an unsympathetic administration. The two Provincial Assemblies which Pitt had set up possessed the power to embarrass but not to nominate or control the executive.[3] The time had now come for the grant of full responsible government. But it by no means followed that British statesmen at home would believe that such was the cure, or have confidence that it could be safely applied immediately after an armed rebellion. Ignorance of Colonial conditions was great, and consistent belief in democracy was rare among the statesmen who had opposed and passed the First Reform Bill. Fortunately Lord Melbourne's Whig government had the happy inspiration to transport to Canada their able but sharp-tempered colleague, Lord Durham. He was both an Imperialist and a democrat at a time when hardly any other person of Cabinet rank was either the one or the other. He and his secretary, Charles Buller, were capable of seeing that full self-government was required, and of saying so very effectively in the famous 'Durham Report.' [1839.]

The problem, however, was far more complicated than

[3] See p. 123, above.

anyone in England realised or than Durham himself knew before he arrived on the spot. He found two nations, French and English-speaking, bitterly opposed to each other as well as to the government. British immigration and farming in the West had now put the French in a very decided minority in Canada as a whole; but in their own Lower Province the French peasants still outnumbered the English-speaking traders and business men. Religious and cultural differences made the schism profound. To establish responsible self-government in Lower Canada would, in that generation, have led only to the breakdown of government, and probably to armed conflict between the two sections of the community. Durham's bold advice was to unite the two provinces in one, and to set up a single elective Assembly with full power over the executive, which would thus be in the hands of the English-speaking majority. This plan was carried out in the Canada Act of 1840. The French protested, but submitted. The new Canadian constitution functioned, with the help of Lord Elgin's shrewd and liberal guidance [1847–54.] until the next great crisis of Canadian history in 1867.[4]

But, in order to understand the circumstances that led to Canadian Federation in 1867, it is necessary to take up the thread of British relations to the United States. Castlereagh, as Foreign Minister, has many claims on the gratitude of posterity, but none greater than his part in the mutual agreement to disarm along both sides of the Canadian border, and in particular to suppress the war navies on those Great Lakes that still divide British territory from the United States. [1817.] Next year, in the same spirit, he began the determination of the boundary westward. This

[4] Though Durham's Report was acted upon in 1840, thanks to Lord John Russell, Durham himself had been most unhandsomely recalled in 1839 by Lord Melbourne, owing to Brougham's intrigues, which were naturally made the most of by the Conservative Peers. Brougham's version of Durham's performance, and his false statement that Durham wrote none of the Report that goes by his name, still find a most inappropriate place in the *Dictionary of National Biography*,—I hope not for ever.

dangerous process, which occupied the joint attention of statesmen at Downing Street and Washington for a generation to come, could never have been brought to a peaceful conclusion if large armed forces and military traditions had existed on either side of the disputed line.

[1818.] In Castlereagh's day, the line was carried forward by agreement from the Lake of the Woods to the summit of the Rockies, along the line of latitude 49°. It was wisely agreed to leave the eventual settlement of the lands between the Rockies and the Pacific still undetermined. That vast region, then all of it collectively known as 'Oregon,' was inhabited as yet only by hunters and trappers of both nations, dependent on the Pacific Coast for their communication with the outside world. The 'joint occupation of Oregon' by the United States and Great Britain kept the peace in these thinly peopled lands, until in 'the roaring forties' the head of the column of American democracy, hot on 'the Oregon trail,' burst over the barrier of the Rockies.

Americans were in an expansive mood. They were conquering nature and peopling a continent with a speed never before known in the world's history. It was a period of the Mexican War and of much tall talk, that represented somewhat crudely a genuine exhilaration in the sense of boundless expansion and a great new destiny discovered. In 1844 a United States Presidential Election was won on the cry of 'fifty-four forty or fight,' implying a territorial claim as far north as latitude 54° 40′, that would have altogether excluded the British Empire from the Pacific Coast. But Canada, too, had her rights of future expansion westward. Peel, one of the most wisely pacific Ministers England ever had, was firm, conciliatory and reasonable. At the very moment when he fell from office, he accomplished a feat as important, perhaps, as the Abolition of the Corn Laws; he obtained an equitable and peaceful definition of the boundary down to the Western Ocean, by the prolongation of Castlereagh's line of latitude 49°. [1846.] The long, invisible border from Atlantic to Pacific is not guarded by sentry boxes and the challenge of rival armaments, but by

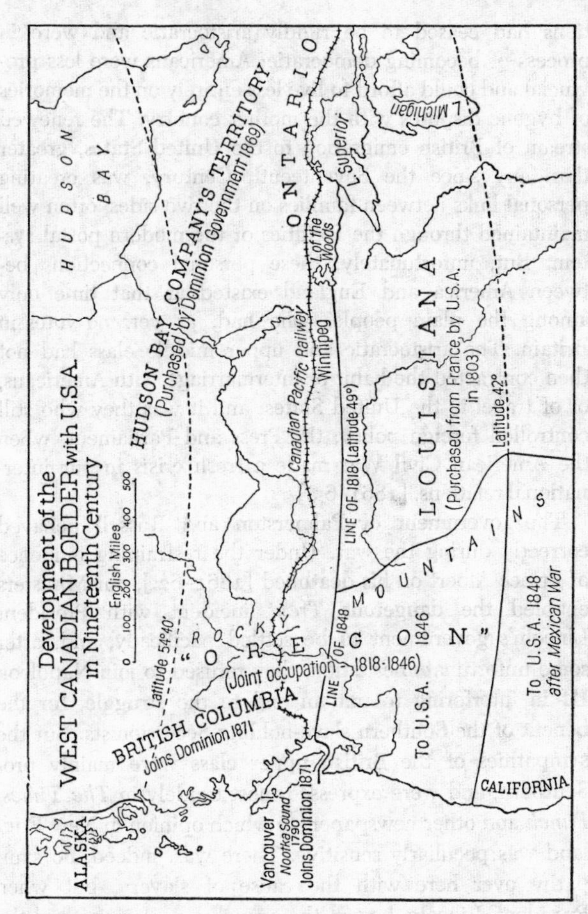

Map 8

the good sense and good feeling of two great communities.

After this triumph of reason and goodwill, it seemed likely that mutual understanding between Great Britain and the United States would move forward steadily out of mutual ignorance and prejudice, bred by the wars and social and religious differences of long ago. British institutions had ceased to be rigidly aristocratic and were in process of becoming democratic; Americans were less provincial and could afford to live less entirely on the memories of bygone disputes with the mother country. The renewed stream of British emigration to the United States, greater than any since the Seventeenth Century, was creating personal links between families on the two sides, often well maintained through the facilities of the modern postal system. But, unfortunately, these personal connections between America and England existed at that time only among the plain people, who had, as yet, no votes in Britain. The aristocratic and upper middle class had not then contracted the habit of intermarriage with Americans, or of travel in the United States; and it was they who still controlled foreign policy, the Press and Parliament, when the American Civil War made a fresh crisis in our international relations. [1861–65.]

The government of Palmerston and Russell behaved correctly during the war. Under the restraining influence of Prince Albert on his deathbed [1861–62.], our Ministers enabled the dangerous *Trent* incident with President Lincoln's government to be settled pacifically, and, after some unfortunate hesitation, they refused to join Napoleon III in interfering to put an end to the struggle, for the benefit of the Southern slave-holding Secessionists. But the sympathies of the British upper class were mainly pro-Southern, and were expressed most crudely in *The Times*, *Punch* and other newspapers to which opinion in New England was peculiarly sensitive. There was, indeed, no sympathy over here with the cause of slavery, but when President Lincoln began the war by declaring that the Union and not Slavery was the issue, many English people did not know enough about America to understand the relation which that statement bore to the whole truth. It was not inexcusable that Englishmen should doubt whether the South could be permanently coerced into membership of the Union. But when Lincoln declared the emancipation of all slaves in the rebellious Southern Confederacy, opinion in England began to swing round to the North. [OCT. 1862.] And from first to last the working classes and the lower middle classes, kept well informed by John Bright, W. E. Forster and others, had been on the side of the Northern democracy against the creation of a Republic based on slavery. After the victory of the North and the assassination of Lincoln, everyone else hastened to take the same side. But so long as the war lasted there was a tendency for British sympathy to divide according as men desired or deprecated the extension of the franchise in our own island.

The North had been deeply incensed by what they took to be British opinion during the struggle; and the South, which had expected more active help, was little better pleased. American feeling took a strong turn back against England, at the very moment when the general trend of development on both sides of the Atlantic was preparing the way for a better understanding between the two peoples. This alienation, due to the accidental circumstances of the Civil War, has not indeed been permanent, but it occurred at a time very detrimental to the progress of Anglo-American understanding. The great influx of Irish hostile to Great Britain, and of Europeans who were of a different tradition and culture, was beginning to take place on such a scale that the prevalently Anglo-Saxon character of the American Republic was, by the end of the century, considerably modified.

The outstanding diplomatic inheritance from the Civil War was that of the *Alabama* claims. Russell, as Foreign Minister, had carelessly permitted that ill-omened steamship to escape from Laird's yards at Birkenhead; she had proceeded to prey upon Northern commerce under the flag of the Southern Confederacy. The irritation of the North against England, after the war was over, expressed itself in the form of excessive claims for damages on this score. The crisis continued grave for several years, but was honourably settled at Geneva in 1872. Gladstone, now Prime Minister, atoned for his unwise expressions of Southern sympathy during the war by consenting to leave the award of damages to the decision of a third party—a great step forward in the history of world-arbitration and peace. In the last decade of the Century, the sharp crisis of the dispute over the Venezuela boundary between President Cleveland and Lord Salisbury was also settled by arbitration; [1895.] and during the subsequent war between Spain and America over the Cuban question, public opinion in England was markedly more favourable to America than was opinion in continental Europe. [1898.] Both these incidents testified to the friendly attitude which British policy and feeling had permanently assumed towards the United States.

The irritation of the Northern States against Britain during and immediately after the Civil War, and the activities of the Irish Fenians on the Canadian border, had warned Canada that her independence was in danger. Fortunately, a generation of full self-government had by that time done its work. The autonomous Colonies of British North America, with the exception of Newfoundland, voluntarily formed themselves into a close Federation, of which the immediate motive was moral resistance to annexationist tendencies in relation to the great neighbour Republic. [1867.] The Canadian statesman to whom Federation was chiefly due, was Sir John Macdonald. Incidentally, the Federation Policy restored to the French Lower Province its separate autonomy, subject now to the bond of general Canadian unity. By this time the British and French communities had learnt to live side by side with diminished friction, and the French had adapted themselves to Parliamentary government.

As a result of successful Federation, the Dominion of Canada has been able to deal with the United States more and more on her own account, and no longer merely through the agency of Great Britain. The new sense of Canadian unity also produced in the decades following Federation, the Canadian-Pacific Railway, which opened the vast regions of the remote West to English-speaking settlement under the British flag. That railway is the spinal cord of the new Canadian nation. [SEE MAP 8.]

Australia in the Nineteenth Century moved in a world remote from outer contact. She inherited no problem like that of the French Canadians. She had no neighbour like the United States. But her history, like Canada's, is that of the formation of a number of separate colonies, divided by great distances of desert, which become completely self-governing in the middle of the century, and by the end of the century have been linked up into an economic unity by long lines of railway. And, as in Canada in 1867, so in Australia in 1901 the time had come for a Federal Union. But the Federal Union of the Australian Colonies is not as close as that of the Canadian. The peculiarity of Australian politics has been the early strength of the Labour party, and the struggle of the democracy with the 'squatters' for the equal division of land and the break-up of great estates. The policy of excluding all coloured races from the continent, and its possible consequences in relation to modern Japan, has in recent years brought the strong nationalism of Australia into a closer sense of outside diplomatic relations with other countries, and of the importance of the British connection. Australia's ideal, which she is determined to maintain even at the expense of rapid development, is an equalitarian society of white men, of high physique and a high average standard of life.

It was Gibbon Wakefield who had brought the public to believe that New Zealand might accommodate other races as well as the Maori tribes. His New Zealand Association, founded in 1837, made the first British Settlements there, only just in time to prevent the annexation of the islands by France. New Zealand, with its one and a half million inhabitants, remains one of the smallest but not the least happy and well-beloved of the British self-governing Dominions.[5]

[5] The population of the self-governing Dominions in our day is: Canada, 10,376,786 (1931); Australia, 6,630,600 (1933); New Zealand, 1,463,278 (1926); South Africa, just under 2 million whites; while Great Britain (England, Wales and Scotland) contains 44,790,485 (1931). Since the War, the Irish Free State has acquired Dominion Status,

The history of South Africa presents points of likeness and of contrast to those of the other Dominions. As in Australia and Canada, the formation of a number of large but isolated communities, widely separated by great spaces of desert, preceded the age of railway connection and of political Federation. As in Canada, the problems of colonization and self-government were complicated by the presence of another European race settled there before the coming of the English. As in the days of Wolfe and Montcalm, so in the days of Kitchener and Botha, there was bloodshed before peaceful settlement was reached. Yet the white population is in a minority of about one to four in the South African Union of to-day, excluding the native Protectorates. Canada is a white man's country, alike by nature and by settlement; parts of Australia could support coloured folk, but policy has reserved the whole continent for whites alone; but South Africa is a land where the European and African races flourish side by side, on the healthy upland plateau of the interior. The white South Africans have been numerous enough to claim self-government and to conduct it successfully; this fact has had constant reactions upon the native problem.

The first stage of British South African history, after the annexation of the maritime station of the Cape of Good Hope during the Napoleonic Wars, was the government of the small community of Boers by British officials near Table Mountain. There was at first the less difficulty because the Boers had not been accustomed to self-government under the Dutch flag, and because there was as yet no large body of British Colonists. But in the third and fourth decades of the Century British immigrants began to arrive in such numbers as to raise difficult questions of language, law and custom. At the same time all slaves in the British Empire were emancipated. [1833.] The Boers did not raise difficulty about emancipation, but considered,

and Ulster responsible self-government: in 1926 Northern Ireland had a population of 1,256,561, and the Free State of just under three million.

not without some reason, that the promised compensation was not paid them in full. In the same years they received inadequate protection in their outlying farms from the raids of the warlike native tribes of the interior. Lord Melbourne's incompetent Colonial Secretary, Lord Glenelg, represented a type of British official of that day who listened too exclusively to a certain kind of missionary on all native questions. These grievances of the border farmers, and perhaps some restless impelling spirit of adventure, were the causes of the Great Trek. The Boers started out, taking their wives and children with them in their ox-waggons, across the veld into the far interior. [1836.] There they lived, after their own free patriarchal fashion, reading their great Bibles, multiplying their herds of cattle, shooting the big game that swarmed around, and watching the native warrior tribes from behind the protection of unerring musket and rifle.

But such isolation could not last long in the Africa of the Nineteenth Century. First in Natal, then on both sides of the Vaal river they were followed up by British and European immigrants of the most various kinds,—missionaries, hunters, farmers, gold and diamond diggers, and capitalist speculators. The clash of the old and new type of white society was repeated again and again in South Africa, in various forms, throughout the century.

For a long time the presence of the warrior native tribes restrained the Boers and British from coming to blows with one another. But after the suppression and pacification of the Zulu warriors by British armies and officials, the Boers felt a little more secure. [1879.] At this critical moment the vacillation of the British governments, particularly Gladstone's, in deciding on a settlement of some kind with the Transvaal Boers, led to the conflict at Majuba. [1881.] Gladstone accepted that British defeat for fear lest the Dutch of Cape Colony should throw in their lot with their blood-brothers beyond the Vaal; and so the Transvaal recovered its independence as the South African Republic. The 'Majuba Policy' was deprived of any chance it had of success, by the development of gold and diamond

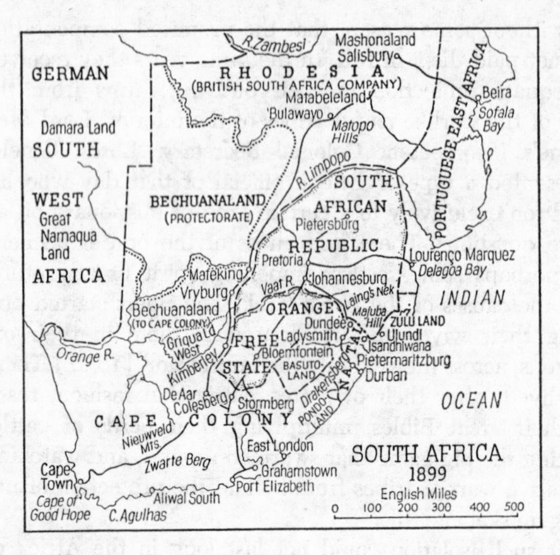

Map 9

diggings in the Transvaal. The scramble for wealth produced a sharper contrast than ever before between the cosmopolitan man of business and the shrewd old Dutch farmer, who wished to exploit the mines without yielding political power in his country to the miners.

At the same time Cecil Rhodes and his Chartered Company[6] were developing new British territories to the west and north of the Transvaal. Rhodesia came into existence. This ambitious thrust into the interior was in part prompted by the fears which Rhodes entertained lest the Germans should spread their territories across the continent from German South West Africa to join Portuguese territory; such a development, if made in time, would cut off for ever the northward advance of the British race. Rhodes, therefore, aimed at establishing in good time a link with the regions beyond the Zambesi, where Livingstone and other British missionaries had in the previous generation showed the way into the heart of Central Africa, and had

[6] See Vol. II., p. 109, note.

shown also how the natives could be led and guided aright. Still further to the north, Britain was in occupation of Egypt. To Rhodes' sanguine spirit, therefore, the Cape to Cairo railway through British territory seemed by no means impossible.

This practical dreamer left a great mark on African geography and history. But not all that he did was what he originally wished to do. He wished to reconcile the British and Dutch races, but he alienated them for a number of tragic years. While he was Premier of Cape Colony, he gave way to his impatience with Paul Kruger, President of the South African Republic, the old-world type of conservative Boer, and in an evil hour planned an armed attack on the Transvaal. 'Jameson's raid' [XMAS, 1895.] united the whole Dutch race in Africa in just resentment and suspicion, enabled Kruger to arm to the teeth, and led up to the second Boer War. For Chamberlain in the Colonial Office at home, and Sir Alfred Milner in South Africa, could see no alternative but to bring the questions at issue at once to a head.

[1899–1902.] The South African War, with its unexpected reverses and its long protraction by the spirited guerrilla resistance of the Boer farmers, had a number of important reactions on the British Empire. It put an end to the somewhat boastful type of Imperialism which dominated the last years of the Nineteenth Century, a spirit which, though it served its purpose in its day to popularize the idea of the British Empire, would have made trouble in the dangerous epoch now approaching. The serious character of this second Boer War made men of all parties take a more sober and broad-minded view of Imperial duties and destiny. It gave a fresh impetus to military efficiency and Army Reform, destined to be of great consequence a dozen years later: if we had won the Boer War too easily we might never have won the German War at all. Finally, it called out the active and enthusiastic help of Canadians and Australasians, who came to South Africa to fight for the cause of the Empire in distress.

[MAY, 1902.] The victory in the field, won by Lord Roberts and Lord Kitchener, led to the annexation of the Transvaal and the Orange Free State. Peace was secured at the Treaty of Vereeniging, where honourable terms were granted to the Commandos who still held out on the desolated veld. The material restoration of the farms was to be undertaken at once by Great Britain, the Dutch and English languages were to be put on an equal footing, and in course of time complete responsible self-government was to be granted under the British flag. All these promises were kept. Responsible self-government was set up as early as 1906 by Sir Henry Campbell-Bannerman, in spite of violent outcries and prophecies of ruin from Balfour, Milner and the Conservatives; the result was the pacification of South Africa. Four years later [1910.] the whole sub-continent was federated in the South African Union, except only Rhodesia and certain native Protectorates. In 1914–18 Generals Botha and Smuts, who had held out to the last against the British armies in 1902, headed the Union of South Africa in the war against Germany, and thereby added greatly to the material and yet more to the moral strength of the Empire, at its moment of greatest danger.

The collapse of the Mogul Empire in the Eighteenth Century, and the reduction of India to an anarchy of warring rulers, chiefs and warrior bands, had compelled the British East India Company to undertake military operations and political responsibilities on the great scale. The process had been hastened by the French effort to drive their European rivals out of India. Lord Wellesley had been the first Governor-General [1798–1805.] to envisage the necessity of going forward till the *Pax Britannica* was everywhere accepted within the circle of Indian States. But although his Maratha wars checked the assaults of anarchy upon the Eastern and Southern portions of the Peninsula, the great sources of unrest in Central India were still left uncontrolled. [SEE MAP 5.] After Wellesley's retirement, an attempt was made to limit British liability and to stop any further advance across India.[7]

[7] See pp. 126–28, above.

But events soon showed the impossibility of leaving confusion to welter on the other side of a long, unguarded line in the vain hope that it would confine itself to agreed limits. The disturbed state of Northern and Central India rendered peace in other parts impossible. Lord Wellesley's forward policy was resumed by Lord Hastings. In his day the Gurkha hillmen of Nepal were reduced by war [1814–16.], and their land has ever since remained our friendly ally, and a great recruiting ground for our Indian armies. Also in the time of Lord Hastings, the Maratha Chiefs and the robber hordes of Central India were finally conquered in the Third Maratha War and the Pindari Wars. [1816–18.] Half a dozen years later, an attack on North-East India by the irruption of Burmese armies into Assam, led to the First Burmese War, [1824–26.] and the beginning of the annexation of Burmah, which was completed in 1853 and 1886. The Burmese, a Buddhist people of Thibeto-Chinese origin, are in no sense a part of the religious and racial mosaic of India proper; but the systems of government applied by the British to India were with modifications applied to this eastward extension of their territory.

After the forward movements and wars of the governorship of Lord Hastings and his immediate successor, there was a pause of some years before the problems of the North-West frontier, and the contact opened out with the Pathans of Afghanistan and the Sikhs of the Punjab led to a fresh cycle of wars and annexations. During this pacific interval, the benevolent side of British rule, and the sense of trusteeship for the Indians was strongly emphasized by Lord William Bentinck and by other able and earnest public servants. Nor, indeed, had the sense of trusteeship been lacking among the British rulers who had dealt in war and annexation, from Clive and Warren Hastings down through Wellesley and Lord Hastings to Metcalfe and the Lawrence brothers. But Lord William Bentinck [1828–35.] was not called on to conquer anyone more formidable than the Thugs, the caste of hereditary murderers on the Indian roads, or to beat down any resistance other than that of the half-hearted defenders of Suttee,—the burning of Hindoo widows. His victories were those of peace.

In 1813 the monopoly of the East India Company for British trade with India had been abolished, and twenty years later its monopoly of British trade with China also came to an end. [1833.] 'John Company' ceased to be a trading concern, but retained until 1858 the shadow of political power, of which the substance had long since passed to the Ministers of the Crown. The new Charter of 1833 embodied one tendency of Bentinck's policy in the words, 'No native of India, or any natural-born subject of His Majesty, shall be disabled from holding any place, office or employment by reason of his religion, place of birth, descent or colour.' But the business of training Indian administrators to render them capable of joining in the work of the British, had yet to be begun. Bentinck and his contemporaries addressed themselves to the task and its problems with an eager and generous zeal.

At this period there was singularly little ill-feeling between Europeans and Indians. The recollection of what had preceded British rule was so fresh that gratitude was still felt. The English and Scots in India were still very few and for the most part select. They were not yet numerous enough to form a purely English society of their own. They were cut off from home by a six months' voyage, often for life. India was their second home. Intermarriage, though rare, was not *taboo*. Colour feeling was not yet as strong on either side as it became at the end of the century. The Indians knew nothing of England or of Europe; their rulers seemed to them strange, invincible men dropped from the skies, more benevolent than most gods or kings whom they knew. Nothing could have made this happy state of things permanent. It is only a question whether inevitable change could have been made better or worse by any system of education for India other than that actually adopted.

It was under Bentinck's rule that the decision was made in favour of English as the medium of education and administration. The controversy was decided by the strong but over-confident arguments of Macaulay, then at Calcutta as a Member of Council. It is difficult to believe that any other language than English could have been permanently accepted. Since India was to be ruled as one, there must be a common official language. And who was going to compel British and Indians, in their dealings with education and government, to employ one of the innumerable languages of the East, arbitrarily selected for precedence over the others?

The teaching of English involved, however, certain dangers which subsequent generations did not take the right means to avoid. An energetic white race, trained in all the uses of self-government for centuries past, and assuming self-discipline and public order as things granted and certain, naturally lays stress in its poetry and its political philosophy on freedom as the crown of life. But these home-bred ideals may have strange consequences when overheard by an audience at the other end of the world and of human experience; there is some truth in the saying that we have attempted in India to 'rear a race of administrators on the literature of revolt.' Mistakes were certainly made in the curriculum of education. But those who argue that all our difficulties of recent years could have been avoided by the simple expedient of keeping Western literature and language out of Indian schools, do not stay to consider how strongly the Indians were even in 1835 demanding to learn English, how much the revival of their own literature and thought since then has owed to contact with Western knowledge, how utterly ungenerous and ultimately impossible it would have been to exclude our fellow subjects permanently from the science and learning of the West, and how dangerous might have been the unsuccessful attempt on the part of government to keep them in ignorance against their own loudly expressed wish.

After the interval of pacific consolidation under Bentinck, the forward movement began again. The wars and settlements of the 'forties decided in broad outline the policy and geography of the North-West frontier. An attempt to bring the mountain tribes of Afghanistan within the radius of British India, led to the famous disaster when a whole army perished in the retreat from Kabul. [1839–41.] It was perhaps a blessing in disguise, for the ultimate peace and safety of the Indian Peninsula have since been found to rest securely on the policy of friendship with Afghanistan as a buffer State, that jealously guards its mountain freedom between the Asiatic possessions of Russia and Britain. Owing to the existence of an independent Afghanistan we have never been in armed conflict with Asiatic Russia.

In the years immediately following this check in the mountain region, the annexations of Sind and the Punjab gave into British hands the great river system of the North-Western plains. The Sikhs of the Punjab were a democratic religious brotherhood, of what we may call 'Protestant' Hindoos, who had long guarded the plains of India against the debouchment of Mohammedan hill tribes, or of invaders from Central Asia. Their great chief, Ranjit Singh, had trained the Sikh warriors in European methods, and had kept friends with the English. [SEE MAPS 5 AND 6.] But after his death this splendid soldiery poured across the Sutlej to attack British India. The ensuing struggle, with battles like Moodkee, Sobraon and Chillianwallah, was as severe as any that the British have ever fought on Indian soil. The victory in war was followed up by the work of the Lawrence brothers in winning the confidence and attachment of the Sikhs by the good government of the Punjab. When therefore the storm of the Mutiny broke, John Lawrence was able to use the newly acquired Punjab, as a place of arms for the reconquest of revolted Oudh. [1857.] Afghanistan also was friendly to the English during the crisis, so that the North-West frontier could be safely denuded of troops till the Mutiny was suppressed.

The Mutiny, as its name implies, was a rising of some of the Sepoy regiments in British pay, including a large part of the artillery. The civilian population was rather a spectator than a participant in the event. The grievances that caused the outbreak were the grievances of soldiers, caused by mismanagement such as that which had undesignedly served out cartridges greased with the fat of the sacred cow and the abhorred pig.

[MAY 1857.] The Mutiny of the Bengal army began at Meerut. Its immediate occasion was unwise severity by incompetent officers, who proved helpless before the storm they had raised. Some of the mutineers made straight for Delhi where there was no British regiment. Delhi fell at once into the hands of the movement; and Cawnpore, after three weeks' gallant defence; and Lucknow, all except the Residency where Sir Henry Lawrence met his death in the defence. It was in this Upper Ganges region that the issue was fought out and won during the summer of 1857, by the British then actually in India and the faithful Indian troops. Their boast that 'alone we did it' is substantially true, though there were many months of severe fighting after the arrival of reinforcements from England. The deeds of Nicholson and the Lawrences, of Havelock and Outram, of Colin Campbell and Hugh Rose, and the little armies which they formed and led, the stories of the Delhi Ridge, the Kashmir gate, and the relief and final capture of Lucknow, re-established the prestige of Britain not only in India, but in Europe also, where the Crimea had exhibited our want of army organization no less strikingly than the fighting qualities of our seasoned troops.

The flame had been stamped out in Central India before it could spread. Most of Bengal, all Madras and Bombay and the North-West had remained loyal. So too had the great Native States like Mysore and Hyderabad. One result of the Mutiny was to put a stop to the course pursued by the over-eager spirit of the Governor-General Lord Dalhousie, of absorbing the territories of protected Indian rulers into actual British territory, in order to enlarge the area of benevolent administration. Indeed Dalhousie's annexation of Oudh, the seat of the Mutiny, had indirectly helped to provoke it. After 1857 the Native States were regarded as essential pillars of the British raj, not least during the political troubles of more recent years which were bred in the provinces directly ruled by Britain.

Although it was a Mutiny of the troops and not a revolt

of the population, the outbreak was related to a dim general uneasiness and fear in the great mass of Indian opinion, at the pace with which Westernization was proceeding. Dalhousie's zeal for reform and progress was seen in many strange novelties—the railways, the telegraphs, and the European standards of efficiency and sanitation.

After the Mutiny these things indeed continued, and India grew accustomed to them. A long period of peace and sound administration followed, the British Government after 1858 replacing the East India Company in name, as it had long done in fact. In 1877 Queen Victoria, on Disraeli's advice, assumed the title of Empress of India.

The memory of bloodshed and racial feud now lurked like a phantom in the secret consciousness of rulers and ruled. Nevertheless, for many years after the Mutiny, the work of good government proceeded without an interruption. Famine and plague were fought by scientific methods. Wealth and population increased as never before.

It was a noble work for the benefit of helpless millions. Yet the bureaucracy, as the useful years went by without incident, contracted the inevitable limitations of any government that is purely autocratic. It considered too exclusively the good work done, and gave too little attention to changes in the political atmosphere. It is possible that the path of the future would have been eased, if hands had been held out from above to the nationalist movement in its earlier and loyal stages, as for instance, to the Indian National Congress in the 'eighties and 'nineties. But when criticism of a mild kind was first uttered, it was too often regarded by the English as sedition, until indeed it became no less.

In the last decades of the century, colour consciousness hardened on both sides. English society in India had become larger, more self-sufficient, more closely connected by short voyages with home. On the other side the educated Indians began to know more of the world across the mountains and the seas, whence the English and others came, and to understand that the phenomenon of white rule was a fact of history and science, not a sending of heaven. The political ideas of nationalist and liberal Europe were terribly familiar to them, mingling in their minds with a racial and conservative revolt against the modern ways of their alien overlords. The Japanese victory over Russia [1904.] affected the attitude of all Asiatics toward white domination. In the new century many of the educated Indians developed an attitude of hostility, and often of sedition and political crime. The anti-English propaganda of the educated was not altogether without effect on the vast uneducated masses of conservative-minded peasantry.

The era of concession from above set in, to meet and control such serious unrest. In the question of the Partition of Bengal, an administrative decision made by a great Viceroy was reversed some years later, in deference to the strength of popular opinion. And the India Councils Act of 1909, the joint work of Lord Minto at Calcutta and of John Morley at Whitehall, enlarged the Legislative Councils by introducing into them a considerable elective element, with powers of consultation and criticism of the actions of the Government. In 1911 George V, as King Emperor, held a great Durbar at Delhi, to which the capital was moved. He was the first reigning sovereign to visit India.

[1914–18.] The Great War of 1914 which immensely stimulated the growth of Dominion self-government, evoked in India claims for equality with the Dominions. Indians felt that Britain could no longer deny to them that right of self-determination for which she professed to be fighting in Europe. In 1917 the British Government announced that its policy was the gradual development of responsible government in India as an integral part of the British Empire; and the Government of India Act, 1919, which embodied the principles advocated by the Montagu-Chelmsford Report on Indian Constitutional Reforms, was the outcome of that momentous declaration. [1919–39.] It provided for a partial responsibility of the Executive to the Legislature in the Provinces, the Central Government remaining solely responsible to the Imperial Government and Parliament, partly because it was felt that matters like defence and foreign relations could not safely be entrusted to the control of an inexperienced Legislature representing a largely illiterate electorate, and partly because the Central Government had to deal not only with British India but with the Native States. In more than one Province the new system broke down because the Nationalists would be satisfied with nothing less than complete autonomy. Unrest took the form of widespread strikes, revolutionary activity, the boycott of British goods, and a civil disobedience campaign organized by Gandhi. In 1930 the Simon Commission Report recommended the establishment, with safeguards, of full responsible government in the Provinces, whilst rejecting the idea of responsibility at the Centre. When, however, some of the Indian princes announced their readiness to enter an All-India Federation, provided that it was self-governing, the Ramsay Macdonald Government declared in 1931 that it would accept the principle of a Federal Executive responsible to a Federal Legislature. After much consultation with Indian opinion the Government of India Act, passed in 1935, provided for the setting up of an All-India Federation consisting of eleven British-Indian Provinces and such Indian States as were prepared to join. Both the Federal and the Provincial Governments were to be responsible to their Legislatures except in the Federal spheres of defence and foreign policy.

Since 1937, therefore, the Provinces have been self-governing, but the establishment of responsible government at the Centre and the realization of an All-India Federation had not been achieved when the outbreak of war between Great Britain and Germany in September 1939 made further constitutional change impracticable for the time being. The plan of a Federal India encountered the opposition of every group whose co-operation was essential. Fearing domination by British India, the Princes showed their reluctance to commit themselves to the scheme, and the necessary number failed to give their consent to it. The Moslem League was afraid that self-government would mean the transference of power from British to Hindu hands. All parties were anxious to co-operate in the task of winning the war, but Congress demanded of the British Government a definite promise of full Dominion status after the conclusion of peace. No such promise could be given without the consent of the Princes, the Moslems and the other minorities, whose separate interests had to be safeguarded. Congress then called upon the eight Congress Ministries in the Provinces to resign, and, responsible government having broken down, the Governors were obliged to set up Emergency Administrations. Communal differences therefore threatened to retard India's constitutional progress and still further to embitter Hindu-Moslem relations.

Finally, however, in 1947–50, India attained complete self-government, in the Hindu Republic of India, and the Moslem Dominion of Pakistan. The British Raj is at an end. And the change has been effected on a basis of friendship between English and Indians.

Our countrymen no longer rule India. But we shall always take a just pride in the great story of how we once controlled that vast sub-continent; how we established the *Pax Britannica* in place of a chaos of violence and war; how for a century and a half the first thought of the governors was the interest of the governed, and how when the time was ripe the Indians, because of what we had done, were able to undertake the task of self-government.

BOOKS FOR FURTHER READING: Egerton, *Short History of British Colonial Policy*; W. A. Dunning, *The British Empire and the United States*; E. P. Adams, *Great Britain and the American Civil War* (2 vols.); Stuart Reid, *Life of Lord Durham* (2 vols.); W. H. Moreland and Atul Chandra Chatterjee, A *Short History of India*, 1936; Lyall, *British Dominion in India*; Chirol, *India* (The Modern World Series, ed. Fisher, 1926); Basil Williams, *Cecil Rhodes*; Ramsay Muir, *Short History of the British Commonwealth*, Vol. II.; Theal, *South Africa* (5 vols.); Pember Reeves, *The Long White Cloud* (New Zealand). See also top of p. 132, above, for Lucas and Wyatt Tilby.

CHAPTER FOUR

The New Reform Era. Gladstone's First Ministry, 1868–74. Disraeli and Modern Conservatism. Gladstone, Egypt, Home Rule. Lord Salisbury's Ministries. The Era of the Jubilees. Social Reform and Imperialism

The victory of the North in the American Civil War and the death of Palmerston together gave the signal for another period of rapid change in the world of English politics. The leader in the new age of transition was Gladstone, who embodied the political spirit of the time with its earnestness, its optimism, its trust in human nature, and its diligent mastery of legislative and executive detail that saved its idealism from running to waste in words. Gladstone completed the transmutation of the old Whig into the new Liberal party, and by the legislation of his first and greatest Ministry of 1868–74 made up the arrears of institutional change overdue. Palmerston's leadership had long imposed delay on the activity of the party whose special function it was to make the pace of progress. Reform now came with a rush, but with no violence, because the resistance made to it was slight.

For at the same time the Conservative party, and therewith the control of the House of Lords' veto on legislation, fell into wise hands. Not without a double personal application, Disraeli in 1868 wrote to the Queen that 'a fund of enthusiasm' 'ought never to be possessed' by a Prime Minister of England–nor, he might with equal relevance have added, by a leader of Her Majesty's Opposition. Certainly the Conservative chief's own sceptical and clear-sighted temper was admirably adapted to the task of 'educating his party' to accept the democratization of our institutions as inevitable, and even to preside over important parts of the process. But Gladstone's more ardent nature was required for the great legislative achievements of 1868–74.

Behind the statesmen of the transition stood the political philosopher John Stuart Mill, whose writings exerted in the 'sixties and 'seventies a wide influence over educated opinion. He brought Bentham's Utilitarianism up to date, and emancipated it from the stricter bonds of the *laissez faire* theory. Mill preached the doctrine of complete democracy in the sense that every man and woman ought to take part not only in national but in local elections. But he knew the limits of the work suited to the democratic machine. He desired to see specialist Departments of State guiding the democracy and keeping politicians properly informed. 'Power,' he said, 'may be localized, but knowledge, to be useful, must be centralized.' The dovetailing of the functions of the Whitehall Civil Service with those of the Downing Street politicians and of the electorate in the country was an essential part of Mill's doctrine of good government. There had been nothing of that in the older Radicalism of Cobbett or the pure *laissez faire* school.

His advocacy of women's rights, in *The Subjection of Women* (1869), though in his own day it was not allowed to affect the political franchise, helped to increase the respect for women's personal liberty, and the belief in the importance of their proper education which characterized the later Victorian age. Mill and Florence Nightingale[1] were the two principal pioneers of the position that women hold in our society to-day.

Mill's treatise *On Liberty* was a plea for freedom of thought and discussion, then much limited by social convention though not by law. The rising generation grew up with this creed of freedom, by no means confined to politics. It was the age of the first heart-searching controversies on Darwin's startling hypothesis of evolution, with its reaction on the literal acceptance of parts of the Bible. *The Origin of Species* and Mill's *Liberty* appeared in the same year—1859. The Natural Science Tripos was being started at Cambridge. [1833–45.] The 'movement' begun at Oxford by Pusey, Keble and Newman, before Newman went

[1] See p. 200, above.

over to Rome, had since gone out from its academic home to meet, and in some cases to blend, with other fresh sources of energy in the Church and country at large. The so-called 'Christian Socialism' of Frederick Denison Maurice and Charles Kingsley began a fresh orientation of the Church in relation to democracy and the social problems of the Industrial Revolution. Modernist theology, under Jowett, Stanley, and Colenso, gained toleration and importance through the Darwinian controversy and the growth of historical method and knowledge. The Church was beginning to contain within her own body something answering to each of the currents of the heady fight going on in the world outside. Much had been gained in knowledge in several different directions—in earnestness yet more. Missionary energy at home and overseas took on fresh life. Selwyn, Bishop of New Zealand in its earliest days of colonization, had an apostolic and democratic spirit which reacted on the Church at home. The merits and demerits of the Church clergy in their relation to the laity were very different from what they had been in the easy-going Eighteenth Century.[2]

The grave abuses in the uneven distribution of Church revenues had been reformed by Peel and the Whigs, and by the Ecclesiastical Commissioners whom they set up after the First Reform Bill. In many different ways, therefore, the Church was newly prepared to stand any assault which might be made on her as a result of the further extension of the franchise of 1867. No doubt many of her exclusive privileges would have to be surrendered, particularly in the Universities. But the resisting power of the Establishment was at once more solid and more elastic than it had been in 1832, when zealous Churchmen had opposed even the First Reform Bill on the ground that it must lead to disestablishment and disendowment.

It would be tedious to enumerate the many other movements of intellectual activity and social change that were

[2] See pp. 28–29, above. For Church history in the 'thirties and 'forties see Dean Church, *The Oxford Movement*, and W. L. Mathieson, *English Church Reform* 1815–40.

stirring in the 'sixties. Among the most important was the organization of the great Trade Unions in the skilled trades, especially engineering, and the growth of the Co-operative movement, which trained so many of the working classes in business habits, thrift and mutual reliance, released them from exploitation by the shopkeeper, and gave them 'a stake in the country.'

The classes newly enfranchised by the Second Reform Bill,[3] in their first use of the vote in 1868, greatly strengthened the Radical element in the party commanded by Gladstone and placed the weapon of a large majority in his active hands. His first Ministry [1868–74.] was the first in English history that can be called distinctively Liberal instead of Whig. In 1868 Conservatism and Socialism were both temporarily in abeyance. It was a mood not likely to last long, but the use made of it by Gladstone in the greatest half-dozen years of his life, went far to equip the country with modern services and institutions, without which she would have been ill-prepared to face the social and imperial problems of days to come. In those years the Universities were opened to men of all creeds, a national system of Primary Education was established, Army Reform was initiated, the throwing open of the Civil Service was completed, the Ballot Act was passed, and the first steps were taken towards the conciliation of Ireland.

The Irish famine of 1845–46, due to the failure of the potato crop, had set going the wholesale emigration to the United States and the Colonies, which by the end of the century had reduced the population of the overcrowded island, in spite of a high birth-rate, from eight to four and a half millions. But for more than twenty years after the famine nothing was done to remedy the wrongs of the Irish peasant in relation to his English landlord. In accordance with the ancient custom of Ireland, the landlord could rackrent and evict his tenants, but he himself put no capital into the land, made no improvements, and left the

[3] See pp. 204–6, above.

small peasant farmer to build and maintain his cabin and everything else on the farm. This system, very different from that of England, was exploited by landlords who were divided from their tenants by race and religion, and who often resided in the neighbouring island, spending there the revenues which their agents wrung from the tillers of the Irish soil.

For twenty years after the famine, Celtic Ireland was prostrate and incapable of agitation. But the relative wealth and importance acquired by the Irish emigrants in the United States and the Colonies, and their organized hatred of England, ere long reacted on the home lands. After the end of the American Civil War, the Fenian Movement, separatist in its objects and criminal in its methods, reminded the English very unpleasantly that the quiescent Irish problem had only been neglected, not solved.

Gladstone was the first statesman to take the conciliation of Ireland seriously in hand. His Irish Land Act of 1870 went a very little way, but it marked the first English recognition of the problem, and he followed it up a dozen years later by more effective legislation for fair rent and security of tenure. [1881.] The land question, kept alive by boycotting and agrarian crime in the days of the Land League, was destined to end in the buying out of the English landlords from Ireland by a Conservative Government. [1903.] But during Gladstone's first Ministry few people in England, except Gladstone himself, understood the real meaning of the Irish land question and its essential difference from the English. [1868–74.] Many Liberals were as much averse as Conservatives to interfere with 'free contract,' which they imagined to exist in Ireland between landlord and tenant.

On the other hand, religious equality was an ideal taken to heart by the intellectual classes trained in the philosophy of Mill, and by the Non-conformists whose effective emancipation had been accomplished by the Second Reform Bill. Their common leader, Gladstone, a High Churchman of the new school, had accomplished in his own mind the wedding of the Oxford religious doctrines with political

Liberalism; his views of Church and State were no longer those he had advocated thirty years before in the book reviewed by Macaulay. In so far, therefore, as Ireland could be conciliated by religious equality, that part of the task was possible in 1869, and it was done. The disestablishment and partial disendowment of the Irish Protestant Church was carried out in a masterly and sympathetic manner by Gladstone, whose known position as an enthusiastic Churchman stood him in good stead during the negotiations. The House of Lords and the Bishops, in a very different mood from that which their predecessors had displayed on Church questions in the 'thirties, made the best terms they could and allowed the Bill to pass.

Gladstone's Liberal Churchmanship, and his political leadership of the Non-conformists and of the academic advocates of religious equality, were of no less importance in the purely English questions of the Universities and Education. The long overdue reform of Oxford and Cambridge by Act of Parliament had first been taken in hand in the 'fifties, when under Gladstone's able management the First University Commission had begun the work. But at that time the Church monopoly could not be abolished. Only as a result of the Second Reform Bill and the election of 1868 was it possible to throw open College Fellowships and University posts to persons of every, or of no, religious denomination. [1871.] London and Durham Universities had already been founded, and in the closing years of the Nineteenth Century and the early years of the Twentieth, a number of other Colleges and Universities grew up all over England and Wales. Scotland was already well supplied.

As University teaching ceased to be the monopoly of a very few, secondary teaching improved and spread. By the end of the century much had been done to amend the backward condition of English middle-class education, which Matthew Arnold had once declared, with oratorical exaggeration, to be the worst in Europe. As education and culture spread among the middle classes, athleticism and the pursuit of pleasures other than the intellectual spread quite as fast. The demand for leisure and amusement grew in all classes with each new decade, as the hard-working mercantile Puritanism of the early Nineteenth Century yielded more and more to new and more varied standards of life, not all of them, perhaps, improvements upon the old.

[1870.] Primary Education was also established on a national basis by the Education Act of William Edward Forster. Where there was no school, a school was set up subject to an elected School Board, the only religious teaching permitted being undenominational. On the other hand, in areas where schools already existed, these 'voluntarily supported' schools were preserved by a largely increased grant from the Treasury, and the Church character that most of them possessed remained intact. The increased grant was a bitter disappointment to the Non-conformists, whose children in rural areas still had to attend these Church schools. But the compromise carried the Bill through the Lords, and if it did harm to the Liberal party by causing discontent in its ranks, it did a great work for the country; it supplied England at last with a population that could read and write, gave training and discipline to the herds of uncared-for children of the slums, and initiated the great educational progress of the next half century.

Gladstone's first Ministry also began the long overdue reform of the Army, and created the modern military system, as distinct from Peninsular and Crimean organization. These reforms are associated with the name of Cardwell, the Secretary for War. Against him were arrayed the vested interests and prejudices of the old Army chiefs, formidably headed by the Queen's cousin, the Duke of Cambridge. But the Government succeeded in carrying a number of very important reforms. They abolished the system of dual control over the Army, definitely subordinating the Horse Guards to the War Office, that is to say the Commander-in-Chief to the Secretary for War. They abolished the system of Purchase of Commissions, which prevented the promotion of men of moderate means. They established the short-service system of enlistment, thereby supplying for the first time a proper Army Reserve. These changes rendered possible a greater efficiency in war in the later years of the century, connected with Sir Garnet Wolseley and put to the test in a number of campaigns against coloured folk in Asia and Africa. The sharper lessons of the Second Boer War gave a stimulus to further changes, which left us in 1914 with an effective Expeditionary Force and a Territorial Army.

The same set of ideas that had led to the abolition of Purchase in the Army, led to the opening of the Civil Service to competition by public examination, completed by Gladstone's action in 1870.[4]

After half a dozen years of activity, Gladstone's first Cabinet had done its work: Ministers could be fitly compared by Disraeli to 'a range of exhausted volcanoes.' For he himself had very shrewdly allowed their lava to exude. The House of Lords had not prevented their policy from taking effect. The work that the country had expected of them was substantially done, and a natural Conservative reaction therefore took place at the election of 1874.

[1874–80.] Thus Disraeli, in his seventieth year, first attained to real power as Prime Minister. The work of his Ministry bore the impress of his own ideas both in domestic and in foreign policy.

At home he was anxious to demonstrate the connection of the new Conservatism with social reform and with conciliation of the working classes. Aided by his able Home Secretary, Richard Cross, he waged war on slums and insanitary conditions with the Public Health Act of 1875 and the Artisans' Dwelling Act. Such measures, and the continuous work of the Local Government Board set up by Gladstone in 1871 to co-operate with the ever-increasing activities of the local authorities, were important palliatives. But bad building and bad town-planning had got such a start in the previous hundred years, that they have never been properly overtaken.

[4] Sir Charles Trevelyan, an Indian and English Civil servant, had a large part in initiating both these movements.

Much less could anything be done to set a limit to the ever-advancing bounds of the realm of ugliness and uniformity, in its constant destruction of the beauty and variety of the old pre-industrial world. Indeed the more prosperous and progressive the country was, the more rapidly did that unceasing work go forward. Man when armed with the machine could not help destroying beauty, whatever the work to which he set his hand.[5]

Disraeli also settled an acute stage of the ever-recurring problem of the rights of workmen in time of strike. In 1867, a judicial decision of the courts had deprived the Trade Unions of the legal position they had enjoyed since the legislation of 1824–25.[6] The courts suddenly ruled that combinations 'in restraint of trade' were illegal. Gladstone remedied this by his Trade Union Act of 1871. But in the same year his Criminal Law Amendment Act rendered picketing and other actions usual in time of strike illegal. The Trade Unionists, incensed with Gladstone, whom they had supported at the election of 1868, largely abstained or supported Disraeli in 1874. And the Conservative Premier in 1875 repealed Gladstone's Criminal Law Amendment Act, and left violence and intimidation in time of strike to be dealt with as part of the general criminal code.

In foreign policy Disraeli renewed the connection between the party he led and the dramatic assertion of British national interests. That connection had not been specially marked since Waterloo. After the Treaties of Vienna, the Tory or Conservative party, that had done so much to make that settlement of Europe, was sometimes more pacific than Palmerston and his followers, because Whigs and Radicals had less veneration for the settlement

[5] It has been well written: 'The Nineteenth Century did not attack beauty. It simply trampled it under foot, with the result that our modern democracy is born atrophied, and has painfully to recover that love of significant form which has been one of the marks of civilized man from the Bronze Age until the Industrial Revolution temporarily destroyed it.'—*Times Lit. Suppl.*, April 25, 1924.

[6] See p. 164, above.

of 1815 and more sympathy with the nations and parties on the Continent who wished to disturb it. Nor had the Colonies interested the Conservatives any more than their rivals, who could boast of Lord Durham. In 1852 Disraeli himself had spoken of 'these wretched Colonies' as 'a millstone round our necks.' But his keen sense of the new situation led him in his old age to appeal to the newly enfranchised British democracy to take a pride in the Empire and an interest in 'spirited foreign policy.' Interest in the Colonies was still only nascent, and was developed much more fully in the following generation, under the leadership of Joseph Chamberlain. Disraeli's principal field of operations was the Near East. His purchase of shares in the Suez Canal for England began the connection with Egypt which shortly after his death led to great developments. And in 1876–78 he and Gladstone, in their angry and magnificent disputation, aroused the passions of their fellow-countrymen over the details of Balkan wars and massacres, which but for these two men of genius would have seemed a far-off battle of kites and crows, and none of England's business.

Disraeli, now Lord Beaconsfield, made the British Government the principal supporter of the Turk in Europe as the barrier against Russian influence; while Gladstone in opposition, by his campaign on the 'Bulgarian atrocities' of Turkey, made one half of British opinion the principal hope of the oppressed Christian races of the East. It was a strange situation, full of danger to our divided land. Fortunately it ended at the Treaty of Berlin [1878.] without war between Russia and Britain. This was Disraeli's 'peace with honour.' He had certainly made England again important in the councils of Europe, and had forced attention to her wishes. But whether the restoration of the liberated Macedonians to the Turkish rule for another generation was precisely what England should have wished, will remain an open question. Many who know the Balkans regret that, since Disraeli was determined, perhaps rightly, that Macedonia should not be added to the newly formed Bulgarian State, he did not in the Treaty of Berlin insist on its being placed under a Christian governor with proper securities for its good government. It is at least conceivable that such an arrangement might have mitigated the ferocity of racial passions in the Balkan cockpit in the Twentieth Century.

The General Election of 1880 put an end to Disraeli's Ministry, and a year later he died in retirement. He had given the Conservative party its orientation in the new world of democracy, by a frank acceptance of changed conditions at home; he had taught the upper classes not to retire to their tents in anger at lost privileges, but to go down into the street and appeal to the masses on grounds of patriotic sentiment and Imperial interest. Gladstone's mistakes in South Africa and Egypt in the following decade, and his Home Rule proposals, supplied material for such propaganda. The principle of appeal from the upper to the lower classes, made on the ground of identity of interest in the nation as a whole, found expression, after Disraeli's death, in the Primrose League, founded in his memory, and in a network of Conservative Clubs and Associations all over the country. In the early 'eighties the idea of 'Tory democracy' received a great stimulus from the brief meteoric career of Lord Randolph Churchill.

At the same time the National Liberal Federation of local Associations, nicknamed the 'Caucus,' was being organized by the other party through the energy of the Radical leader, Joseph Chamberlain, whose political power was rooted in his personal control over the local politics of Birmingham. Democratic appeal and elaborate mechanical organization were entering into the electoral methods and political programmes of both parties. New forms of influence and of veiled corruption were arising in place of the old, new forms also of idealism and devotion to the public service. The thoroughness of modern organization and party propaganda at least secured that Parliamentary government should not fail in Great Britain for want of popular interest in elections and in politics. And the presence of real dividing principles, the rival interests of classes, and great questions like Home Rule, prevented the highly organized two-party system from becoming in England a mere lifeless machinery, representing nothing but a struggle for office.[7]

[1880–85.] Gladstone's Second Ministry was not so triumphant an affair as his First. In 1880 the Liberal party had not, as in 1868, a definite political philosophy of its own, nor an agreed political programme. It was borne into power by reaction against Disraeli's 'Jingoism,' and by vague democratic aspirations not yet formulated into any clear programme of social reform. And it was at once faced with unavoidable problems in Ireland, Egypt and South Africa, about which, in the year 1880, Liberals, like other Englishmen, knew little and cared less. Gladstone indeed knew and cared about Ireland, and his Land Act of 1881, giving fair rents and security of tenure, was a real measure of amelioration. But it did not solve the land question, still less break up the formidable union of land agitation with the political demand for Home Rule, which Parnell's new policy of 'obstruction' was forcing on the notice of the British House of Commons.

[1884.] The principal achievement of the Ministry was the Third Reform Bill, which extended Household Suffrage to the county constituencies. The agricultural labourer and the miner were at last enfranchised. Till then their conditions of life had received all too little attention. The attempt of Joseph Arch to start Agricultural Labourers' Trade Unions had failed in the previous decade for want of political power behind it. The agricultural labourer had been ill-used even in times of prosperity, and he fared still worse in the years of agricultural depression, due to the great increase of American importation in the late 'seventies.[8] His enfranchisement in 1884 combined with other economic and social circumstances to initiate a slow, continuous improvement in his lot, but not before the villages

[7] The changes of this period in British politics are coldly and severely analyzed in Ostrogorski's *Democracy and the Organization of Political Parties,* Vol. I.

[8] See p. 191, above. Between 1881 and 1921 the proportion of the population engaged in agriculture fell from about 12 to about 7 per cent.

had been desperately depleted by the 'rural exodus' to the towns. The social history of rural England in the Nineteenth Century is in many respects a chronicle of disaster.

The Parliamentary enfranchisement of the rural labourer soon led to the establishment of elective local self-government for the country districts. Hitherto they had been not only judged but administered by the patriarchal rule of the nominated Justices of the Peace. The Conservative Government in 1888 set up elected County Councils; and in 1894 the establishment of Urban and Rural District Councils and Parish Councils by the Liberal Government completed the machinery of rural democracy. Judicial powers and public-house licensing were still left to the Justices of the Peace, but their great administrative powers passed to the new elected bodies.

The neglect of the South African problem in the first months of Gladstone's Ministry led to the Majuba tragedy.[9] The Egyptian affair began more brilliantly. The breakdown of Turkish and native government in Egypt, where European countries had many financial and personal interests, led to the occupation of Egypt by the British troops under Wolseley, victorious over Arabi at Tel-el-Kebir. [1882.] France had refused at the critical moment to participate, though Egypt had hitherto been more under French than English influence. British control in Egypt began, greatly to the material benefit of the Egyptian peasant. The Nile valley prospered, ruled by the all-potent 'advice' daily given by Sir Evelyn Baring, Lord Cromer, to the Khedive's government. The French regarded our presence there with jealousy, and many unpleasant incidents resulted, until the important agreement with France on Egypt and other subjects was made by Lord Lansdowne in 1904.

But closely attached to the Egyptian question was the Sudanese, and it was here that Gladstone came to grief. While the lower reaches of the Nile held the ancient civilization of Egypt, its upper reaches contained the barba-

[9] See p. 219, above.

rism of the Sudanese tribes, at that period organized under the Mahdi and his successors as the centre of slave-raiding in the interior of Africa, and a constant threat to Egypt. Any conscientious ruler of Egypt, or indeed any Power sincerely interested in the fate of Africa as a whole, must needs aspire to deal with the plague-spot of the Sudan. But the time was not yet. Egypt had first to be set in order, and her financial and military resources built up.

But in the course of the necessary withdrawal of Egyptian garrisons from the Sudan, Gladstone's Government made errors. Spurred on by William Stead, the father of modern sensational journalism, the Ministry selected for the work Charles Gordon, a strange and single-minded hero fit for any service except that of initiating retreat. Instead of successfully evacuating the Sudan he was soon shut up in Khartoum, besieged by the Mahdist hordes. The British Government failed to send the relief expedition until too late. Gordon perished [JAN. 1885.], and with him perished much of Gladstone's influence over his own countrymen at home. In Africa the defeat made less difference. The Sudan would in any case have been evacuated at that time. Only after Cromer had done his work in Egypt, was Lord Salisbury's Government able to conquer the Sudan with the British and Egyptian armies under Kitchener in 1898.

The General Election of 1885 resulted in a great defeat of the Liberal party in the boroughs, largely owing to Gordon and Khartoum. But the newly enfranchised agricultural labourer cast his vote for the party to whom he owed it, in the hope of obtaining some real improvement in his miserable lot. Lord Salisbury therefore did not obtain a clear Conservative majority with which to govern the country. The notable consequence was that the balance of power at Westminster lay in the hands of a strange man who, though himself of Anglo-Saxon origin, regarded British Liberals and Tories with a cold, indifferent hatred. Charles Stewart Parnell had established the iron discipline of his personal ascendancy over the Home Rule party from Ireland, numbering eighty-five members of the new British Parliament. Henceforth, so long as the Union of 1801 was maintained, Irish affairs must clearly be a controlling factor in British politics, as they had not been in the early and middle parts of the century when the Irish Representatives were many of them attached to one or other of the two British parties. Politics could not go on as before. Either the two British parties must unite against Parnell, or one of them must come to terms with him. Gladstone came to terms with him, and introduced a Home Rule Bill. [1886.]

In the light of subsequent events, many in our generation will be disposed to consider such a decision natural and even obvious, and to wish that the question of Irish self-government could have been settled then in peace, instead of in 1921 after a series of horrible events. But it is difficult to say whether the cause of Irish conciliation was retarded or advanced by Gladstone's proceedings. The speed of his *volte-face* on a subject of such immense importance bewildered and exasperated the British electorate. The Home Rule question broke up the Liberal party and greatly weakened it for twenty years to come, while Conservatism became closely identified with Unionist doctrine for Ireland. Above all, Gladstone's acceptance of Parnell's claim to have Protestant Ulster as a part of the new Ireland, was more than an error in tactics. It flew in the face of racial and political possibilities.

The Conservative party had been courting the Irish vote not without success during the election of 1885. But it seized the opportunity given it by Gladstone's compact with Parnell to appeal to British national feeling. Home Rule was read in the light of Khartoum. The growing Imperialist sentiment of the *fin-de-siècle* did not recognize Home Rule for Ireland as an essential part of the new creed of Empire, in spite of much support for Irish Home Rule in the self-governing Dominions oversea. The passions aroused by the Home Rule controversy in England, marked by such episodes as the publication in 1887 of forged 'Parnell' letters in *The Times*, rendered rational statesmanship by an agreement of parties impossible. Yet nothing else would have served the case.

The reaction against Gladstone and Home Rule was strong enough at the election of 1886 to secure an independent Conservative majority over Gladstonian Liberals and Irish combined. There followed an era of strong Conservative government under Lord Salisbury in alliance with the Liberal Unionists, especially with Joseph Chamberlain, who became the champion of the new Imperialism. In that way the country was ruled until after the Boer War at the end of the century, with the exception of the three years of Liberal rule (1892–95). The Liberals and Irish under Gladstone then forced a Home Rule Bill through the Commons by a majority of thirty-four. It was thrown out by the Lords, and in the election of 1895 the country ratified their action. This event gave to the Conservative chiefs a new idea of the function of the Upper Chamber in modern politics, more ambitious than that adhered to in practice by the cautious Peel and Disraeli. The consequence in the following century was that as soon as the next big change in democratic opinion took place, a contest between the two Houses led to a very grave constitutional crisis, such as had been conspicuously absent from our politics since 1832.

The defeat of Home Rule at the polls in 1895 was definitive for a number of years to come, and there was a temporary lull in Irish affairs. The Conservative Ministry who had previously relied on coercion to govern Ireland, developed a policy of 'killing Home Rule by kindness.' They enlarged local self-government, and, by buying out the English landlords, ended the Irish land question, at least in its old Cromwellian form. But the political demand for Home Rule, or something more, remained unabated. In the Twentieth Century the national demand for self-government was so deeply implanted in the mind of the Irish Celts, that it survived not only the fall and death of Parnell (1890–91), but the subsequent removal of the land grievance—the man and the question which had first given it power seriously to disturb the politics of the British Empire.

[1898.] Gladstone died in retirement in his eighty-ninth year. The impassioned efforts of 'The Grand Old Man' for Irish Home Rule had been the most dramatic and extraordinary part of his life, but the least successful. It is possible that the Liberal party, and the politics of the Empire as a whole, would have developed more naturally towards the end of his life, if they had been left by him to the men of that generation. Gladstone's immense activity overshadowed friends and foes, and pushed them into positions not of their choosing. But, viewing his life down its whole length, many will conclude that he did more than any other man to adapt the machinery of the British State and the habits of British politicians to modern democratic conditions, without a total loss of the best standards of the older world. The legislation of his First Ministry had done most to modernize our institutions. The Second and Third Reform Bills largely resulted from the lead he had himself given the country after the death of Palmerston. He had interested the new democracy in Parliamentary government by constant popular appeals, not to sensationalism or self-interest, but to men's reasoning faculties and their sense of right. His reasoning may often have been defective and his appeals to moral indignation may have been too often and too easily made, but on the whole his habit of carrying public questions in their serious aspect before the tribunal of great popular audiences was a fine and fruitful example, made at an important period of transition in our public life.

The government of Great Britain by Lord Salisbury's Conservative Ministries [1886–92., 1895–1902.] in alliance with the Liberal Unionists, covered a period of trade prosperity and, until the Second Boer War,[10] of peace with civilized peoples. Good relations with the Continental Powers were maintained on the basis of the 'splendid isolation' of Great Britain. The other Great Powers, pre-

[10] See p. 221, above.

paratory to the great act of world-destruction in our own day, were already dividing themselves into two camps, arming in nervous rivalry—the Triple Alliance of Germany, Austria and, at that time, of Italy, against the Dual Alliance of France and Russia. Great Britain remained outside both these groups, but owing to the hostile attitude of France as our colonial rival in Asia and Africa, and to the continual dread of Russia's intentions towards Afghanistan and India, Lord Salisbury was upon the whole in a relation of greater friendliness to the Germanic Powers. But always a certain uneasiness attended the relations of a government based on Parliamentarism and popular rights with the great militarist bureaucracy created by Bismarck; the new leaders of the German destiny inherited an instinctive distrust of the influence of British political institutions. But the general orientation of British policy was not affected by this *malaise* until Kaiser William's admiration of the British Navy led him to build a rival fleet—a development that only became dangerously noticeable in the following century. Under Lord Salisbury's management, the African continent was divided among the Great Powers by peaceful agreement. The interior of the Dark Continent was now in rapid process of exploitation by Europeans armed with modern means of locomotion, and protected by modern knowledge of tropical medicine.

At home the last two decades of the century, and of Queen Victoria's reign, whether under Liberal or Conservative Ministries, were years of social and administrative progress, particularly in the direction of what was known as 'municipal socialism.'[11] Baths and wash-houses, museums, public libraries, parks, gardens, open spaces, allotments, lodging houses for the working classes were acquired,

[11] In 1888 the Conservative Minister, Mr. Ritchie, passed his County Council Act, which not only set up popularly elected bodies to rule the counties, but enlarged the existing machinery of urban democracy by turning the largest cities into County Boroughs, and by erecting the elected London County Council to govern all London except the old 'City' area.

erected or maintained out of the rates. Tramways, gas, electricity and water were in many places municipalized. It was also a great period of voluntary effort, of 'Settlements' like Toynbee Hall, and of a very general awakening of all classes to the terrible consequences of 'environment' in the slums, in 'the richest country in the world'—as England was then still accounted. The scientifically guided Christian inspiration of Canon Barnett; the statistical investigations of Charles Booth and his helpers into the real facts of London life and his reasoned advocacy of Old Age Pensions; the social side of 'General' William Booth's work of redemption through the Salvation Army, and Church work on similar lines; the civic patriotism of the new London, and its activities initiated by John Burns of Battersea and the Progressive party of the London County Council in its early years; the investigations and 'Fabian' tactics of the Sidney Webbs, to manœuvre instalments of socialism out of Liberal and Conservative governments and parties; the more militant life breathed into Socialism by Henry George's *Progress and Poverty* and by Hyndman's Social Democratic Federation; the extension of Trade Union activity from the highly skilled to the ill-paid and unskilled trades signalized by the Dockers' strike of 1889,—all these and many other movements and forces indicated that the social problem was not at its end but at its beginning, and might well in the coming century devour the other aspects of political life.

Meanwhile, apart from the conscious action of politicians or of social reformers, the continual and ever-increasing rapidity of the Industrial Revolution was year by year silently transmuting social habits, obliterating old distinctions of rank and creed, and turning a Bible-reading people with ideals based on reminiscences of rural or burgher life and a hierachy of classes, into the city population that we know. A significant portent was observed in the growth of Harmsworth's *Daily Mail,* catering for the new half-educated democracy of all classes, in a fashion quite different from that of the more solemn political organs which had satisfied the Victorian *bourgeoisie.*

At length, in January 1901, the figure passed away that had presided over the changing scene during a period of transition longer and no less momentous than the reign of George III himself. 'The Queen' had reigned so long that in the minds of her subjects the Monarchy had become female in its attributes. All through her long reign—alike before, during, and after her married life, alike in her period of Whig and her period of Conservative preferences, in dealing with Ministers to whom she was attached and with Ministers whose policy she abhorred and whose personality she disliked—Victoria had with fixed steadiness of principle adhered to a settled constitutional practice of her own. She always insisted on knowing what was being done; she compared it in the vast store-house of her memory and experience to what had been done in the past; if she disagreed, she protested; if the Minister still adhered to his decision, she gave way. But not all Ministers adhered in every case to their first decisions, particularly in questions of appointments or in the phraseology of documents. The Queen's practice of this method for more than two generations of men, definitely fixed the position of the Crown in the Constitution, so that the storms of the Twentieth Century, which have raged round so many other institutions, have left the Monarchy unchallenged. Victoria's successors, by evincing a more complete absence of party predilection than she showed herself, have further smoothed the path of constitutional kingship in the new age.

At the same time, since the idea of a Federation of the Parliaments of the Empire has failed to materialize, the Crown has been left as the sole official bond of the whole Imperial fabric. Here, too, the Queen was in her element. In her latter years she admirably filled and greatly enjoyed her new position as Empress of India and as head of a great association of free peoples, which was proclaimed and dramatized by the Imperial pageantry of her two Jubilees. [1887, 1897.]

Victoria was possessed in a high degree of queenly instincts and dignity, but they were softened and popularized by a mind and an emotional nature of great simplicity. In herself she was not very different from her female subjects in humble stations of life—except that she was also a great Queen. She was not at all an aristocrat; the amusements and life of the aristocracy and their dependents and imitators meant little to her. She was above the aristocracy, not of it. With the other side of her nature she was a simple wife and widow-woman, who would have been at home in any cottage parlour. So, too, the intellectual and artistic currents of the age flowed by her unnoticed—except when Prince Albert was there to instruct her. The common people understood her in her joys and sorrows better than they understood those who stood between themselves and her, raised on the platforms of aristocracy or of intellect.

For these reasons, political and personal, the coming of democracy had, contrary to general expectation, coincided with a revival of popular affection for the royal office, disjoined as it now was from pretensions to direct political power.

BOOKS FOR FURTHER READING: *Queen Victoria's Letters*; Morley's *Gladstone* (2 vols.); Buckle's *Disraeli* (6 vols.); Winston Churchill's *Lord Randolph Churchill* (2 vols.); John Bailey, *Some Political Ideas and Persons* (on Queen Victoria and Disraeli); John Stuart Mill, *Autobiography*; Francis Darwin, *Charles Darwin*; Lytton Strachey, *Queen Victoria*; Redlich and Hirst, *Local Government in England* (2 vols.); Lady Gwendolen Cecil, *Lord Salisbury*; Mrs. Dugdale, *Balfour*; Barry O'Brien, *Parnell*; Stephen Gwynn, *History of Ireland*; Webb, *History of Trade Unionism*; Beatrice Webb, *My Apprenticeship*; Warre Cornish, *The English Church in the Nineteenth Century* (2 vols.); Herbert Paul, *History of Modern England* (5 vols.); J. A. Spender, *A Short History of Our Times*; R. C. K. Ensor, *England 1870–1914* (Oxford Hist. of Eng.), 1936.

E. Halévy, *History of the English People*, for the whole Nineteenth Century; also Clapham, *Economic History of Modern Britain*.

CHAPTER FIVE

Balfour's Ministry. 1902–5

The close of the Nineteenth Century, the South African War, and the deaths of the Queen and of Lord Salisbury, coincided so nearly in time as to mark the end of an epoch. The Victorian age had been a long period of ever-increasing prosperity at home, of gradual, uninterrupted, pacific transition from the old to the new society, and of peace and security for Britain in her most important foreign relationships.

But the first two decades of the new century involved the world in the greatest catastrophe of modern times, and even before that catastrophe had taken place, the relations of nations, races and classes had taken on a hard and hostile aspect. Man's power over nature far outstripped his moral and mental development. In a single generation came the motor-car, wireless telegraphy, and the conquests of the air and of the world under the sea. Such inventions, and the application on a colossal scale of older processes of steam and electricity, were perpetually transmuting the economic, social and international fabric before it had time to solidify; speed and mechanism destroyed the older habits of life and thought in our island, and began the suburbanization of the rural landscape; throughout the world, nations and races were linked up too suddenly for their peace; and national ambitions found ready to their hands new weapons of conquest and self-aggrandisement which have proved the means of mutual destruction.

The South African War,[1] about which the Liberal party had been divided in opposition, left the Conservatives with a large majority after the Khaki election of 1900, to begin the business of the new century. The two leading Ministers were Arthur Balfour, Salisbury's nephew and successor in

[1] See p. 221, above.

the Premiership, and Joseph Chamberlain, who as Colonial Secretary had done so much to arouse the British Empire to a state of self-consciousness.

Balfour's Act of 1902, inspired by the wisdom of the great civil servant Sir Robert Morant, added another storey to the edifice of National Education begun in 1870; it handed over the responsibility not only for elementary but for higher education to the County Councils and County Boroughs. In this way Secondary Education for the first time received proper financial support, and was co-ordinated with the rest of the national system. The new local authority—the Education Committee of each County Council—was able to devise broader schemes of policy than the old School Boards, which had often administered too small an area.

The reform has resulted in a great enlargement of secondary schools, and the erection of a 'ladder' by which able students of small means can ascend through them to the Universities. Improved Secondary Education has raised the average standard of work and intelligence at Oxford and Cambridge by opening them to many more able men of all classes; and it has been the making of the new Universities that sprang up apace in the new century, at Liverpool, Leeds, Sheffield, Birmingham, Bristol and Reading, in addition to London, Durham and Manchester Universities founded in the previous century but come to full maturity in our own.

But no change in English Education could take place without fierce controversy over its religious and sectarian aspect; Balfour's Act placed the Church schools and the Roman Catholic schools, partly supported by voluntary subscription, under the control of the new County Education Authority, in return for adequate maintenance to be given them out of the rates. But the Non-conformists and others resented the support of denominational schools by means of rates levied on all, particularly since so many of the Church schools lay in rural villages where no other teaching was available to Dissenting parents. This controversy helped to reunite and revive the Liberal party, which had been divided during the South African War into 'Little Englanders' and 'Imperialists.'

[1902.] Balfour, who for all his philosophic detachment never wanted courage to hold a course, pushed through this unpopular Bill, and in later years the House of Lords prevented his settlement from being seriously altered by Liberal Governments. In the post-war world the outcry against its working has died away. For one thing, the control exerted by the County Education Authority over the Church schools has proved more real than Liberals expected.[2] Moreover the public attitude to religious controversy has been altering rapidly in the last fifty years. Church and Dissent are less hostile to one another, in presence of an increased falling away from religious observance of any kind. The growth of the new Paganism has made Christians kinder to one another. The Church clergy arouse less antagonism than of old, because they are less apt to regard themselves as the rulers of the society in which they live. They are kept in check, no longer by Non-conformist hostility, but by their own sensitiveness to the atmosphere of a new age more indifferent to ecclesiastical claims and social pretensions. Trollope's Archdeacon Grantly would think it a sad world. It is possible, however, that religion in some respects has gained in influence though it has lost in power. Church, Chapel and Sunday School are less attended, and the Bible is less known than it was before the Education Act of 1870; but the wireless brings religion into many homes. It is difficult to analyse the new situation. There is less aggressive anti-clericalism but more indifference than in the later Victorian era.

This diversion of the nation's interest into new channels has had its reflection in politics. The political aspect of the quarrel between Church and Dissent had been the life blood of the Whig and Tory, the Liberal and Conservative

[2] As a result of the storm of opposition, the Bill of 1902 finally passed in a form whereby religious instruction in Church Schools was placed under the authority of the Managers as a whole, thereby putting an end to its exclusive direction by the parson of the parish.

factions, from Charles II to Victoria. In our own day the reassortment of parties on a basis of industrial and social questions only, with no reference to religion, was the prime reason of the disappearance of the Liberal and the advent of the Labour party in its place after the War. Class-consciousness has superseded chapel-consciousness. The excitement over Balfour's Education Bill was the last party fight on the old ecclesiastical lines.

Another great reform of Balfour's Ministry was the Irish Land Purchase Act of 1903. It set up a machinery, oiled by a large loan on generous terms from the British Government, by which the ownership of most of the land of Ireland has passed from the Protestant landlords to the native peasant farmers. This peaceful revolution did not, as Balfour hoped, prevent the resurgence of the demand for political self-government or quench the national aspirations of Irishmen. But it smoothed out one of the chief complications of the Irish question, which, if left unremoved, might have rendered even such settlement as we have now attained, or any agreed settlement at all, impossible in the days to come.

At this stage, the waning fortune of Unionist Conservatism was put to a hazard calculated either to check or to precipitate its ruin. Joseph Chamberlain, with a vigour unmatched since Gladstone's advocacy of Home Rule, preached the doctrine of Protection, renamed Tariff Reform. [1902–5.] The motive that first impelled him to this audacity was the desire to link the Dominions to the Mother Country by a system of Imperial Preference. Without it, he believed, the bonds of Empire would ere long be relaxed. The difficulty was that Great Britain could not give effective preference to Canada and Australasia without placing a tax on foreign foodstuffs, to be remitted in the case of Dominion products. And in England popular tradition had a vague but hostile memory of the old 'Corn Laws'; greybeards told tales of the 'hungry forties,' when taxed bread was scarce on their parents' tables.

Imperial Preference, therefore, was a bad election cry.

Moreover, after the South African War, the country had had enough Empire for awhile; so Chamberlain's Preferential Tariff, in the hands of his insular fellow countrymen, was soon moulded by the Conservatives into a scheme of which the prime object was the protection of British goods. This aroused the enthusiasm and opened the purse strings of many British manufacturers. But their zeal was suspect to the consumer, especially to the working man with his family budget to consider. Free Trade doctrine was very strong in all sections of the community; it had behind it fifty years of unchallenged authority and custom; caution and tradition, usual mainstays of the Conservative party, supported the Liberal economic thesis. Moreover the prosperity of British commerce under the Free Trade system was not yet shaken. Joseph Chamberlain in his lifetime was beaten by the still obstinate prosperity of our staple industries. He could prophesy their ruin, but its coming was delayed.

Indeed, the great interest that most required protection in the first years of the new century was agriculture. Ever since 1875 foodstuffs from America and all the world had come flooding into Great Britain on a scale never foreseen in the day of Cobden and Peel, when prices had been steadied, not smashed, by free importation from Europe. But, with the prairies and the pampas developed as Britain's food farm, it was becoming impossible to grow food at a profit in the island. English farm hands, badly paid and housed even in good times, were now deserting the land for the cities at an appalling rate. Great Britain was on the way to become urbanized altogether, unlike any other country in the world. How could a check be put to this catastrophe, which would be irremediable when once complete? The protection of British agriculture was the proposal that politicians were most afraid to advocate, though something might be done under cover of Colonial Preference. The Free Trade system under which Britain had so long flourished had little regard for agriculture. Food was the currency in which foreign nations and our own Dominions paid for British manufactured goods. And cheap corn and meat was of great value to the wage-earning community. The absence of a democratic peasant-proprietorship like that of the European Continent made it difficult to advocate agricultural Protection. The field labourer, long ill-used by the farmer, scarcely knew whether he wished agriculture to be protected; he could slip off to the nearest town or mining district and get a better wage and eat his cheap food there. The most effective popular appeal of Chamberlain's opponents was the unsavoury memory of the old Corn Laws, the fear of dear foodstuffs and the cry of the 'small loaf.' So it was only after the First World War had shaken party traditions and old economic doctrines, and the German submarine had shown the use of the plough in Britain, that an attempt was made by subsidies and control of imports to maintain food production within the island and so save a little of what is still left of country life, while securing by statute a minimum wage to the field labourer. That all life in Britain should become urban and suburban, while her fields fall back to jungle, would be a horrible disaster, for strategic, human and social reasons more important than any purely economic consideration.

To return to the situation of 1902–25, Balfour's position as head of a party divided against itself by Chamberlain's propaganda, was one of extreme difficulty. Half the veterans of Salisbury's Cabinets, and the young intelligence of the party, Hugh and Robert Cecil and Winston Churchill, were fighting for Free Trade. Yet the zealots of Tariff Reform were converting the great majority of active Conservatives behind Balfour's shrugged shoulders. His acute and sceptical intellect already occupied the middle position between the full Protectionist and the full Free Trade doctrine; this opportunist detachment is the most usual attitude of Englishmen to-day, but was regarded between 1902 and 1906 as a dishonest and laughable subterfuge. But Balfour was always singularly indifferent to public opinion, and his perfectly sincere belief in a middle way, although it then made both sides angry, admirably suited his purpose, which was to hold the Conservative party together as long as possible. Eventually he would have to follow Chamberlain because most of the party was following him, but he would do so as slowly and for as short a distance as possible. He would continue in office and carry out certain measures of home and foreign policy which had nothing to do with Tariff problems, in spite of the fury of Free Traders and Protectionists. He would be the stillness in the midst of the tornado. So he held on to office till December 1905, though his party had been in disruption and the credit of his government gone for several years. No doubt the refusal, continued for so long, to face the new issue at an Election made the crash worse when it came.

Chamberlain had failed in his effort to make the working classes see their interest in his new programme. His great campaign had set Englishmen thinking hard about economic questions, but many of them thought Socialism instead of Protection. Affinities govern politics: the slogan that 'Tariff Reform means work for all' was discredited not always on purely economic arguments, but because Chamberlain's allies had for so many years of power passed so little 'working class legislation'; their new zeal to cure unemployment by tariffs was therefore suspect.

Moreover Labour was in these years growing 'class-conscious' and determined to act politically for itself. The effective rise of the Labour party took place at this time. It had only two representatives in the House of Commons when the century ended; one of these two was Keir Hardie, in his 'deer-stalker' cap conspicuous among the Victorian 'toppers.' As late as 1900 the great working class constituencies, even the mining districts, refused to 'vote labour,' and returned either Liberal or Conservative candidates.

Then came the blow of the Taff Vale decision in 1901, whence much of our recent political history takes its origin. The Judges once more undid the work of former Parliaments, and destroyed by a legal decision the rights that Trade Unions had held for a generation under Gladstone's

Trade Union Act of 1871. The Taff Vale case was carried up to the final Court of Appeal in the House of Lords, when the Law Lords decided that a Trade Union, though admittedly not a corporate body, could be sued in its corporate capacity for damages alleged to have been caused by the action of its officers; and that it could be sued not merely for criminal acts of its agents but for acts, not unlawful, which caused loss to others. This entirely new and unexpected interpretation of the Act of 1871[3] by the Law Lords of 1901 struck at the very heart of Trade Union action. Under the Taff Vale judgment, Trade Unions durst not, under peril of losing all their funds in damages, take any strike action to raise wages or to prevent the lowering of wages. Naturally employers took advantage of the new state of things between 1901 and 1906.

The Conservative government would probably have been wise in Conservative interests if it had at once legislated to put back the law on Trade Union liability to the place where everyone had supposed that it rested for thirty years past. To judge by his conduct on a similar occasion, Disraeli would certainly have done so. But the great industrial employers, formerly divided between the Liberal and Conservative parties, had, since the Home Rule split, nearly all of them gone over to the Conservative party. The Liberal party was now in a position to take up the Trade Union cause and profit by a labour alliance. But the Conservative party was not. Balfour's government shelved the issue by appointing a Royal Commission which was to report after the next General Election.

At length in December 1905 Balfour resigned, Sir Henry Campbell-Bannerman formed a Liberal government uniting all sections of the party, and unusually strong both in old and young talent. The new Ministry went to the country in January 1906. Labour ran a host of independent candidates, and in other constituencies gave its vote to Liberal candidates who pledged themselves to give Trade Unions complete immunity from legal proceedings.

[3] See p. 240, above.

The result of the General Election was like an earthquake. There had been nothing approaching it since the destruction of the old Tory party in the first election after the Great Reform Bill, and that had been the consequence of an entirely new electoral system. In 1906 the net Liberal gain was 273. The Liberals in the new Parliament numbered 397; the Irish Nationalists 83; the Unionists who had ruled the last Parliament were reduced to 157. And, most significant of all, a Labour party of 50 members had suddenly sprung into existence.

The overturn, which took everyone by surprise, was significant of a greater tendency to mass emotion in the large modern electorate, bred in great cities, and less tied up by party traditions than the old. There have been other such elections since. Moreover the issues of 1906 had all been unfavourable to the late government—the Education Act, Protection, Taff Vale, and the recent introduction of indentured Chinese Labour into the South African gold mines, which seemed a sorry outcome of the great Imperialist War. But behind all these things was something more fundamental. A new generation had arisen, wanting new things, and caring more about 'social reform' at home than about 'Imperialism' in Ireland, South Africa or anywhere else.

Whatever party or doctrine would be the ultimate gainer, the old forms of Imperialism and Conservative Unionism were never again to hold power. Protection, indeed, had a future. But the Conservatism that held power after the First World War, as an alternative often preferred to Labour governments, was liberal in its outlook on Irish, Egyptian, South African and Indian questions, and semi-socialist in its outlook on the duties of the State to the working class. Meanwhile until the War the Liberal Party bore rule for the last time, in close though uneasy alliance with Labour, and left a deep impress on social legislation.

Balfour's last great reform before leaving office in 1905 had been the establishment of the Committee of Imperial Defence. It was developed by Asquith's government as a means for laying plans for the possible event of war. Its functions are consultative only; it provides the Cabinet with information and advice, and its decisions can only be carried into effect by Parliament or by Departments of State. As it is not an executive body, its composition is fluid. The Prime Minister summons whom he thinks fit—generally the Secretary for War, the First Lord of the Admiralty, the Foreign Secretary, any Dominion Prime Ministers who may be in England, and the technical advisers required for the questions under discussion at each particular meeting. The Committee has, however, a Secretary of its own, whose permanence in a constantly changing body gives him great importance. Sir Maurice Hankey, as Secretary of the Committee of Imperial Defence after 1912 and Secretary of the Cabinet after 1916, left his impress on our growing institutions.[4]

The importance of the Committee of Imperial Defence is two-fold. It enables the problems of army, navy, air force and home front to be considered together in their mutual relations and as parts of one general policy, of provision for possible war. And it enables the responsible statesmen of the Dominions to meet the home authorities in confidential discussion and concert plans for the defence of the Empire as a whole.

[4] It is only since December 1916 that the Cabinet has had a Secretary present at its meetings, a Secretariat and regular agenda papers. The change took place first when, under stress of war, a smaller body, the 'War Cabinet,' took the place of the larger Cabinet. When the ordinary larger Cabinet was restored in the autumn of 1919, the Secretariat was kept.

CHAPTER SIX

The Last Liberal Government. December 1905 to May 1915

For ten years Great Britain was ruled, for the last time, by a Liberal Government. Its leaders were men of unusual personality and power. There was Haldane, the soft-spoken lawyer-philosopher, who won the confidence of the soldiers and reformed the Army; John Morley, the veteran of the Radical intellectualism of the last century, who was now on behalf of the British Government to cope with the new problem of national self-consciousness in India; there was Edward Grey, remote, firm and sadly serene at the Foreign Office; there was young Winston Churchill looking round for his kingdom; and there was Lloyd George, on whom time and great events should fix many diverse labels, mutually contradictory but all true. And coming on there were such able administrators and legislators as Herbert Samuel, Walter Runciman and Reginald McKenna. The working classes were represented for the first time in a Cabinet, by John Burns, a personality hewn out of old English oak. For a decade all these men most astonishingly held together, for two successive Prime Ministers knew their business: Campbell-Bannerman, an easy-tempered but shrewd Scot, who saw quite through the souls of men, started his team of colleagues in harmony; won the confidence of the raw and restive legion of Liberal recruits in the House; pacified South Africa by reversing the policy of Milner and granting responsible government before it was too late[1]; then died in 1908, his tasks accomplished. He was succeeded by Asquith, a Yorkshireman of high integrity and unshakable nerve, with a skill in advocacy learnt in the law and applied to politics, sound judgment to choose well between the opinions of others, and a rare skill in manipulating discordant colleagues.

[1] See p. 222, above.

The great achievement of this last Liberal Ministry was the initiation of measures of social reform on a scale beyond all precedent. Old Age Pensions, on a non-contributory basis, helped to empty the workhouses, to give happiness to the old and relieve their loyal sons and daughters of part at least of the burden of their maintenance. [1908.] Democratic Budgets shifted more taxation on to the wealthy. Workmen's Compensation, Miners' Eight Hours, Medical Inspection of Children and the Children's Bill, the Town Planning Act, the Sweated Industries Act, measures of Unemployment and Health Insurance, and the Small Holdings Act for rural districts formed part of a vast programme of laws placed on the Statute Book. Such measures, implemented by municipal bodies, and extended by the work of Care Committees, Play Centres, Boy Scouts, Adult Education and other such activities outside the harsh discords of politics, together with constantly advancing medical science and practice, have in the present century, in spite of the War, raised the standard of children's health and happiness, reduced the death-rate and prolonged the average of human life by several years, and begun a more even distribution of the national income and opportunities for happiness.

The function of Local Government has undergone immense extension under modern democracy. It is looked to now not merely to remove public nuisances, to supply sanitation, lighting and roads, but to act for the personal benefit of the individual citizen. It is to Local Government, controlled and aided by the State Offices in Whitehall, that the poorer citizen is beginning to look to supply the house he lives in; the electric light and gas he uses; free education for his children—from infant schools to University scholarships; medical clinics and isolation hospitals; books from the free library; baths and swimming; cricket fields and 'green belts' of open country for his Sunday walks; trams or buses to take the family to work or school; and a hundred other benefits to make life kind.

As Sir William Harcourt said as far back as 1894, 'we are all socialists now.' At any rate, by whatever name you call it, this system of State assistance to the life of the poorer citizens is a great fact of modern English life. Its principal instrument is found in elective local bodies, empowered by successive Acts of Parliament, helped financially by Treasury 'grants in aid' of rates, and kept up to mark by government Inspectors.

This system, originated in the middle of the Nineteenth Century, has been growing faster than ever in the Twentieth. In the Rating and Valuation Act of 1925, in the Local Government Act of 1928 we see the Central Power taking more and more control of local government. There is an ever-increasing tendency of the Minister and Department at Whitehall to direct the action of the local authorities on a single national model. The national model is enforced on the local authorities not merely by Acts of Parliament, but also by elaborate regulations which modern Acts of Parliament allow the Minister to make departmentally by acts of administrative legislation. 'Delegated legislation' it is called, because Parliament by Statute delegates to the Minister (of Health, Transport or Education) the power to make subsidiary rules to be enforced on the local authority as if they were laws.

Local authorities are becoming more and more the agents of Central Government in carrying out a national policy for the benefit of the poorer citizens, largely at the expense of the richer citizens, through the local rates and the national taxes that go to make up the grants-in-aid. Under this system the elected local authorities have more powers, but less independence, than of old. They cannot refuse to carry out these multitudinous duties imposed by Act of Parliament or by the regulations issued by the Minister. The days have indeed long gone by since the local benches of Justices of the Peace in 1795 introduced a new national policy of rates in aid of wages, the 'Speenhamland system,' without any reference either to Parliament or to any Minister or Department at Whitehall.[2]

[2] See pp. 146–47, above.

In future every government, whether called Conservative, National or Labour, must be at least half socialist. The last Liberal government recognized this fact, and applied great legislative and administrative ability to meet the needs of the new social and economic scene. [1906–15.]

The Liberals, who had ceased to be in the main a middle-class party, could only maintain themselves so long as the working class would vote for their candidates. In the very first days of the new Parliament, the degree of Liberal dependence on Labour opinion was made dramatically clear. As a result of the General Election, the Taff Vale decision must be reversed—but on what terms?

The Liberal government in 1906 introduced a Bill based on the Report of the Commission appointed by Balfour,[3] on which Mr. Sidney Webb and others had sat. The Bill, as those Commissioners had advised, would have left Trade Unions suable, but only when illegal acts had been done by their express orders, or by 'some person acting under their authority.' At once the Trade Union world was up in arms demanding complete immunity for their funds; repeated experience of the hostile ingenuity of Judges had filled Labour with a profound distrust of the law courts in cases where Trade Union rights were concerned. Those rights as held under the laws of 1825 and again of 1871 had been taken away by legal decisions, after long years of secure enjoyment. And so it might be again. The Labour members in the House, and a large number of Liberal members who had pledged themselves at the Election to make Trade Union Funds immune from legal actions, declared that the Government's Bill was not enough. Campbell-Bannerman surrendered and accepted the demand for complete legal immunity of Trade Unions from actions for torts, though their individual members breaking the law of course remained subject to penalties. The new Bill passed both Houses, for Balfour refused to divide against it on third reading in the Commons and this agreed signal was obeyed by the Lords; they let it pass, while they threw

[3] See p. 260, above.

out the new Government's Education and Licensing Bills.

It was thus already shown in 1906 that Labour was the strongest element in the progressive or left-wing side of politics, stronger than the 'old Liberal' interests, Non-conformity and Temperance. The Lords had not dared to challenge Labour, although all the Conservatives and many of the Liberals regarded legal immunity as a dangerous privilege for bodies so powerful as the amalgamated Trade Unions of the Twentieth Century; miners, railwaymen and transport workers were becoming organized on a national instead of local basis, and bade fair to be each 'a State within the State.' And now they were rendered in large measure exempt from the control of law.

At the same time, by encouraging the rejection of distinctively Liberal measures such as the Education and Licensing Bills, the Conservative leaders put the House of Lords again in the forefront of politics, a position from which the prudence of Disraeli had preserved it. Under his wise direction, the Lords had allowed Gladstone to put on the Statute Book all his large programme between 1868 and 1874, including even the Disestablishment of the Irish Church, and the Conservatives had consequently won the next General Election. And in the 'eighties the Lords had restrained their natural impulse to act as a partisan body on a level of authority with the House of Commons. But in 1893 they had won popularity by the bolder course of throwing out Gladstone's Home Rule Bill; their complete success on that occasion, endorsed by the verdict of the country at the next Election, misled Chamberlain, Balfour and Lord Lansdowne into supposing that the Lords could play the same game in the more democratic Twentieth Century against a much more formidable government backed by a vast majority.

Their strategy in deserting Disraeli's caution was fundamentally at fault; but in the years 1906–8 their tactics were clever and at first successful. They passed the measures in which the working classes were most interested, but humiliated the Government by refusing to pass the measures about which its Liberal supporters specially cared.

The Liberals seemed already reduced to impotence within two years of their triumphal entry into power. The bye-elections began to turn heavily against the Government. A Conservative reaction was on foot, and a little patience would have met its reward. But the Peers had no patience, and at the instigation of the party leaders, proceeded to commit the greatest tactical error in modern politics. They threw out Lloyd George's Budget of 1909.

This new interpretation of the constitutional function of the hereditary Chamber in matters of finance amounted to a claim on its part to force a General Election whenever it wished; for a Government unable to raise taxes must either resign or dissolve. In future all Parliaments not to the liking of the Lords could be dissolved at their will. The rejection of the Budget was also a breach with the custom of the Constitution, of which Conservatives should above all regard themselves as the guardians. Neither Disraeli nor Lord Salisbury would have dreamt of such a proceeding as to invite the Lords to reject the Budget of the year. The Twentieth Century was not a time for an hereditary Chamber to claim powers it had not exercised even in the aristocratic Eighteenth. But it was in vain that King Edward VII warned the Opposition leaders of the danger of the course on which they were set.[4]

But a tendency to violence and excitement had already invaded the mind of the new Century. Militant Suffragettes, Labour Unions, Irish parties, and foreign military potentates were not the only people to be subject to its

[4] It had been agreed in Charles II's reign that the Lords could not amend a money Bill, but could throw it out. But since the custom had arisen of putting all the year's taxes in a single Budget Bill, the Lords had never thrown out a Budget. They had thrown out a separate money Bill, Gladstone's Repeal of the Paper Duty Bill, in 1860, but passed it in the following year when he put it into the Budget. The Lords in 1909 claimed that the Valuation Clauses of the new Land Tax in the Budget were not proper to a finance Bill, and that the Budget could not therefore claim the customary privilege of unchallenged passage through their House.

influence. The Tariff Reform movement was being carried on in an atmosphere of perpetual excitement and anger; the new type of newspaper lived on sensation; Lloyd George's shrill demagogic note was new in speeches delivered by Ministers of the Crown; and the Peers caught the contagion of violence.

[1909.] Lloyd George's Budget was unpopular with the upper class, justly, in so far as it proposed new Land Taxes in an ill-conceived form which proved on trial to be impracticable; and less reasonably, because it made a very moderate increase of direct taxation of the well-to-do. There was to be a graduated income tax at about a quarter of what it is to-day (1937) and corresponding death duties, to pay for Old Age Pensions and a very necessary increase in the Navy. If the Opposition had waited, they could have won the next Election and repealed the Land Taxes. But they urged on the Peers to reject the Budget, the very thing which Lloyd George most desired. He made ample use of his opportunity; his harangues at Limehouse and elsewhere sharpened the edge of controversy and aroused the democratic passions. It was the grand electoral issue for the Liberals—'Shall Peers or People rule?' The Peers defended themselves by claiming that they had only referred the Budget to the People, and that the land valuation clauses were not proper to a Budget: but they were on the defensive; the Opposition had lost the advantage of attack.

Meanwhile Asquith and his other colleagues appealed more quietly to the moderate men, who had been drifting back to the Conservative allegiance, but who were shocked by the disregard of constitutional custom by the Lords. At the same time the Liberal Ministers were able to rally the Labour and the Irish forces to a joint effort to limit the Lords' power of veto. Another issue at the Budget elections was Tariff Reform: it was urged by Conservatives as a method of raising money preferable to the increased direct taxation necessary under a Free Trade government.

All these issues were brought to a head together by the fight over the rejected Budget and over the Parliament

Bill: that measure proposed to prohibit the Peers from either amending or rejecting money Bills, and to change their absolute veto on other measures to a suspensory veto for two years. The country was twice consulted in 1910—once under King Edward, and once after his death under the new King, George V—with the result that in both elections a majority of about 120 was secured by the Liberal-Labour-Irish combination.[5] The Liberal party was therefore master of the Lords, but at the mercy of its own allies. George V, after the second election had confirmed the result of the first, compelled the Peers to pass the Parliament Bill [1911.], by using, at Asquith's behest, the same method of a threatened creation of Peers *en masse* as William IV had, at Grey's dictation, employed to pass the First Reform Bill. Again the prerogatives of the Crown had proved the weapon of the democracy, a fact which helped to move the working classes still further from Republican doctrine.

But 1911 was not, like 1832, the end of the worst trouble. For opinion in the country was much more evenly divided than in that famous year of old, when the Lords had little save their own constitutional powers with which to maintain the fight. The Home Rule question now came up in earnest, for under the Parliament Act the Peers could no longer defeat it, but only delay its passage. The disestablishment of the Church in Wales, the long-standing demand of Welsh Non-conformity and of the majority of the Welsh members, was also now a practicable proposition, heaping yet more fuel on the fire of men's wrath.

Unhappily the worst exacerbation of parties in Great

[5] The interval between the elections of January and of December 1910 was largely occupied, after Edward VII's death, by a conference behind closed doors between the chiefs of the two parties in the attempt to solve the House of Lords and other problems by agreement. It failed after months of discussion. Both Edward VII and George V made strenuous efforts to avert the clash between the two Houses; Victoria had succeeded on several such occasions, as in 1868 and 1884; but the temperature from 1906–14 was too hot for royal mediation.

Britain—a mixture of old constitutional and denominational with new social and financial antagonisms—corresponded in time with the climax of the older and more intense antagonisms of race and religion in Ireland. The prevailing spirit of the day was wrath and violence: many even of the female advocates of Votes for Women—the most important of the many political cross-currents of that distracted era—resorted to organized outrage on persons and property to advertise their cause, with the result that their cause lost ground. The women who made outrage a method of persuasion were distinguished by the title of 'Suffragettes' from the law-abiding women suffragists. Labour troubles, too, were acute and strikes constant; individual strife between the vast national organizations of capital and labour in mines and railways were a new feature of life in the last years before the War. As in the Middle Ages, great corporations were threatening to become stronger than the unorganized community.

But Lloyd George, the stormy petrel, loved to ride such waves. It was in the midst of these furies, concentrated largely upon his head, that he passed the complex and unpopular Health Insurance Act [1912.], a contribution scheme to insure the whole working population against sickness, which has since proved a blessing to the working classes, and no ill friend to the doctors, who at first looked at it with natural misgivings, sharpened by political prejudice. Two of the most valuable of the social reforms of the Twentieth Century, Balfour's Education Act of 1902 and Lloyd George's Insurance Act of 1912, were highly unpopular and injured the Governments that passed them; both were rendered possible by the work and wisdom of the great public servant Sir Robert Morant, and by the stubbornness of the two Ministers who forced them through Parliament. Though Balfour and Lloyd George were mutual opposites in politics, character, tradition and intellect, they both liked to go out in a storm. It seemed impossible in 1912 that they should ever be friends. But strange things were lurking behind the clouds ahead.

The passing of the Parliament Act had opened the way

for the placing of Home Rule on the Statute Book; instead of absolute rejection, two years' delay was the worst the Lords could now do against any measure sent up to them. In these circumstances, the two parties in Britain should have united to dictate to the two communities in Ireland a reasonable settlement—Home Rule, with the Protestant part of Ulster excluded. But tempers were so raw after the Parliament Act struggle, that it was difficult for good sense to break in. Ireland, whose case had long demanded impartial consideration as an Imperial problem, had for a whole generation been used as the stalking horse of British party interests and passions. The Conservative party, now led by Bonar Law, more stubborn on this issue than even his predecessor Balfour, openly encouraged Ulster to arm for resistance under Sir Edward Carson's sincere and dogged leadership. The Liberal Government on their side ought to have announced that the six Protestant counties of Ulster should be allowed to contract out from Home Rule. That is what Asquith intended to happen, but he did not say so clearly, for fear of losing Redmond's votes on which he now depended in the Commons. On neither side was British statesmanship in this matter on a level with the circumstances, and Nemesis descended upon all concerned. It is true that at late last the issue as between parties in England had been narrowed down to the degree and method of 'contracting out' of Home Rule to be permitted to the several Counties of Ulster. But even so there was not final agreement, and meanwhile the passions aroused in Ireland were by this time so strong—Sinn Fein gaining ground on constitutional Nationalism, and Orange feeling worked to its height, and both sides illegally armed—that civil war seemed unavoidable. Then suddenly, in August 1914, a greater quarrel and a more terrible danger reunited in a week Liberal with Conservative, capital with labour, man with still unenfranchised woman, and even, for a few months of tense and novel emotion, Ireland with England and Orange with Green.

CHAPTER SEVEN

End of Isolation. Lansdowne and Grey. The Ententes with France and Russia. Haldane's Army Reforms. Europe's Drift to War. 1914

From Canning to Salisbury the 'splendid isolation' of Great Britain served her interests well. She avoided a whole series of continental wars—except the adventure of the Crimea, which was of her own seeking and the consequences of which were easily liquidated. In the then state of scientific invention and warlike armament, the Navy was still her sure and sufficient shield, and for a hundred years after Trafalgar no Power attempted to build a rival fleet. The Balance of Power in Europe was adequately adjusted without Britain's make-weight, and the independence of the small countries of the Rhine Delta was not seriously threatened. During the Franco-Prussian War of 1870, Gladstone had, in pursuance of the terms and the policy of the Treaty of 1839,[1] announced Britain's intention to take arms against either French or German violation of Belgium's neutrality, and on that occasion the warning was enough. In spite of Colonial difficulties with France, and Asiatic difficulties with Russia, Salisbury in the 'eighties and 'nineties saw no necessity to attach our fortunes to those of the Triple Alliance of Germany, Austria-Hungary and Italy. We stood by ourselves alone, safe behind the shield of supreme naval power. But some, including Chamberlain, were beginning to be anxious.

With the new century, and the jealousies and hatreds let loose by the South African War, the period of 'splendid isolation' came to an end. The first steps on the new road were taken by Lord Lansdowne as Foreign Minister under Balfour. To their thinking, the number, size and ubiquity of armed forces by land and sea all over the world rendered it necessary that we should have at least some defined

[1] See p. 181, above.

friendships. An understanding with America would have been preferred, but her traditional policy of isolation rendered it out of the question. So the Japanese Alliance was made [1902.], originally to counterbalance the advance of Russia on to the shores of the Pacific, and to prevent the partition of China by Russia, Germany and France, which America disliked as much as we, but would do nothing active to prevent. The Japanese Alliance also enabled us to dispense with the creation of an immense naval establishment in the Pacific. Britain's friendship served to keep the ring for the rise of the first 'coloured' Great Power, to which the other European Powers were hostile. Japan's triumph over Russia in war [1904.] had many reactions upon India and on the world at large. Ten years later, the Japanese, faithful to their alliance with us, safeguarded the waters and coasts of the Far East against German designs during the First World War, besides giving effective help in the Mediterranean.

More important even than the Japanese Treaty was the simultaneous evolution in our relations with France and the German Empire respectively. The state of the Balance of Power in Europe was again giving cause for anxiety. Germany was more and more overshadowing Europe by her unparalleled military preparations, based on ever-increasing population, wealth and trained intelligence; and moreover she was adding to her predominant army a fleet built in rivalry to our own. To Britain the sea was the primary consideration of her very existence, as it was not to Germany. It was this naval rivalry which altered Britain's attitude to the European Powers.

During the last twenty years of the Nineteenth Century we had been in constantly recurring danger of war with France or Russia, owing to the clash of our interests with theirs at various points in Asia and Africa. In the first years of the new century it was felt that the dangers of such a war, with the power of Germany on the flank of the combatants, were too great to be any longer risked. If Germany had been ready to make friends with Britain and share the business of guarding the *status quo* and the peace of the world, a German Entente might have been made. But tentative suggestions of this kind by Chamberlain and others had been rejected by Germany; and her growing hostility to us and her naval rivalry were evident. There was therefore no alternative but to remove by agreement our specific causes of quarrel with the French Republic and the Russian Czar.

In 1904 Lord Lansdowne settled the outstanding differences between Great Britain and France in Egypt, Morocco, and Newfoundland by a Treaty of Agreement on these points, and so permitted the growth of the *entente cordiale*, not yet an alliance, and not on our part hostile to Germany —unless indeed Germany would have it so. King Edward VII's popularity in France during his holiday visits helped to make an atmosphere propitious to the new friendship, but he had nothing to do with the initial choice of the policy by his Ministers.

Sir Edward Grey succeeded Lansdowne at the Foreign Office in December 1905. It was a moment of European crisis, though the English people, intent on its General Election, scarcely knew it. Germany was threatening France on the question of Morocco. A clause in Lansdowne's agreement with France of the year before pledged us to support France diplomatically on that issue, in return for her recognition of our status in Egypt. Grey, in agreement with the Prime Minister Campbell-Bannerman, implemented this promise, and stood by France on the Moroccan question. The other nations of Europe, except Austria-Hungary, took the same line at the Algeciras Conference early in 1906, and so did President Theodore Roosevelt on behalf of the United States. Germany receded.

There had been more behind than the Moroccan question. Germany had resented Lansdowne's settlement of Anglo-French quarrels in 1904 and wished to show France that she could not depend on England; Grey showed her that she could. It was the testing of the Entente. If the return of the Liberals to power in December 1905 had meant, as a large part of the Liberal party wished, the return of Britain to her old isolation, France could not have resisted, and must either have fallen in war or become the vassal of Germany. Russia at that moment was crushed by her defeat in the war with Japan, and was ripe for internal revolt. Germany aimed at drawing first Russia and then France into her orbit. Britain would then be at her mercy. We were no longer in a position to defy a united Europe as in Nelson's day; submarines, aircraft and long-distance guns were depriving us of our insular safety. Yet the danger of such a European combination under German leadership was actual. In July 1905 the Kaiser and the Czar had met in the Czar's yacht off the Baltic island of Björkö, and had there signed a Treaty which put Russia on the side of Germany, by an agreement avowedly aimed against England, and as dangerous to her as Tilsit.

The Treaty of Björkö had indeed been torn up, but its policy might be renewed at any moment, and then France would be forced to follow suit, if Britain's pledge of support to her proved valueless. Grey's action over the Moroccan crisis prevented any such development. After Algeciras (1906) France and Russia both saw that Britain's friendship was worth having.

Grey could not, however, positively pledge England to convert the diplomatic support promised by the Lansdowne Agreement into military support, in case of war. The English people would not be pledged beforehand, until a *casus belli* arose. Grey had not the power to turn the Entente into an Alliance, any time between 1906 and 1914. Moreover even if his colleagues, his party and his country had consented to an obligation so definite—and that was far from being the case—Grey's own view was that a pledge to take part in the next war might encourage France and Russia to more intransigent policies and engage us in a struggle not essentially defensive. All that Grey had either the wish or the power to do was to let Germany know the great likelihood that England would stand by France in arms, if France were attacked. This he did.

On the other hand, war had been so near over the Moroccan issue, that in January 1906 Grey had sanctioned 'Military Conversations' between the British and French staffs. To contemplate a contingent possibility of British intervention and yet have no war plan ready would have been madness, for while Britannia was fumbling with her sword, the Germans might be in Paris in a month. The Military Conversations of January 1906 were amply justified, as events of August 1914 were to show. Campbell-Bannerman ought no doubt to have told his Cabinet about them at once, but both he and Grey regarded them as a purely departmental question. In that view they were wrong: they should have told the Cabinet. But it would have been a far more unpardonable mistake not to have any plans for a war that might break out and destroy France in a few weeks, if England had made no preparations to come at once to her help.

On the basis of the Military Conversations with France in 1906, was built up Haldane's great army reform of the next years. The Military Conversations arranged a detailed plan for the immediate despatch of an Expeditionary Force to France in case a war should arise in which England decided to take a hand. One part of Haldane's Army Reforms of 1906–12 was the creation of such an Expeditionary Force of 150,000 men of all arms, ready at a moment's notice to go to France by routes prearranged with the French authorities. It was this preparation that enabled our forces to arrive just in time to save Paris from the German onrush in 1914.

Haldane also created the Territorial Force, turning the old 'Volunteers' and 'Yeomanry' into effective fighting units. Kitchener, on service abroad, did not realize that the amateurishness of the old 'Volunteers' was a thing of the past, and when called to the War Office, in 1914, refused to make use of the Territorial organization. But he used the men whom it had trained.

In the same years the Officers' Training Corps was established in a General Staff to think out military plans. The army at last had an official 'brain.'

In 1907 Grey made an Anglo-Russian agreement to remove the specific causes of quarrel with Russia, as Lansdowne three years before had removed the causes of quarrel with France. With German unfriendliness and naval power increasing every year, it would have been the height of folly to drift into war with Russia. Yet unless the Persian question were settled by agreement, war would come on that issue. The Russians had Northern Persia already in their grip, and designed to push on to the Persian Gulf and to the Afghan frontier; we had old and great interests on the Gulf, and the protection of the independence of Afghanistan was regarded as essential to the safety of India. The Persians could not defend themselves against Russia. We had either to leave all Persia and the Gulf to the Russians, or fight a war with them on behalf of Persian independence, or else come to an agreement as to our relative spheres of influence. Grey chose the latter course, in which he was warmly supported by Campbell-Bannerman and by Morley as Indian Secretary. But the Anglo-Russian agreement was attacked by the advanced half of the Liberals and by the Labour party, as showing neglect of Persian interests and friendliness with the autocracy of Russia. This section of opinion was unwilling to increase armaments, yet anxious to pursue a policy in defence of Persia which must have led to a war with Russia—with Germany and the German fleet on our flank.

Grey's Anglo-Russian agreement was the only possible course consistent with our own safety. Yet it was a bad best. It prevented a Russo-German Alliance like that of Björkö which would have overwhelmed us, but it gave to the German public the sense of being 'encircled.'

The charge that Great Britain deliberately fostered a policy of 'encirclement' of Germany, though often repeated in that country, does not stand any test of truth. Grey, in the earnest pursuit of better relations, offered Germany outlets into Asia and Africa, by the Bagdad railway agreement and the agreement that Germany should have her share in case of Portugal's sale of Colonies. That was not 'encirclement.' Moreover in the part that Grey so often played as disinterested mediator in the Balkan troubles, he carefully discouraged the creation of a Balkan or a Slav bloc against Austria-Hungary, and he declined to oppose the dominating influence that Germany herself acquired at Constantinople.

Politically, therefore, there was no encirclement. And militarily it was precisely Germany's central position that gave her such immense and almost decisive advantage when war came. The encirclement, such as it was, was of Germany's own making. She had encircled herself by alienating France over Alsace-Lorraine, Russia by her support of Austria-Hungary's anti-Slav policy in the Balkans, England by building her rival fleet. She had created with Austria-Hungary a military bloc in the heart of Europe, so powerful and yet so restless that her neighbours on each side had no choice but either to become her vassals or to stand together for protection. The accident that the Teutons lay between the French and the Slavs put the Germans by the nature of geography in the centre of a 'circle,' thereby rendering their military power all the more formidable. They used their central position to create fear on all sides, in order to gain their diplomatic ends. And then they complained that on all sides they had been encircled. When Bismarck, in evil hour, made the Alliance with Austria-Hungary, he began a system that ere long caused the Franco-Russian Alliance to follow. Germany thus began the fatal system of Alliances which prevented the 'localization' of any future quarrel between two great European powers, and in the end dragged more than half the world into a war begun on a Balkan issue.

By 1914 Grey had removed by agreement every specific cause of quarrel between England and Germany; but neither he nor any man could remove the fact of the overgreat German power which in case of European war bade fair to destroy the independence of France and Belgium, and face England with a Continent united under vassalage to Berlin. As the years 1906–14 went on, the increase of the German fleet in rivalry to ours, and crisis after crisis of sabre-rattling on the Continent, partially awakened the English people to the dangers of the situation. But at no moment was the nation willing to convert the Entente with France and Russia into Alliance. Everyone was alarmed by Germany and her fleet, but this country was unwilling to decide beforehand what her action would be until the actual occasion should arise.

There were two storm centres whence war might break loose over the world—the Balkans and Morocco. In 1911 a second Moroccan crisis arose out of the Algeciras settlement of 1906. The dispute was known as 'Agadir,' after the Moroccan port to which the Germans sent a warship. After several weeks of danger, during which Britain again supported France, the affair was settled by compromise: France secured the recognition of the rights she claimed in Morocco by ceding some Colonial territory elsewhere to the Germans.

The Agadir settlement of the Moroccan question removed the last direct cause of dispute as between France and Germany themselves. But their allies might yet fall out and drag them into war. For there remained the Balkans, and in the Balkan question was involved the fate of the Austro-Hungarian Empire: its rule was extended in Bosnia over Yugo-Slavs, and the free Yugo-Slavs in Serbia therefore desired the break-up of the Empire of the Hapsburgs, in order to unite their nationals under their flag. The hostility between Vienna and Belgrade was intense. And Germany thought herself obliged on every occasion to support her ally Austria-Hungary, and Russia to support the Slav interest in the Balkans.

[1912.] Crisis after crisis arose in this region, each time nearly leading to a world war. The expulsion of the Turks from Macedonia and Thrace by the armies of Serbia, Greece and Bulgaria was long overdue and in itself desirable, but it greatly increased the tension between Austria-Hungary and her southern neighbours. For Serbia, after her victory over the Turks, emerged as a military power of proved value, her ambitions now directed northwards to free all Yugo-Slavs still under Austrian rule. To maintain the threatened territories of the Empire intact, the rulers of Austria-Hungary thought it incumbent on them to crush the Serbs. War on this issue was just averted in 1913 because Grey used his good offices as mediator, and Germany on that occasion helped the work of peace. Next year the outcome was different.

The atrocious murder of the Austrian Archduke Francis Ferdinand at Sarajevo on June 28, 1914, was closely connected with the agitation conducted in Serbia for the redemption of Bosnian Yugo-Slavs. It was inevitable that Vienna would exact guarantees that this agitation should come to an end. Unfortunately the statesmen and soldiers in charge of Austro-Hungarian policy were determined not merely to get such guarantees, but to seize the opportunity of the Sarajevo murder to annihilate Serbia by war, even at the risk of the interference of Russia, whom they trusted Germany to keep off. Germany was therefore deeply concerned and her rulers ought to have insisted on their right to be consulted by their ally. Unfortunately the Kaiser and his Chancellor, Bethmann-Hollweg, though not really desiring war, gave Vienna a 'blank cheque' on July 5 to send what Ultimatum she wished to Belgrade.

When the Ultimatum appeared on July 23, it surprised the Kaiser and the whole world by its extravagance: such demands had never been made of an independent State: yet Serbia did accept nine-tenths. A European Conference could easily have bridged the remaining difference. Grey urgently pressed on Germany the necessity of such mediation. But the Kaiser, though he had not approved of his ally's Ultimatum, refused any Conference at all and declared that the question was a local affair between Austria-Hungary and Serbia with which neither Russia nor any other country was concerned. Such words meant war, for Russia's whole policy would be stultified by permitting the destruction of Serbia's independence; she began the slow process of her mobilization. Germany, by this time in the hands of her military men who could think only of their time-tables of war, sent Ultimatums to Russia and to her ally France. At the beginning of August the huge strength of the German armies rolled, not eastward against Russia, but westward against France, through innocent Belgium.

Thus the quarrel, though it had broken out on Eastern questions which did not concern Britain, threatened at the very outset to put an end to the independence of France and Belgium, in circumstances which would have prevented those countries from ever raising their heads again, otherwise than as vassals of Germany. The victory of the Central Powers would have meant the subjection of Europe to an Empire better calculated to survive and rule in perpetuity than ever Napoleon's had been. The very virtues of the German people, as the servants of their rulers' ambitions, made the danger of permanent slavery for Europe extreme.

Sir Edward Grey had made every effort to avert the war, and thereby helped to win for Britain and her Allies the moral sympathy of a large part of mankind, particularly in America. But when those efforts failed, self-preservation dictated that we should not permit the Channel Ports, the Netherlands, and indeed all Europe, to fall into vassalage to a power that was already openly our rival at sea. The violation of Belgian neutrality and the invaders' treatment of Belgian resistance was a drama that brought home, on a wave of generous emotion, the dreadful facts and necessities of the hour to the unwilling mind of the British public, which craved for nothing but peace.

Up to the moment of the invasion of Belgium, in the first days of August, British opinion had been divided as to the necessity of taking part in a European war. Neutralist feeling at the end of July was very strong, especially in the City, in the North of England and in the Liberal and Labour parties. Half the Cabinet, headed by Mr. Lloyd George, was neutralist. It would therefore have been utterly impossible for Grey, as is sometimes suggested in the retrospect, to threaten Germany with our participation in war a day earlier than he did. Any premature attempt in July to commit Great Britain to fight would have led to the break-up of the Cabinet, and the division of the country at the moment of its greatest peril. Such a disaster nearly occurred, and was only averted by the wisdom of Asquith, who held together his colleagues and his countrymen. In that week of tumult and alarm, the heated mass of opinion might have exploded into fragments flying in opposite directions. The danger of national division came to an end as a result of the actual invasion of Belgium, and on August 4 Great Britain went to war as a united country on behalf of her Treaty commitments to protect Belgian neutrality. Belgium was not the only reason why we had to fight or perish; but it was the reason why we were able to strike as a united people, in time, but only just in time, to prevent the fall of Paris and the Channel Ports into the German power.

CHAPTER EIGHT

The First World War. 1914–18

A brief summary of the leading events of the War may be a useful prelude to remarks on its general characteristics.

The long-prepared plan of the German war lords was to hurl their main attack through neutral Belgium upon Paris, crush the French resistance at a blow, and then turn round and deal with the more slowly mobilizing forces of Russia. It came within an inch of success. The French Generals, Joffre and Foch, instead of preparing to meet the coming blow at the north of their line, began a rash offensive in Lorraine that was bloodily repulsed. Meanwhile the German armies trampled across Belgium, punishing resistance with a calculated 'frightfulness' that was meant to terrorize enemies and neutrals, and sounded the new, ruthless note of modern war. [AUG. 1914.] The treatment of innocent Belgium rallied England to join the fight as a united nation, and struck answering chords in America.

The British military chiefs, who had been left unacquainted with the French plans, had taken a more correct view of German intentions than their allies. The 'Expeditionary Force' prepared by Haldane, nearly 100,000 strong, crossed the Channel without the loss of a man or of a minute, and stood in the path of the main German advance as it emerged from Belgium. The British were overwhelmed by enormous superiority in numbers, but fought delaying actions at Mons and Le Cateau which at once established the reputation of our soldiership in the new war.[1] Then followed the British 'retreat from Mons'; the French also were falling back along the whole long front, and the Germans confidently expected to enter Paris in another week. All seemed lost, but then happened, for very natural causes, the 'miracle of the Marne.'

Joffre and Foch, after the great error which had cost France so dear in the first month of the war, kept their heads in apparently desperate circumstances, and brilliantly retrieved the situation by a counter-attack, taking advantage of the want of communication between the different German armies which had advanced at different speeds. The invaders were defeated by the French and British at the Battle of the Marne and forced to retreat from the neighbourhood of Paris. [SEPT. 1914.] But they dug themselves in on enemy territory, retaining Belgium and a large slice of France, including 80 per cent. of her coal and almost all her iron. But the Channel ports were left outside the German lines, so that the allied armies in France were in direct communication with England and her supplies. In that posture matters remained for the next four years. 'Trench warfare' had begun. The opposing lines from the Channel to the Swiss border, though often swaying and sagging deep, first one way then another, never actually broke until the autumn of 1918. But to maintain that western deadlock, there were poured out, in constant attack and counter-attack, millions of lives and the accumulated wealth of the past century of European progress.

Could the deadlock in the West be broken by operations in the East? The Russian masses had invaded East Prussia

[1] The Kaiser denied that he had ever used the phrase attributed to him at this time about 'the contemptible little British army.' But the humour of the 'Mons veterans,' the original Expeditionary Force of August 1914, demanded that they should continue to call themselves 'the old contemptibles,' and as such they will always be remembered by their countrymen. A. E. Housman's *Epitaph on an Army of Mercenaries* also refers to them.

in the early weeks of the war and so contributed to the result of the Marne by drawing off two German army corps from the West. But even before these supports could arrive, the battle of Tannenberg had been fought [AUG. 30, 1914.]: the invaders of Prussia were defeated with a loss of 300,000 men, at the hands of Hindenburg and his Chief of Staff, Ludendorff, henceforth the two heroes of Germany's war.

After Tannenberg the war between the armies of Russia and those of Germany and Austria-Hungary was continued on a gigantic scale. There was less of trench warfare in the East than in the West. For three years the struggle swayed forward and backward over great stretches of country, chiefly over the prostrate body of Poland.[2] Sometimes the Russians had success, but they were fatally handicapped by their want of arms and supplies, due to the primitive civilization of their country, and the ineptitude and corruption of the Czarist government, staggering to its final doom. If the British could have obtained a direct and easy route to Russia her deficiencies in armament might have been better supplied. But the Baltic was closed, and the attempt failed to open a route through the Dardanelles into the Black Sea.

The year 1915, with the attack on the Dardanelles and Constantinople, was indeed the one chance that England had of achieving victory by any method save exhaustion of the combatants. Success at this strategic point might perhaps have shortened the war by two years. Turkey had joined the Central Powers, [OCT. 1914.] thereby involving England in an immense increase in her liabilities, for she had to defend against the Turks not only Egypt and the Suez Canal by operations in Palestine, but the Persian Gulf and its oil supplies by operations in Mesopotamia. Moreover the entry of Turkey into the war tempted Bulgaria to avenge her own griefs by an attack on Serbia. If

[2] As a result of the World War Poland in 1919 came back into existence as an independent nation, because her German and Russian oppressors, though on opposite sides, had both been defeated.

Bulgaria marched on the enemy's side, the defence of Serbia against the overwhelming forces of Austria-Hungary would become impossible. But if, before Bulgaria threw in her lot with the enemy, England could force the Dardanelles and the capture of Constantinople, Bulgaria would almost certainly take our side instead, and the whole of the Balkan States would be mobilized against Austria-Hungary. For these reasons the attack on the Dardanelles was attempted. But it failed, with the result that Bulgaria joined the Central Powers, [NOV. 1915.] Serbia was overrun, and for the next three years the French and English armies would do nothing but hold on to the Macedonian port of Salonika as a base for future advance, if and when the enemy power should begin to fail.[3]

On the other hand Italy, in May 1915, entered the war on the side of the Allies, and a 'trench warfare' of a kind similar to that on the Western front was established in the foothills of the Alps, holding so large a part of the Austrian forces that the worse consequences of the failure in the Balkans were avoided. Austria-Hungary survived till 1918, but was unable, owing to the Italian pressure, to help Germany on the Western front, or to push the advantages gained in the Balkans and in Turkey.

The British Cabinet, led by Asquith, had ably conducted the initial crisis of the war. A financial crash had been avoided, the country had been rallied in a united Home Front, the navy had done its initial work well, the Expeditionary Force had been landed promptly and safely in France. The Dardanelles was the one great failure, due to divided counsels, resulting in premature and ill-supported attempts that gave the enemy warning. Soldiers, sailors and statesmen must all share in that responsibility. If no

[3] The idea, held by some, that an attack from Salonika in 1916 or 1917 would have brought down the Austro-Hungarian Empire, overlooked the fact that Germany, holding the inner line, could send troops and supplies to the Balkans far more quickly than France and England. But when the attack on the Dardanelles had been made in 1915, Germany had not then been in a position to send troops there direct across hostile and neutral territory.

man was the hero of the occasion, no man was solely to blame.

Apart from the Dardanelles the affair at sea had been well managed. The Expeditionary Force had reached France safely and at once; enemy cruisers had been hunted down and destroyed in all the seas of the world. The Japanese Alliance secured the Far Eastern Seas. Admiral Sturdee sank Spee's German squadron off the Falkland Islands in December 1914. The Grand Fleet under Jellicoe was provided with quarters at Scapa Flow, which proved safe even under modern conditions of submarine work; thence for four years it watched the enemy Grand Fleet in its harbours on the North German coast; the situation corresponded to Nelson's watch off Toulon, but owing to modern conditions the watch had to be conducted at a much greater distance. Only once the German Fleet emerged in force and the Battle of Jutland ensued. [MAY 1916.] The result of that action, which involved severe losses on both sides, was that the German Fleet escaped, but that it never attempted to put to sea again.

The same year 1916 saw much slaughter but no real change upon the Western front. The great attempt of the Crown Prince's armies to end the war by breaking through the French defence of Verdun failed after long months of effort. The first large-scale offensive of the newly raised British armies on the Somme also gained no substantial ground.

After Jutland the Germans turned their attention to the submarine campaign, which in April 1917 had attained such success that England was in danger of starvation and the allied cause of collapse. But the situation was saved in the following months by the heroism of the merchant service, the application of new scientific instruments to the location of submarines, the convoy system, and the entry of the United States into the war as a result of the submarine campaign against her own shipping. [APRIL 1917.] Meanwhile the British 'blockade' was wearing down the stubborn resistance of the German peoples.

Indeed it is not improbable that Germany would have

been defeated in 1917 if Russia had not that year gone out of the war as a result of her Bolshevik Revolution following on her repeated defeats in the field, due largely to governmental incompetence. The period between Russia's retirement from the struggle and the advent of the American armies in Europe in the summer of 1918, was one of great danger for the Allies. In April 1917 the French offensive at Chemin des Dames proved a disastrous failure, and there was talk of mutiny and revolution. The pressure on France was relieved by the tremendous offensive of Haig on the Ypres front in the gloomy battle of Passchendaele, fought all autumn long in rain and mud; after frightful losses it registered little positive advance. The tragic and dangerous year 1917 was cheered at Christmastime by the capture of Jerusalem from the Turks by the British army under Allenby advancing from Egypt. In the following year Allenby conquered all Palestine, entered Damascus and destroyed the Turkish military power. It was in these campaigns that 'Lawrence of Arabia' won his great reputation as leader of Arab irregulars.

The year 1918 would see the gradual arrival in France of the armies now being raised and drilled in America. If Germany had been wise she would have negotiated for a tolerable peace before they arrived. But her military men would not cut their losses, and were still for 'world conquest or downfall.' The destinies of Europe were in the hands of Ludendorff, who underrated the potentialities of American military power, and who hoped to conquer France beforehand by a great offensive in the spring. Owing to the falling out of Russia the Germans had for the moment a superiority in numbers in the West which tempted them to their ruin. Mismanagement, partly due to Lloyd George's distrust of Haig's tendency to attack, left the British force in France weaker than it need have been when the sudden blow fell upon it in March 1918. Perfect weather helped the Germans in their last mighty effort, which thrust back the English and the French very much as in September 1914. Paris and the Channel Ports were again in imminent danger. But the spirit of resistance in the French and British armies was not broken, and with the approach of summer they were cheered by the constant arrival of regiments of young Americans, eager for the war which had become so fearful a burden to the surviving veterans of Europe. The tide turned. A better co-operation between the allied armies was at length secured by making Foch Commander-in-Chief.

But the glory of the counter-offensive that ended the war lay chiefly with the decision of Haig and the efficiency of the British Army. The British Government did not expect the war to end till 1919 or even 1920, and to the last Lloyd George remained suspicious of Haig's love of the offensive, which this time at any rate proved right. The old saying that the English only win one battle in a war, the last one, is not really true, but has a certain verisimilitude in the light of the events of August to November 1918. Ludendorff's offensive in the spring had exhausted Germany and used up her spiritual and material power of further resistance, sapped by our naval blockade. On the Italian, Turkish and Balkan fronts the allies of Germany were defeated and put out of action. Turkey and Bulgaria were conquered. Austria-Hungary dissolved, by a series of revolutions, into her component racial parts. Even Ludendorff's iron nerve was broken and he demanded an armistice. The flight of the Kaiser to Holland, the German revolution and the Armistice of November 11 followed.

Some points of comparison of the First World War with the conditions and methods of the Napoleonic Wars may be a not unfitting way to end this book.

First, there was the difference of geographical situation. Jacobin and Napoleonic France attempted to conquer Europe from the base of its North-West angle; the Germanic powers made the same attempt from the more formidable strategic centre which gave to them 'the inner line' of battle against all comers—Russian, Balkan, Italian, French and English-speaking. Britain's communications with her allies in the East, particularly with Russia, were therefore more liable to interruption by the enemy. Also, in case the enemy won the war, it would be far more easy for the 'Central Powers' to hold Europe and Western Asia in permanent subjection than it would have been for the successors of Napoleon, who could not have kept the Germans down for ever, even if the battle of Leipzig had gone the other way.

As regards the strategy and tactics of the two struggles, Britain's part in both was to supply the money and maritime power of the Alliance, and to blockade the enemy by sea. But in the later war we also undertook another duty: we 'paid in person,' sending over armies numbered in their millions, and counting our dead at a million and our wounded at over two million in the four years. In the French wars from 1793 to 1815 our military effort, though important, had been small, and our average annual loss of life not above five thousand. Against Germany our average annual loss of life was nearly two hundred and fifty thousand. We found it necessary to make the greater military effort on the later occasion, partly because of the more formidable strength and geographical position of the 'Central Powers'; if once we allowed the Germans to overrun all Europe as Napoleon had done, we should never get them out again.

But our fuller participation in the war by land was dictated also by the changes in military and naval weapons and tactics, which had already shaken the old security of our island position. The possessor of the Channel Ports could, by long-distance guns, aeroplanes and submarines, threaten our existence much more formidably than Napoleon and his flat-bottomed boats at Boulogne. So the British people themselves, as soldiers, took a leading part in the decisive operations of the war. The modern Leipzig and Waterloo consisted of a continuous battle, fought day and night for four years along a line hundreds of miles long. Modern financial credit, and means of transporting men, food and warlike stores, enabled the opposing nations to maintain millions of fighters continuously in the trenches, year after year, on each of the principal fronts.

The most marked difference between the two wars lay

in armaments and tactics: the long Napoleonic wars began and ended with the Brown-Bess musket and close-order fighting of British line and French column. Invention continued all the time to be applied by England to industry, but was not applied by any country to war. Wellington's weapons and tactics were much the same as Marlborough's, Nelson's ships much the same as Blake's. Napoleon recognized the relation to war of modern administration and organization, but he was fortunately blind to the military possibilities of modern science. But on the later occasion the methods of warfare, which in 1914 began with all the latest mechanical appliances and in Germany at least with the fullest national organization, were revolutionized several times over in the course of four short years. Not only did trench-warfare take the place of the war of movement, but the development of aerial and submarine warfare on a great scale, and the invention of gas-warfare by the Germans and of tank-warfare by the British, are changes without any parallel among the slow-witted and unscientific wars of Napoleon. Science was harnessed, and the whole civil population was mobilized. Our ancestors in war time had lived safe behind Nelson's shield, happily producing Scott's lays and novels, Wordsworth's poems, Constable's and Turner's pictures; but now the civil population of Great Britain was fain to devote its whole energy and brains for four years to the business of slaying and being slain.

In the days of Pitt and Castlereagh we increased our Colonial Empire at the expense of France and her allies, and we did so again at the expense of Germany a hundred years later. But the Colonies had taken no part in the earlier struggle, for in Pitt's day the First British Empire had already been lost and the Second was still in its infancy. A hundred years later it was fully grown. There was indeed no machinery of Imperial Federation to bid the Empire march into line, but by free individual choice, Canada, Australia, New Zealand, and Anglo-Dutch South Africa took each its full share in the whole long contest. Between them they raised overseas contingents of a million and a half men. When the war was over, each Dominion insisted on a full recognition of its nationhood. They claimed individual representation in the League of Nations, and the right to retain those German colonies they had themselves taken in war. And finally, in 1931, the Statute of Westminster has given legal force to the long-established custom that the Parliament of Great Britain should legislate for the Dominions only at their own request. Laws affecting the succession to the Crown can be altered only with the concurrence of each of the Dominions, and the King can take no advice about appointments or other action in the Dominions except from Dominion statesmen. In the post-war world it is no longer Parliament but the Crown that links the Empire, in symbolism, in loyalty and in law.

India in the time of Pitt and Bonaparte had been the scene of the final struggle against French influence among the native courts and armies. But India in 1914–15 sent over great bodies of troops, enthusiastic to take part in the European contest. Unfortunately in India, Egypt and Ireland the protracted and deadly character of the War gave rise to unrest and political exacerbation of which the early months had shown no sign.

The attitude of Britain to Ireland during the War was at heart friendly and very different from the spirit of 1795–1800. But there was sad mismanagement. The golden moment in the autumn of 1914 was missed when Kitchener refused to make sympathetic use of the first outburst of Irish Nationalist readiness to volunteer for service overseas. In Easter 1916 the Sinn Fein rising in Dublin was followed by the execution of its leaders, which turned them into martyrs of the Irish people and hastened the conversion of the island from Redmond's Home Rule Policy to the Sinn Fein demand for a Republic. This change of opinion was complete by the end of the War, and led, after a disgraceful and bloody interlude, to the Treaty of 1921, which established the Irish Free State as a Dominion; the six Protestant counties of Ulster had, a few months before, obtained a Home Rule system of their own together with representation in the Westminster Parliament.

After the War, Egypt became an independent State, though in close alliance with Great Britain. And India was set on the path of self-government. For although the Empire was governed after 1918 mainly by Conservative statesmen, their Imperial policy was extremely liberal. The old methods of Anglo-Saxon domination were shown, during the War, to belong to a bygone age. South Africa was saved and the neighbouring German territories overrun by the Dominion force under Botha and Smuts, who only a dozen years before had been our enemies in the field.

Relations with the United States during the War were subject to somewhat the same general conditions as in Napoleon's time, but owing to wiser management and a better spirit, took an opposite turn. On both occasions, the interests of England as the great blockading Power necessarily clashed with those of the neutral merchant Power, desirous of sending her goods as usual to the European market. But whereas the Perceval Ministry had acted as though war with the United States were a matter of indifference, and had idly drifted into that catastrophe, no such mistake was made by Sir Edward Grey, who sacrificed points of real military value in permitting the passage of cotton and other articles of value to the enemy, in order to prevent an early explosion of American opinion against us. The Germans did the rest. Owing to the careful methods of British blockade-diplomacy, the pro-Ally feeling in the United States and the German submarine attack on American persons and shipping were given time to operate, and draw the great neutral into the contest on our side.

Blockade conditions differed in several vital respects from those of Napoleonic times. It is true that our blockade of the enemy's principal Fleet, though conducted at long distance from Scapa Flow, was at least as effective as Nelson's close watch off Brest and Toulon in stopping all chance of invasion and in paralysing the enemy's great ships. But the Napoleonic privateers and frigates that skirmished against British commerce in spite of Nelson, were as nothing to the German submarine, which in the latter part of the War threatened to starve England into surrender. New methods of fighting the new danger were devised and carried out with a scientific efficiency wholly modern, and an old-fashioned skill and courage at sea of which the Royal Navy and the Merchant Service had not lost the secret.

England no longer fed herself, as in Napoleonic times, and the command of the sea was therefore more than ever essential to her very life. But neither, it appeared in the event, could the Central Empires feed themselves for an indefinite period. As the British blockade tightened, especially after the American entry into the War enabled the stranglehold to be increased diplomatically and navally, Germany and Austria began to starve outright. Since the Industrial Revolution, European countries had ceased to be self-supporting in proportion as they were highly civilized and modern. The economic fabric by which the modern millions lived was too international and too delicate to survive for long the injuries done by acts of scientific war. It survived them after a fashion for four years, during which the accumulated wealth and civilization of a hundred years were used up. When the dreadful four years came to an end, Europe was ruined, materially and morally, and made very little recovery. Nothing but the removal of the fear of yet another such war could have enabled the freedom and elasticity of higher civilized life to be resumed. And another war came.

A remarkable contrast appears between the Napoleonic and the German wars, as regards the position of the working classes and the relations of Britons to one another. Pitt and Castlereagh fought the French as constitutional statesmen, by and through the House of Commons; but it never occurred to them or to any of their colleagues that the common people required, in time of national peril, any management or consideration beyond anti-Jacobin repression and the silencing of Parliamentary Reformers. Nor, as regards the mere winning of the War, did this reckoning prove wrong. But the dangers of the Home Front in 1914–18 had to be met by very different methods. Early in 1918, while the War was still raging, the Fourth Reform

Bill was passed by general consent, giving what was practically Manhood Suffrage, and a large instalment of the new principle of Woman's Suffrage; the cessation of outrages by the Suffragettes, and the splendid war work done by women in the factories and elsewhere, had converted many objectors to their enfranchisement. The element of Dictatorship was perhaps stronger than in Pitt's time, as regards the relation of the Government to the House of Commons. But the English Cabinet Ministers of 1914–18 had always to appeal deferentially to the people. For they knew that if munition workers slacked or stopped work, it was no longer in the power of 'magistrates and yeomanry' to make them go on. Since 'the lower orders' had developed into an enfranchised and partially educated democracy, only persuasion could effect what repression had accomplished in the days of the Luddites. In the struggle with Jacobin France, the war-time specific was Combination Acts to suppress Trade Unions; in the struggle with Germany it was the raising of wages to an unprecedented height, and inducing leaders of the Labour party to enter the Coalition Cabinet. The hardships of wartime did not, as a hundred years before, fall with their greatest force on the fortunes of the wage-earner. So long as the common danger of the War lasted, the spirit of brotherhood in the British people of all classes, both at home and in the field, was at any rate much deeper and more widely spread than during the wars against Napoleon.

If Constantinople had been taken in 1915, it is possible that victory might have been obtained in two years, by mobilizing all the Balkan States against the Central Powers, and opening a free channel of supply to Russia. But Kitchener and the Cabinet failed to give proper timing and support to the spasmodic naval and military attacks on the Dardanelles, and the great opportunity of shortening the War was lost. In consequence of that failure, decision was only reached after a gradual process of exhaustion on the Western Front by the slaughter of millions, and the slow starvation of Austria-Hungary and Germany by the British blockade. When Russia fell out of the Alliance owing to the Bolshevist Revolution in 1917, her place was taken, only just in time, by the United States, unable any longer to condone the sinking of American ships by German submarines.

A Coalition War Ministry of Liberals and Conservatives had been formed under Asquith in the second year of the War. An ultimate though not an immediate consequence of the failure at the Dardanelles in 1915 was the fall of Asquith in December 1916. With him went a liberal element which might have been most useful at the peacemaking, but could not survive the stresses of war. Asquith had many qualities as a Prime Minister in war time, but he needed a great military adviser and he had not found all that was needed in his Secretary of State for War, Kitchener of Khartoum. Kitchener roused the country to an early perception of the length and magnitude of the struggle, and conjured up the voluntary enlistment of 'Kitchener's armies' in the early months, while the country was still unwilling to submit to conscription. He was indeed a great personality and had a great hold over the public imagination, but he had not the elastic mind necessary for the conduct of a world war under modern scientific conditions.

The man who rose to the height of the occasion, at least in the opinion of great masses of his countrymen, was Lloyd George. His activity as Minister of Munitions had made good the original deficiencies of the War Office. His imagination was always at work, his energy was contagious, and the state of courageous excitement in which he dealt with one war problem after another gave more confidence to the man in the street than the exasperating calm of Asquith's stoicism. There will always be divergent opinions as to Lloyd George's contribution to the victory, but at least his activity and courage helped to give confidence to the country and energy to its leaders in the last two grim years.

EPILOGUE

The Aftermath

When at last the German line gave way before Foch's strategy and Haig's attack, and victory came with unexpected suddenness in November 1918, England and France were called upon in an instant to switch their minds from the fierce mood of war to the prudence, foresight and generosity that peace-making requires. It took long years before France could think sanely, but in a year or two England had recovered her usual good nature but scarcely her good sense; unfortunately the peace had to be made in the first six months, while the war passions were still aflame in every land. Nor was Lloyd George the man to risk his great popularity and spend his immense influence in a struggle against the passions of the hour, which always had an undue influence on his susceptible and mercurial mind. Moreover the circumstances under which he had replaced Asquith as Prime Minister had led to a breach between him and the major half of the Liberal party during the last two years of war; the Armistice found him in political alliance with the proprietors of certain popular journals, then fiercely calling out for vengeance on German war crimes. And so at the General Election of December 1918 Asquith's followers, who would have stood for moderation in peace-making, were deliberately proscribed by Lloyd George and annihilated at the polls; the Liberal party was rent and destroyed, and has never recovered importance, for the Labour party in later elections step by step took its place.

In the General Election held in these circumstances between the Armistice and the peace-making at Versailles, a House of Commons was returned pledged to make Germany pay for the War. Lloyd George held a huge majority —and the huge majority held Lloyd George. After tying this millstone of a mandate round his own neck, he went to Versailles to help Clemenceau and Wilson give peace to the world. [JAN.–JUNE 1919.] France, who had suffered more, was yet more intent on vengeance than England, and Wilson, meaning well, understood little of realities in Europe, or of opinion in America.

Wilson and Lloyd George prevented France from permanently occupying the German part of the left bank of the Rhine; they obtained this only by a promise that America and England would guarantee the frontiers of France against attack, a promise which America refused to ratify; consequently England also declined this obligation for awhile, thereby losing for some years all control over the policy of France towards Germany, and at the same time encouraging Germany to revive her ambition of conquest.

Upon the whole, the drawing of European boundaries was not ill done at Versailles. The new Europe consisted of a number of States based on the real principle of nationality. Indeed, the States that became the heirs of Austria-Hungary, had been formed by the act of their own populations, as a result of the last stage of the War, before ever the statesmen met at Versailles to confirm the change. It was the War, not the Peace, that destroyed the Empire of the Hapsburgs. In 1920, as a result of a war with Soviet Russia, Poland rashly expanded her eastern frontier far beyond the 'Curzon line' approved and guaranteed by England.

The treatment of Germany by the victorious Allies erred in two respects. In the first place no effective system of inspection was enforced to prevent the war chiefs in Germany from secretly preparing rearmament. And at the same time nothing was done to make the new German Republic popular with the German people. It should have been the first object of England and France to enable it to survive as a peaceful democracy. But the German nation was humiliated by the dictation of terms on the hardships of which she was not even permitted to plead before the victors; she was forbidden to unite peacefully with Austria; she was excluded from the League of Nations; in the matter of Reparations she was treated in a manner so fantastic as to help to exasperate her without benefiting her creditors.

At the same time the League of Nations was set up and was closely associated with the terms of the Treaty. But England alone of the Great Powers gave support to the true spirit of the League, and made some effort to remedy the grievances of Germany, particularly as regards Reparations. The mood of the unhappy General Election of December 1918, having dictated the Treaty, soon died out in the placable breasts of the English, who hastened to disarm and put the war memories behind them, trusting with too complete a confidence in the power of the maimed League of Nations to avert the natural consequences both of the War and of the Peace.

America retired into herself. Having been instrumental in pledging Europe to the policy of the League of Nations, she refused at the last moment to join it. Nor would she any longer co-operate in any practical way to preserve peace. It was a vicious circle: her withdrawal made the European anarchy worse, and the European anarchy has made her more determined than ever not to interfere in Europe again. She even withdrew from the Reparations Commission, where her support would have enabled England to restrain France; the French were therefore able to find a quasi-legal excuse for their rash invasion of the German territory of Ruhr in 1923, England vainly protesting. The outcome was the Germany of Hitler. The other main cause of the rise of the Fascist and Nazi forms of government has been the simultaneous imitation of and reaction against Communism, to which doctrine the success of the Bolshevist Revolution in Russia gave a great impetus throughout the Continent. The outcome of the War was to destroy liberty, democracy and parliaments in the greater part of Europe. And the Nazi form of government, based on wholesale torture and massacre, was so immeasurably worse than anything in the experience of modern Europe, that its reality and implications were not believed in England until in 1940 it had extended its frightful operations over almost the whole Continent.

In the years that followed the signature of the Peace Treaties, English policy had the one merit of goodwill, but showed neither foresight nor firmness. Nothing really effective was done to appease German opinion in the earlier years while appeasement was still possible, nor until very late to prepare for the storm when the storm became only too probable.

The English people, in a natural reaction after four years' experience of the unspeakable horrors of modern 'total' war, regarded pacifism and unilateral disarmament as a method of securing peace, and hailed the League of Nations as a machine for making all safe by some magic or automatic process not clearly defined. Alas, if England intended the dictates of the League to be respected, she should have put herself in a position to enforce them, for no other nation had both the strength and the will. If she meant to remain a European power, she should have armed as others were arming. Even after the Nazi Revolution of 1933—an event ominous enough in all conscience—Germany was allowed, without any corresponding effort on our part, not only to build up her great army again but to obtain a temporary predominance in the air, to militarize the Rhineland contrary to Treaty, and to make upon it the Siegfried Line to block us out of Central Europe. At the same time Italy, whose geographic position controlled our other contacts with Austria and the Balkans, was driven into the arms of Germany by the feeble application of 'economic sanctions' against Mussolini's Abyssinian aggression (1935–36): England in that fatal affair would neither abstain from interference nor threaten to fight in earnest. Europe was sacrificed to Abyssinia—and in vain. Meanwhile no serious effort was made to come to an agreement with Russia for the restraint of Nazi German aggression.

Future historians will have the unenviable task of dividing the blame for a long series of errors between the successive governments of the country and the ever varying moods of the opposition and public opinion which those governments too often weakly followed. It was early in 1939, on Hitler's occupation of Prague in violation of the

Munich agreement of a few months before, that the British people and Government woke up to the dread realities of the situation into which they had been drifting for twenty years. Even then the pace of rearmament was by no means what the crisis required, and the union of parties and full development of war effort was only effected after six months of actual war. At length England faced supreme danger with her old courage, of which she found the symbol in Winston Churchill.

So the isolationist movement in America and the pacifist movement in Britain between them handed the world over to its fate, by permitting the 'unnecessary war' as Winston Churchill called it. After the First World War the States of Europe had been free and independent; even Poland, Czecho-Slovakia, Hungary, the Balkan and Baltic States enjoyed independence, because the war that ended in 1918 had resulted in the defeat both of Russia and of Germany. Therefore Europe was free, and would be free to-day, if there had been no second war. That war (1939–45) resulted in a second defeat of Germany but in the triumph of Russia in the East. Many of the States for whose freedom we fought against Germany have now lost it to Russia. And the material and moral devastation in Europe is without precedent in any war that history records.

The Twentieth Century has been kept in perpetual movement and unrest by the headlong progress of inventions, which hurry mankind on, along roads that no one has chosen, a helpless fugitive with no abiding place. The motor age has changed life even more than the railway age, and now the air-age is changing it again, with atomic power or what-not to follow. Life in great cities has divorced most Englishmen from nature. And the disappearance of craftsmanship and the substitution of mass production by machinery has taken out of men's lives much of the joy and pride of work. But there has been a very great advance in education; and broadcasting is effecting an intellectual change which it is too early yet to estimate. It is hard to cast the balance of the vast account. The most encouraging feature is that, in spite of the frightful handicap of the First World War and its consequences, the material well-being of the majority of the inhabitants of this island was greater in 1939 than a generation before; and the Second World War has been waged by the British people with a manifestation of ability and morale even greater, perhaps, than that shown by their fathers in the First. There is therefore a hope that in the end man may use his new powers to make his life fuller and happier than of old, if only an escape is found from totalitarian war and violence.

In these short volumes I have tried to set down some aspects of the evolution of life upon this island, since the ages when it lay as nature made it, a green and shaggy forest, half waterlogged, while here and there, on the more habitable uplands, the most progressive of the animals gathered his kind into camps and societies, to save himself and his offspring and his flocks from wolves and bears and from his fellow-men—down to the very different scene of our own sophisticated times. In the earlier age, man's impotence to contend with nature made his life brutish and brief. Today his very command over nature, so admirably and marvellously won, has become his greatest peril. Of the future the historian can see no more than others. He can only point like a showman to the things of the past, with their manifold and mysterious message.

SOME LEADING EVENTS BETWEEN THE TWO WORLD WARS

1918 (DEC.). Lloyd George's General Election.

1919 Treaty of Versailles.
League of Nations set up.
Britain disarms, France and Italy do not.
Montagu-Chelmsford reforms establish Dyarchy in India: disturbance and repression: Gandhi.

1920 United States Senate prevents America entering into League of Nations. America refuses to guarantee French territory and therefore Britain follows suit. 'Ulster' obtains a separate Parliament (DEC.).

1921 War against Sinn Fein ended by Treaty in December: Irish Free State set up as a Dominion.

1922 Turks drive Greeks out of Asia Minor: Britain stops Turks at the Straits.
Fall of Lloyd George Ministry.
Mussolini establishes Fascism in Italy.

1923 French occupy the Ruhr.

1924 First Labour Government, dependent on Liberal vote, lasts eight months.

1925 (DEC.) Locarno Treaties: temporary relaxation of European tension.
Germany joins the League of Nations.

1926 General Strike and Miners' Strike.

1927 Disarmament Conferences fail.

1928 Local Government Act.

1929 Second Labour Government, dependent on Liberal vote, lasts two years.

1931 World Slump and Financial Crisis.
(AUGUST) Break-up of Labour Ministry.
National Government formed and wins General Election against Labour.
Statute of Westminster gives new legal status to Dominions.

1932 Unemployment question acute: gradual, partial recovery.

World Economic Conference fails. Japan defies and leaves League of Nations about Manchuria.

1933–34 Hitler establishes Nazi rule in Germany. Leaves League of Nations, repudiates obligations of Versailles Treaty and rearms Germany.

European tension again becomes acute.

1935 Jubilee of King George V.

Act of Parliament gives Responsible Self-government and Federal constitution to India.

Mussolini attacks Abyssinia, a member of the League of Nations.

1936 League 'economic sanctions' fail to save Abyssinia.

Hitler re-occupies Rhineland.

Treaty with Egypt as an independent Nation.

George V dies, succeeded by Edward VIII (JAN.–DEC.), who abdicates. George VI succeeds.

Spanish Civil War begins.

British rearmament begins slowly.

1938 March. Hitler annexes Austria.

September. Munich. Hitler occupies defensive frontier of Czecho-Slovakia.

1939 March. Hitler enters Prague.

September. Hitler attacks Poland.

Second World War begins.

LIST OF MINISTRIES

1770–82	North (Tory, King's Friends).
1782	Rockingham (Whig).
1782–83	Shelburne (King's Friends and Chathamites).
1783	Coalition of North and Fox (Whigs and Tories).
1783–1801	Pitt (Chathamites and King's Friends, gradually becoming Tory; Conservative Whigs join in 1794).
1801–04	Addington (Tory).
1804–06	Pitt's Second Ministry (Tory).
1806–07	Ministry of All-the-Talents (Whigs and Tories).
1807–09	Portland (Tory).
1809–12	Perceval (Tory).
1812–27	Liverpool (Tory), becoming more liberal in policy after 1822.
1827	Canning (Liberal Tory).
1827	Goderich (Liberal Tory).
1828–30	Wellington-Peel (Tory).
1830–34	Grey (Whig).
1834	Melbourne (Whig).
1834–35	Peel (Conservative).
1835–41	Melbourne (Whig).
1841–46	Peel (Conservative).
1846–52	Russell (Whig).
1852	Derby-Disraeli (Conservative).
1852–55	Aberdeen Coalition (Peelites and Whigs).
1855–58	Palmerston (Whig).
1858–59	Derby-Disraeli (Conservative).
1859–65	Palmerston (Whigs and Peelites, Liberals).
1865–66	Russell (Whig and Liberal).
1866–68	Derby-Disraeli (Conservative).
1868–74	Gladstone (Liberal).
1874–80	Disraeli (Conservative).
1880–85	Gladstone (Liberal).
1885–86	Salisbury (Conservative).

1886	Gladstone (Liberal).
1886–92	Salisbury (Conservative, supported by Liberal Unionists).
1892–94	Gladstone (Liberal).
1894–95	Rosebery (Liberal).
1895–1902	Salisbury (Unionist).
1902–05	Balfour (Unionist).
1905–08	Campbell-Bannerman (Liberal).
1908–15	Asquith (Liberal).
1915–16	Asquith (Coalition).
1916–22	Lloyd George (Coalition).
1922–23	Bonar Law (Conservative).
1923–24	Baldwin (Conservative).
1924	MacDonald (Labour).
1924–29	Baldwin (Conservative).
1929–31	MacDonald (Labour).
1931–35	MacDonald (National).
1935–37	Baldwin (National).
1937	Neville Chamberlain (National).
1940	Winston Churchill (Coalition).
1945	Attlee (Labour).
1950	Attlee (Labour).
1951	Winston Churchill (Conservative).

INDEX

ANCHOR BOOKS

ECONOMICS

ANATOMY OF A METROPOLIS—Edgar M. Hoover and Raymond Vernon, A298
COMPETITION AND MONOPOLY—Mark S. Massel, A386
THE CORPORATION TAKE-OVER—Andrew Hacker, ed., A465
CORPORATIONS IN CRISIS—Richard Austin Smith, A475
ECONOMIC PHILOSOPHY—Joan Robinson, A415
THE ECONOMY, LIBERTY AND THE STATE—Calvin B. Hoover, A241
THE ERA OF TYRANNIES—Elie Halévy, Robert K. Webb, trans., A463
THE EXPLODING METROPOLIS—Editors of Fortune, A146
FREE MEN AND FREE MARKETS—Robert Theobald, A447
THE GUARANTEED INCOME—Robert Theobald, A519
INTERNATIONAL POLITICAL COMMUNITIES, A488
INTRODUCTION TO ECONOMIC REASONING—Marshall A. Robinson, Herbert C. Morton, James D. Calderwood, A338
JOURNEYS TOWARD PROGRESS: Studies of Economic Policy-Making in Latin America—Albert O. Hirschmann, A448
LABOR AND MANAGEMENT IN INDUSTRIAL SOCIETY—Clark Kerr, A401
THE MANPOWER REVOLUTION: Its Policy Consequences, Excerpts from the Senate Hearings Before the Clark Committee, ed. by Garth L. Mangum; Foreword by Senator Joseph S. Clark, A522
MARKETS IN AFRICA: Eight Subsistence Economies in Transition —Paul J. Bohannan and George Dalton, eds., N39
METROPOLIS 1985—Raymond Vernon, A341
THE ORGANIZATION MAN—William H. Whyte, Jr., A117
ORIGINS OF SCIENTIFIC ECONOMICS—William Letwin, A462
QUIET CRISIS IN INDIA—John P. Lewis, A383
THE RED EXECUTIVE: A Study of the Organization Man in Russian Industry—David Granick, A246
STRATEGY AND STRUCTURE: Chapters in the History of the Industrial Enterprise—Alfred D. Chandler, Jr., A461
TWO WORLDS OF CHANGE—Otto Feinstein, ed., A396
UNION DEMOCRACY—Seymour Lipset, Martin A. Trow, and James S. Coleman. With a foreword by Clark Kerr, A296
THE URBAN COMPLEX: Human Values in Urban Life—Robert C. Weaver, A505